OUR FUTURE IN ASIA

OUR FUTURE

BY ROBERT AURA SMITH

IN ASIA

NEW YORK · 1940 · THE VIKING PRESS

First published in October 1940

FOREWORD

THE opinions and judgments expressed in this book are my own. They do not represent, in any sense, the editorial opinions or policy of my employer, the *New York Times*.

It is a great pleasure to acknowledge, gratefully, the large amount of cheerful assistance from many persons that has made this book possible. First of all I should like to mention the consular agents of both the United States and Great Britain, who have been unfailing in their courtesy and whose help has been invaluable. Similarly, the representatives of the Department of Commerce have provided much useful material, and the office of the United States Trade Commissioner in the Philippines, as everyone in the Far East knows, is an indispensable, competent, and co-operative adjunct to anyone who is trying to find the economic facts about our relationship to the Far East. The United States Chamber of Commerce has also been very helpful in providing convenient statistical abstracts of our foreign trade.

It is an extraordinary pleasure to pay a debt of gratitude, also, to my former colleagues on the *Manila Daily Bulletin*. The quality of the *Bulletin*'s reporting makes Philippine fact-finding easy. I should be remiss if I did not add an appreciation of the encouragement that I have received from my colleagues on the foreign desk of the *New York Times* and did not add a special word of gratitude for the assistance of Mr. John S. Chalmers.

For the three maps of the South China Sea I am indebted to the skill and always friendly co-operation of Mr. Russell J. Walrath, cartographer of the *New York Times*. The map of Philippine

mineral resources is reprinted through the courtesy of *Asia* maga-
zine.

The difficulties of copy reading were overcome with the stalwart
assistance of Miss Geneva Crumb.

Finally, it should go without saying that none of this book
would have been written without the monumental help of my wife,
whose observations of the Asiatic scene have been called upon,
constantly, to supplement and to check my own judgments.

Situations are changing rapidly in East Asia. There will undoubtedly be fresh "incidents" while this book is on the press. It
cannot hope, therefore, to be abreast of the latest headlines. It does
attempt to show the main streams of policy on which those headlines are based.

ROBERT AURA SMITH

New York, August 20, 1940

CONTENTS

Page

FOREWORD   v

INTRODUCTION   1

I. OUR STAKE IN THE SOUTH CHINA SEA—1
    Strategy and Profit   7

    The Age of Rubber; Filling the American Sugar Bowl; The
    Ubiquitous Coconut; Where We Get Our Tin; Imports and
    National Defense; More Than Defense Items; Sellers Also Buy;
    The Value of an Outpost

II. OUR STAKE IN THE SOUTH CHINA SEA—2
    Economic Geography   28

    Hong Kong; Manila, "The Pearl of the Orient"; "Paris of the
    Far East"; Surabaya, South Seas Metropolis; Batavia, Spice Coun-
    ter of the World; Singapore, at the Asiatic Crossroads; Economic
    Tug of War; Meeting a Market Crash; Tennis Shoes for Fifteen
    Cents

III. OUR STAKE IN THE SOUTH CHINA SEA—3
     Our Political Neighbors   46

     Life-line of the Netherlands; Functions of a "Protectorate"; How
     Malaya Is Ruled; The Philippines: Democracy in Embryo; Far
     Eastern Stability

IV. THREATS TO THE STATUS QUO—1
     The Question of Empire   55

     Shortening the Defense Line; Wanted: an Empire Mind; In
     Defense of Empire; A New "White Man's Burden"

V.   THREATS TO THE STATUS QUO—2
     Native Nationalism   71

     Nationalism in Malaya; Changes in Netherland Rule; Outpacing
     the Filipino

Contents

Page

VI. THREATS TO THE STATUS QUO—3
     The March of Aggression   79

     The Threat to British Malaya; Menace to the Philippines; Neth-
     erland India's Status Quo; The Blank Check to Japan

VII. OUR PHILIPPINE VENTURE—I   91

      A Self-Contradictory Policy; Creating an Economic Dependency;
      A Problem in Centralization; How to Dynamite "Preparation";
      The Motives behind Independence; The Grinding of the Axes;
      The Fruits of Panic; What Do They Want?; Portrait of a Pa-
      triot; The Vexed Question of Race; The Philippine "Politico";
      Hand-Cut Heaven; Liberty vs. Independence: Round One

VIII. OUR PHILIPPINE VENTURE—2   122

       Uses for an Army; The Ebb-Tide of Confidence; MacArthur
       Restates His Case; A Touch of Skepticism; Concerning "Rational
       Reasons"; Armed Against What?; Advance Guard of Invasion;
       Japan Becomes Generous; More Than a Soldier's Job; The Naval
       Base Problem; Air Bases of the Future

IX. OUR PHILIPPINE VENTURE—3   147

     Our Fifth Customer; Mining Enters the Picture; Chromium and
     Foreign Policy; The Basis of Taxable Wealth; Where the Empire
     Mind Comes In; Blowing Hot and Cold; Wanted: A Face-Saving
     Formula; Prestige and Sovereignty; How to Reduce Risks; Security
     in the Long View

X. OUR LEGAL POSITION IN ASIA   169

    The Nine-Power Pacific Treaty; A Basis for Discussion; The Va-
    lidity of Obligations; The Kellogg-Briand Treaty; Our Naval
    Treaties; The Trade Treaty of 1911; Tokyo Gets Worried

XI. OUR RELATIONS WITH CHINA   183

     Abraham Lincoln Paraphrased; The Attack on Inequality; What
     Is "Exploitation"?; Another Sort of Investment; New Vistas in
     China

Contents

Page

XII. OUR RELATIONS WITH JAPAN 197

Our First Treaty with Japan; The First "Gentlemen's Agreement"; Another Setback to Pride; On the Day-to-Day Basis; Fighting a Holy War; Possibility of an Embargo; No Time Like the Present; Time Works Both Ways; When a War Is Not a War; Japan Will Strike Back; Paying for Having a Conscience; Backfire in Asia; Several Ways to Jump; The Case for the Embargo; We Violate Our Own Policy; Blood on Our Hands; Caution Versus Outrage

XIII. JAPANESE EXPANSION AND AGGRESSION 239

The Pressure Is There; Impatient Patriotism; The Tanaka Memorial; Still Before the Public; A Declared Political Policy; Communism or Russia?; Chinese New Dealers; "The New Order in East Asia"; The Reply of General Chiang; The United States Reaction; Behind the "Yen Bloc"; Oriental "Culture"; "A Monroe Doctrine for Asia"; A Reply from Washington; A "Spokesman" Out of Turn; Some Differences in Doctrine; "Friendly to Japan"; Window Dressing for Aggression; Russia in the Picture

XIV. THE DEFENSE OF THE SOUTH CHINA SEA 278

Five Naval Bases; Strength of the Air Arm; Avoiding an Understanding; An Ode to Chestnuts; To a Dynamic Policy; We Are Not Helpless

INDEX 297

MAPS

Geography of South China Sea Area   Page 6

Products of South China Sea Area   33

Mineral Deposits in the Philippines   93

Colonial Expansion of Japan   241

OUR FUTURE IN ASIA

INTRODUCTION

ALONG with three great Western empires—the French, the British, and the Dutch—we of the United States had worked out in southeastern Asia in recent years a stable and secure status quo. The established order there has now been challenged. We face the passing of that area into different hands.

Today we are forced to decide whether that order in the East is worth preserving. Our first problem, therefore, is to ask ourselves what our position in southeastern Asia really is; how vital it is to our well-being; whether or not we need and want it; whether or not we can and will fight to keep it. Our future in Asia depends on what we propose to do about the status quo in the South China Sea. It may have much to do with our future elsewhere.

In the United States we have tried to keep ourselves remote from the European conflict. We have tried to wrap ourselves in a hemispheric quarantine against the spread of war. Our object has been the preservation, so far as possible, of our chosen way of life. Many have believed that we could keep ourselves aloof because we had no geographic frontier within the line of attack. But it has become increasingly clear that we can hope for no such immunity in Asia. There, in the Philippines, we have a political frontier. In China, Indo-China, Netherland India, and Malaya, we have an economic frontier.

In a large sense the war in the West and the war in the East are one. On each front a dynamic force has appeared with the avowed object of disrupting international structures and substituting a new world order, redistributed for the benefit of different regimes and a different way of life. The colonial world of the East has been a factor in the stability of the way of life that is now under assault in the West. The size, the riches, the peaceful character of the colonies surrounding the South China Sea, and their relationship to Western freedom, have invited aggression and redistribution. The destruction of the mother countries was, from the beginning, the avowed purpose of the National Socialist and Fascist Revolution in Europe. The collection of a sizable part of the loot, once the world's democratic empires were fully disorganized, became the Japanese conception of a new world order.

For years we have been discussing, somewhat academically, the problem of Japanese southward expansion. It was always an "if and when" proposition. That time has passed. The expansion is begun; the problem is laid at our door.

Politically, southeastern Asia embraced, in the late summer of 1940, the Asiatic colonial outposts of what remained of three European democratic empires, and of the United States. French Indo-China was already under direct attack. British Malaya was the Far Eastern redoubt of the British Empire, which was fighting for its life at home. Netherland India had become the new capital for an economic empire whose seat of government had shifted from The Hague to Batavia. The Philippines were an American outpost, from which our own legislation has committed us to beat a precipitate and inglorious retreat in 1946. That was the political status quo in the South China Sea.

Economically, southeastern Asia possesses world control of rubber and of tin; one-fourth of the world's oil; all of the world's manila hemp; all of the world's quinine; the major producers of the world's tungsten and antimony; the greatest exporters of rice; the world's control of copra and coconut oil; the largest chromite deposit and the sixth gold producer in the world. Those products of the southeastern Asiatic market comprise with its purchases a foreign trade of a billion and a half dollars annually.

It is that political and economic position, and the interest of the United States in it, which are now under attack.

We have had ample warning, both that the attack was coming, and that the struggles in northwestern Europe and in southeastern Asia were intimately related. Japanese "intervention" in North China coincided suspiciously with democratic "non-intervention" in Spain. Japanese cruisers were going into the Gulf of Tongking to shell the southwest coast of China at the same time that Generalissimo Francisco Franco was going into Madrid and Chancellor Adolf Hitler was going into Vienna. The strategic island of Hainan off the coast of French Indo-China was occupied by the Japanese at about the same time that Munich brought "peace in our time." Spratly Island, about a rifle shot off the coast of Borneo, was occupied at the time Prague was over-run.

The collapse of the French in June 1940 sent the "manifest destiny" of Japan into high gear and precipitated the most astonishing paradox in a world that had become full of them. A Chinese democracy announced to the world that in the name of self-defense it would fight against aggression by another Oriental people for the preservation of the stability of French Indo-China. China would help to defend a colonial outpost of a Western democracy, taken from the Chinese Empire by Western force less than sixty years ago!

Aggression has made strange bedfellows when the Chinese army fights the battles of the Western world.

And yet this need not be surprising. The needs of the Western world and the development of its political structures had built up around the South China Sea a productive and stable status quo. The life-lines of Western empires went into those colonies, and their products in turn went into the markets of the world. They represented a peaceful, established, orderly, non-predatory economy, organized for profit.

World revolution, as instigated by the Nazis and then belatedly adopted by Mussolini and the Japanese, was aimed precisely at such structures. Men and parties that despise democracy, eschew economics, and are mobilized against a world commerce in terms of gold, were on the march to destroy existing structures and to redistribute the basis for profits.

"Smash and grab" had already reduced most of Europe. "Smash and grab" was just beginning to get warmed up in Asia.

It is a natural tendency of the human mind to restrict its horizons wherever possible. For that reason, perhaps, confronted with this dynamic threat to almost all of the organized political economy of the world, the people of this country have thought in terms of defending our continental limits and our hemispheric frontier.

When we thought of defending our trade relationships against outside invasion, we thought naturally of trade with South America. When we thought of penetration and aggression, we thought of Nazi deals with Brazil and Nazi plots in Uruguay. But while this was going on we were being faced with the equally dynamic threat to a political and economic position vastly more important than mere hemisphere defense.

Our connection with southeastern Asia makes our ties to South America look like child's play. We buy more from three colonies on the South China Sea than we do from all of South America combined. While we contemplate lightly throwing away our Philippine position, our trade with the Philippines has systematically outranked our trade with Brazil, or Argentina, or any other South American country, for the last fifteen years.

There has been some discussion as to what would happen if and when an invader brought his airplanes and tanks within the continental limits of the United States. There is still not enough discussion of what has already happened under an invasion of airplanes and tanks that is cutting into the life-lines of American trade and the American political future in Asia.

It was a startled American public that heard two years ago that our frontier was on the Rhine. We have seen that frontier vanish. We are perhaps just beginning to realize that our frontier has been on the Yangtze since 1937, and that we have a frontier on the South China Sea.

Events in Europe have taken many decisions out of our hands. We still have an opportunity to make some of the decisions in respect to Asia.

The object of this book is to examine some of the bases upon which those decisions must be made, and to assist, if possible, in the development of a more realistic approach to the possibilities of our future in Asia.

Geography of South China Sea Area

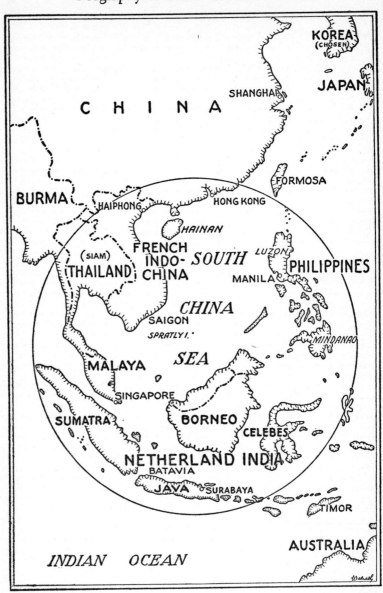

CHAPTER I

OUR STAKE IN
THE SOUTH CHINA SEA—I

Strategy and Profit

ON A map of Eastern Asia set a pair of compasses, one leg in the center of the South China Sea, the other extended to the scale of 1,000 miles, and draw the circle. Enclosed in this circle is the battle-ground of America's future in Asia.

Within this circle are the three most southerly provinces of China, French Indo-China, the Philippines, most of Netherland India, British Malaya, Thailand, and part of Burma. The area so enclosed is 3,141,600 square miles. That is roughly the area of the continental United States. Two-thirds of it, however, is water, and on the remaining one-third lives a population of 130,000,000, again just about the population of the United States. That population is made up of about 20,000,000 Chinese and 110,000,000 Malays.

The largest population group is that of Netherland India, roughly 66,000,000. The land area of the Netherland Indian Archipelago is something more than 700,000 square miles, or about three times the size of the state of Texas. But more than 40,000,000 persons, of that 66,000,000, live on one island, Java, which is about the size of the state of Kansas.

The next population group in size is that of French Indo-China. In an area of 277,000 square miles, or about the size of Texas plus Massachusetts and New Jersey, there live a little more than 20,000,000 persons. They are predominantly Malay, but with strong Chinese intermixture.

Our Philippine Archipelago contains the next largest population. There are 16,000,000 Filipinos living on a land area of 115,000 square miles. That is about the size of New York, Pennsylvania,

Delaware, Maryland, New Jersey, Connecticut and Rhode Island.

The Kingdom of Thailand (Siam), about as large as California and Indiana, has a population of about 7,000,000.

British Malaya is the least densely populated of these colonies. It has an area about the size of Nevada and a population of 4,-500,000.

The circle on the map takes in a segment of South China about the size of Florida with a population of about 20,000,000.

These are diverse countries and diverse peoples, but they have a curious homogeneity. They are united first of all by race. All except the Chinese are Malay. In addition there is a basic similarity in these countries in living conditions, climate, economic structure, and political position. There is a common outside danger.

They have an additional unity, from the American point of view, in their relation to our economic needs and our strategic raw materials. Our Philippine outpost brings us within that circle, physically. Our dependence upon southeastern Asia for important raw materials and for certain markets brings us within that circle, economically.

Any drastic modification of the pre-war economic and political structures in the region of the South China Sea is a matter of vital concern to the United States from considerations of both strategy and profit. For both necessities and comforts we are dependent, to a greater degree than is often realized, upon our continued access to the area of the South China Sea.

We like to think of ourselves as potentially, if not actually, self-sufficient. There is, no doubt, a large part of our population that honestly believes that we could be easily self-contained within our continental limits. But the recent emphasis upon national defense has shown that this would be possible only if we were to acquire, in advance of any hostilities, large stores of some important war materials. And in addition such self-sufficiency would require a radical, and at some points very unpleasant, alteration of our standards and ways of living.

In spite of the fact that our whole economic structure as a nation is organized on the basis of having surpluses for export, we are at the same time the second largest consuming nation in the world in the field of foreign trade. We are not only great sellers; we are great buyers. The imports of Great Britain, and of Great Britain alone, exceed those of the United States.

Those imports naturally give a conspicuous place to tropical products, since it is those products that either cannot be produced at all within our continental limits or cannot be produced as economically as they can be purchased abroad.

Over the last ten years, for example, the seven major imports of the United States were, in order: rubber, sugar, coffee, paper and pulp, vegetable oil, raw silk, and tin. Of these only paper and pulp, which we import from Canada, and raw silk, which we import from Japan, are not tropical in origin. The other five are major export products of the South China Sea area. And raw silk too is of course identified with our Asiatic interests.

THE AGE OF RUBBER

It should hardly be necessary to point out why rubber is of the utmost importance in our foreign trade and in our national life. The United States is the largest importer and consumer of rubber in what is truly "the rubber age."

Rubber heels on our millions of shoes; rubber tires, at least four to the car, on our millions of automoblies—those are only the beginning. Rubber insulation on electric wiring in the country with the most electric wiring; rubber in telephones, in both wires and instruments, in the country with the most telephones. Rubber in refrigerators, washing machines, garden hose, door stops, fountain pens, golf balls, underclothing, toy balloons, sanitary goods, and streamlined trains.

Our luxury in living is primarily the luxury of rubber.

It is no wonder that even in a bad year, such as 1939, rubber made up one-twelfth of our total purchases, with the modest figure of

$178,000,000. It is no wonder that when we look to life-lines in trade our first look should be at our rubber supply.

That rubber life-line, of course, leads straight to the South China Sea.

More than four-fifths of the world's rubber is handled over the wharves of Singapore. Not all of this is produced in British Malaya, even with its 3,250,000 acres of rubber plantations, since Singapore is also the clearing house for the large rubber production of Java and Sumatra, and is a buying and shipping market for Indo-China and the Philippines. Netherland India produces about one-fourth of the world's rubber supply; British Malaya more than one-half.

Our dependence upon this import is our first tie to the South China Sea area. Our trade with Singapore is the economic life-line not only for our automobile industry but also for many other industries involved in making life worth living in the United States.

Since this life-line extending to a relatively remote part of the earth is dangerously threatened, attention naturally turns to the possibilities of reducing this dependence by replacement. Two such possibilities have been suggested. The first is to derive our necessary imports of rubber from Brazil; the second is to develop the manufacture of rubber substitutes from materials that can be had within the United States.

Brazil's present role in the world's rubber supply has possibly been a matter of some considerable misapprehension among Americans. The production of rubber is so closely identified with images of the Amazon, dugout canoes, and piles of rubber on the wharves at Para, that there is a tendency of think of Brazil as the most important source of the product.

At one time this would have been quite correct. But the demand for rubber changed, and the source changed. The dugout canoe, the open fire (and incidentally a disastrous mode of tapping trees) gave way to plantation methods. But even after this trend set in, Brazil, being first in the field, dominated the picture. In 1912, for example, world production of rubber was 114,276 long tons. Of this, Brazil produced 41,619 tons, or 40 per cent. Other American production amounted to almost 15,000 tons.

By this time, however, the cultivation of rubber had been introduced in southeastern Asia and 17,498 long tons were produced. Of these, roughly 15,000 were British and the remainder came from Netherland India, Siam, Indo-China and the Philippines.

That was just at the beginning of the great expansion in both production and consumption. That expansion coincided almost exactly with the decline of Brazilian production and the gigantic growth of Asiatic production.

In 1937 world production was 1,135,398 long tons, and of this, Far Eastern production was 1,108,717. British production in Malaya and Borneo accounted for slightly more than half of the total. The significant factor here is that Brazilian production had dropped more rapidly in the relative than in the positive picture. The Brazilian output in 1937 was one-third of the 1912 level, and its total volume was 15,576 long tons. This would have been a respectable part of the 1912 world production; in 1937 it was just about a rubber band in a tire factory. It was actually 1.3 per cent of the world output or not quite enough to supply the normal needs of the United States for three working days.

But, it is urged, we could shift the center of gravity in rubber production and again make Brazil the leader in the field. That is true; we probably could. Rubber will grow in Brazil. But it takes seven years to bring a rubber tree into production and it requires large investment and large-scale organization to lay out a plantation. Consequently, while it is theoretically possible for the United States eventually to procure a major part of its rubber in this hemisphere, such a move would require long-range planning, very large capital investment, complete co-operation of other American states and a very considerable lapse of time before the volume of present Far Eastern production could hope to be challenged.

We might not have the seven years and the millions of dollars to put into the project at the present time.

Development of another producing area commensurate in size

with the Singapore area would, moreover, inevitably produce so great a surplus as to wreck the world market structures. It would necessarily be a cut-throat operation in which the United States would deliberately undertake to divest the Eastern producers of their importance in order to bring the source of supply within this hemisphere. It could be done, but the price that would be paid would obviously, on several counts, be very high.

The other possibility that has been much discussed recently is the manufacture of rubber substitutes. Probably the layman has suffered some false optimism on this point. Substitutes can undoubtedly be manufactured if it is imperative to do so. But the manufacturers themselves have not suggested that this would be a desirable course of action except as a military necessity. It has not been suggested that the substitute product would be either cheaper or better than natural rubber.

It is also a mistake to assume that the substitution could be made overnight. Large volume production is required and substitute manufacture has not yet been organized on a large scale. In 1939, for example, the rubber substitute output was 1,700 tons. Our rubber consumption in the same year was 590,000 tons. Manifestly an increase in substitute manufacture to meet such a large need would be a major operation requiring a considerable lapse of time and a very large capital investment.

At the very best it would be much more expensive and much less satisfactory to supply our rubber needs by means of substitute products than to continue to use the already developed product that nature supplies.

There is a further objection to any plan of displacing our entire natural supply with a domestically manufactured substitute. Such an operation would necessarily be a part of precisely the type of autarchy to which we have taken so much exception in the field of government and trade.

To be self-contained may, under some conditions, be a military necessity. We have not accepted the theory that it is good economics or a good way of getting along with our neighbors in the world. It is suggested that we are obliged to fight fire with fire. But that does not justify starting the fire if it is not imperative. It is the interchange of products that makes for satisfactory life among nations. The attempt to free itself entirely from this interchange is one of the marks of the very type of regime that we have pledged ourselves to oppose.

Thus while the production of rubber substitutes may be a tremendously important anchor to windward in times of international danger, it is just the sort of anchor that we hope we shall not have to use. If we can sustain our natural source of supplies, without too great hazard, we shall be better off economically and politically.

Filling the American Sugar Bowl

Next on the list of essential imports is sugar. The United States, using annually more than six million tons of sugar, is the largest consumer in the world. We are dependent for more than two-thirds of that sugar upon off-shore production.

We do not get the bulk of our sugar from the area of the South China Sea, but that area contains two of the world's most important sugar producers: Java and the Philippines. The United States is taking, at the present time, 850,000 long tons each year from the Philippines. We make up the remainder of our off-shore volume from Hawaii, Puerto Rico, and Cuba.

Again, in regard to sugar, it would be possible for us to produce within our continental limits a somewhat larger quantity than we now do. Domestic beet sugar is another of those anchors to windward. Beet sugar production is, however, relatively uneconomical. It is even more costly than cane production plus transportation. Moreover, it requires a type of back-breaking labor that most Americans refuse to do, and the result has been the importation of Mexicans, the use of immigrant labor, and the use even of child labor.

It might be possible, if it were necessary, for the United States so greatly to increase the acreage planted in beets that we could free ourselves from dependence on off-shore sugar production, but it would be a costly operation to the consumer. Fortunately there seems to be little reason to do this, since Cuban sugar production, near at hand, can be so easily expanded.

The relation of the South China Sea area to this sugar problem is not so much a question of having supplies to meet our own needs. It is rather the fact that Java and the Philippines combined have enough potential production capacity to break the world market at any time the powers controlling them decide not to concur in limitation by agreement. Java, for example, has produced only one-third of its sugar capacity for more than fifteen years. Philippine production could be doubled in the course of two seasons. It is greatly to the interest of the United States to have this production in friendly and co-operative hands, since sugar producers in this country and elsewhere in the world feel that no profit is to be gained by overloading the market.

The situation in the South China Sea in respect to coffee, the next major import, is somewhat analogous to the situation in sugar. We buy relatively little of our coffee from Java; most of it we get from Brazil. But Java is the world's third producer. In 1937, for example, Netherland India turned out 217,969,000 pounds under adverse conditions. So while coffee is not a product for which we depend upon Asia, it is a matter of importance to our whole market structure. The volume of production, present and potential, in the South China Sea area may vitally affect coffee producers in Brazil and their relation to the American consumer.

The next item in our import trade, paper and pulp, is our major Canadian import, and the disposition of the countries surrounding the South China Sea will have little effect on it.

THE UBIQUITOUS COCONUT

Our fifth import is vegetable oils. And to the United States that means, primarily, coconuts.

When I first went out to the Far East I had, I suppose, an average American point of view. When I thought of coconuts I thought of those festive occasions when, like other American small boys, I was allowed to pay a nickel for a coconut down at the corner store. We brought it home and admired its "face." (We weren't so far wrong at that. In some of the Polynesian dialects the word "ko-ko" means "head," just as it did in American slang before "bean" replaced it.) We carefully drove two nails into the eye-holes and drained the milk. Then it was tapped all around to loosen the meat from the shell and finally ceremoniously opened.

I thought of that painstaking process many years later when I saw brown-skinned Filipinos down in Batangas "opening" coconuts, splitting more than twenty-five to the minute with one blow of a bolo, and laying them out to dry to make copra.

If anyone had asked me about the commercial significance of the coconut at the outset of my travels, I might have thought rather vaguely about those bushel baskets of coconuts in the corner store and also about coconut layer cakes and possibly about the "coconut candy" that we saw from time to time before the candy bar was a major article of trade. If I had asked my wife, she might have told me about a really good shampoo or about coconut oil in a lipstick or a face cream.

But even if I had known that, I should not have been able to explain that road down through Tayabas, bordered by miles upon miles of coconut palms stretching back from the road as far as the eye could reach. Rivers covered with floating rafts of coconuts. Barge-loads of sacks of copra pulled up on a mechanical conveyor at Opon.

Coconut cake and lipstick would not explain why the United States, even in a bad year, imports more than $50,000,000 worth of copra and coconut oil and may at any time double that figure.

The ever-present coconut—where does it go? Into the American soap kettle, first of all. It is brought, in the form of oil, in huge tankers that ply the Pacific. Their advertisements in the newspapers read, "Deep tanks for coconut oil." The making of soap is its most important use, but there are many others.

About 25 per cent of our imports go into the making of oleomargarine. They even called it "coconut butter"until the label law stopped that practice. Vegetable shortenings, confectionery, lacquers, even some processes for the tanning of leather use coconut oil. Now it is being used in the manufacture of plastics, where it competes with its formerly invincible Asiatic rival, the soy bean.

In addition to oil, the milling process produces by-products that are a vital element in world trade. Copra meal, for example, is used for stock food, and copra cake is a fertilizer.

Coconuts that are not milled for oil may be dried and shredded to produce desiccated coconut, familiar in candy bars and cakes.

We get our copra and coconut oil, of course, from the South China Sea. Coconuts grow all over the tropics, but the area of the South China Sea is the greatest concentration of copra making and collecting and of coconut milling. The Philippine production is the best organized, and exceeds the other South China Sea areas in volume. Singapore, however, is the collecting station for many diverse areas, and controls the copra market, except for Philippine shipments to the United States. Singapore quotations are the accepted standard.

The field of vegetable oils has been a big economic battle-ground in the United States. Many of the oils are interchangeable. Cottonseed oil, for example, will do many of the things that coconut oil will do. Domestic animal fats, particularly dairy fats, displace coconut oil at some points. Palm oil and palm kernel oil also occupy a conspicuous place in the economy of fats.

A peculiar property of coconut oil, not shared by the others (with the possible exception of babassu from Brazil) is its lauric acid content. This is what makes good soap lather in hard water, and that in turn is what makes the supply of coconut oil important to the largest consumer of soap in the world.

Some American domestic interests, such as cottonseed oil producers and dairy farmers, have found it desirable to exclude as much coconut oil from our markets as possible. We now have a Federal excise tax of five cents a pound on all imported vegetable oils. The Philippines, incidentally, enjoy a differential of two cents a pound. Copra, however, the raw material from which coconut oil is made, is on the American free list and is likely to continue there because of the important function that this oil fulfills.

The coconut has also a military significance. Coconut oil is one of the best sources for glycerine, and glycerine, of course, is essential to the manufacture of many types of explosives. It is a curious side-light on the military function of coconut that coconut char is one of the most important elements in the manufacture of gas masks.

There seems to be general agreement that an acute shortage of fats is almost as serious a military handicap in the long run as the shortage of metals or fuels. The United States is apparently in no danger of suffering from a quantitative shortage. If, on the other hand, it were cut off from its coconut sources it would suffer qualitative losses that would necessitate the use of very unfit substitutes.

One of our major interests in the South China Sea area is, therefore, the maintenance of continued access to the most important coconut-producing area in the world.

The next important item in this Far Eastern picture is raw silk. This is the major factor in our trade with Japan, since our purchases of silk make possible Japan's purchases from us. Under normal conditions, quite the most important of those Japanese purchases has been raw cotton. This interchange of American raw cotton for Japanese raw silk is one of the best and most stable bases imaginable for peacetime trading operations. The normal course of this interchange has been interrupted by Japanese wartime economy. It will be of great advantage to the United States, however, and to Japan, if this pacific flow of goods can be resumed. At this point, also, then, our political relationship to Japan has a vital effect on the import trade picture.

WHERE WE GET OUR TIN

Now we come to the last of these major American imports, tin. Here again the United States is the world's largest consumer. We buy more than one-third of the world's total output. In 1939 our tin imports amounted to about $70,000,000 and constituted a little more than 3 per cent of our total purchases. Our quota in 1940 was substantially increased.

The area of the South China Sea is by far the most important tin producer in the world. British Malaya alone produces more than one-third of the world's total tin supply and Netherland India almost one-fourth. Tin is shipped into Singapore also from Burma, Thailand, and Indo-China. It goes to some of the world's largest tin smelting plants, at Singapore and Penang. There are other large smelters in the Singapore area, and that is not surprising, since this part of the world accounts for 71 per cent of the world's total tin supply. Of the 208,220 long tons produced in 1937, for example, southeastern Asia supplied 148,151 long tons.

Access to this supply is, of course, a matter of the utmost importance to the United States both from the standpoint of the character of our whole civilization and from the standpoint of national defense.

But, it is often suggested, we could get our tin from Bolivia, without the necessity of crossing the Pacific. We could, of course, if three things were different. First of all, Bolivia would have to produce enough to satisfy our needs; second, it would have to be smelted; and third, Bolivia would have to want us to get it.

The first factor is perhaps the most significant. We usually think of Bolivia as a great tin-producing area, but again taking 1937 for a comparison, we find that Bolivia turned out only 25,074 tons. This was only 12 per cent of the total world production, and we were buying three times that amount.

The second factor, smelting, could no doubt be met by the requisite investment. At the present time the smelters do not exist in this hemisphere to handle a greatly increased Bolivian output. The smelters do exist in southeastern Asia.

The third factor is the attitude of the Bolivian government, which has already taken steps to check tin expansion. All metals must now be marketed through the Central Bank of Bolivia, and the government will control any further exploitation. Conservation, not expansion, is the Bolivian slogan. After the experience of the American oil companies with confiscation in Bolivia it is doubtful if there will be any great desire to pour American capital into the country to build up tin production when the marketing of that production must be, from the outset, completely at the mercy of the local government.

This examination of our seven greatest imports should show the necessity for a Far Eastern policy that will assure the continued flow of goods that are a vital part of our standard of living and of our safety. Asia is the largest supplier of goods to the United States. Our normal purchases from the Asiatic countries are more than a billion dollars annually. More than a third of these, moreover, come from the Philippines, Netherland India and British Malaya. Our national interest in that circle on the map should be obvious.

IMPORTS AND NATIONAL DEFENSE

Our dependence upon imports of certain essential materials has become more generally a matter of common knowledge with the emphasis that has been placed upon national defense. It is only in recent years that we have thought so clearly about the importance of access to raw materials in any defense program.*

About two years ago the Army and Navy Munitions Board made public its classification of raw materials under the heads of strategic, critical, and essential. Strategic raw materials are those, imperative for national defense, that are not produced in sufficient

---

* It would be an unpardonable oversight not to mention at this point the public service that was done by Dr. Brooks Emeny in his splendid book The Strategy of Raw Materials. This book has become basic reading for anyone interested in the economic side of national defense.

quantity within the continental limits of the United States. Strategic materials, then, are the key to our dependence on imports for defense.

Critical materials are those, of the utmost importance to defense and to national stability, for which our sources of supply are reasonably assured but for which the greatest care must be taken to safeguard sources and accumulate reserves.

Essential materials are those in which we appear to enjoy self-sufficiency or ready access but which are of the utmost importance to the prosecution of a war.

The strategic materials, our first line of economic defense, wherein we are not self-sufficient, are: aluminum, antimony, chromium, coconut char, manganese, manila fiber, ferrograde, mica, nickel, optical glass, quartz crystal, mercury, quinine, rubber, silk, tin, tungsten, and wool.

There are eighteen of these materials. Of the eighteen, ten are major products of the South China Sea area. We have already noted the place that rubber and tin occupy in our trade with that part of the world. Other items are equally important to our defense.

Manila fiber, for example, is essential to naval construction, and it is a world monopoly of the South China Sea area. Quinine, without which defense against malaria is impossible, is a world monopoly controlled by Netherland India. The world's largest known chromite deposit is in the Philippines. Production of manganese in the Philippines has multiplied 600 per cent in the five years 1935–39. One of the world's most important nickel mines was opened up in 1937 in Celebes. The southern part of China, enclosed within our circle, is the world's most important producer of tungsten and antimony. Philippine ores are being analyzed at the present time for both ferrograde and aluminum content. The ore of the gigantic Philippine chromite deposit, for example, runs roughly 38 per cent alumina. This content, up to the present, has been quite incidental to the chromic oxide content, but it is not unreasonable to suggest that when utilization is made of the millions of tons of Philippine chromite the alumina can be recovered as a by-product affording a source of supply quite as important as bauxite.

Out of eighteen strategic materials, then, only six are not intimately identified with our future in the South China Sea; for four we are overwhelmingly dependent on that area, and at least a half-dozen more are likely to come into the world picture as development, exploration, and a specific interchange of goods in that part of the world increases.

More Than Defense Items

But our interest in the products of the South China Sea does not stop with these strategic materials. This area is also a very important source of many products on the list of critical and essential materials, such as asbestos, coffee, kapok, cutch, camphor, copra, iron, lead, palm oil, petroleum, shellac, and sugar.

In some cases we actually derive our major imports of these products from fields already developed in the South China Sea area. Some of them are of the utmost importance from the military point of view. Others, as we have noted, support our standard of living.

The normal need for some of these items may be unfamiliar to American readers, but their place in trade is frequently of an importance measured not simply by their dollar value. The extent of our dependence upon this part of the world for some of these products is of most significance.

Take kapok, for example; it has a very important place in American industrial life, in the manufacture of mattresses and life preservers. The United States normally imports between 8,000 and 14,000 tons of this product. The value of these imports in 1939, for example, was a little more than $2,000,000. Eighty-eight per cent of our total supply of kapok was derived from Netherland India, and most of the remainder came from the Philippines.

We seldom think of sago or tapioca as big items in world trade, yet in 1939 we bought well over $5,000,000 worth of tapioca, and again 88 per cent of it came from Netherland India.

Of pepper the United States is the largest consumer in the world, and our imports for 1939 amounted to about $3,250,000. We got 96 per cent of this from Netherland India.

For its porch furniture the United States uses the world's supply of rattan. We import about a quarter of a million dollars' worth every year. Eighty-seven per cent of it comes from Netherland India and most of the remainder from French Indo-China and the Philippines.

In recent years the United States has become increasingly a consumer of palm oil. Our source of supply was, up to the last fifteen years, primarily West Africa. For example, less than 4 per cent of the 139,000,000 pounds of palm oil that we used in 1925 came from the Far East, while almost 80 per cent came from Africa or the United Kingdom. By 1939 the source of our imports had shifted radically, and we got 84 per cent of our palm oil from Netherland India alone. The United States, the most important market for the increasing production of palm oil, takes approximately half of the entire output.

Of all vital commodities that are also of strategic military value, the one for which we are probably most dependent on the Far East is quinine. We are the world's largest consumer, using approximately 2,000,000 pounds a year of the cinchona bark from which quinine sulphate is made. This is a Netherland Indian monopoly; in 1939, for example, 99.4 per cent of our imports of this essential product came from there.

For these several products the United States is almost entirely dependent upon the Netherland possessions in the South China Sea area. For still other supplies that region is relatively important. Netherland India supplied, for example, 28 per cent of our 1939 imports of crude rubber and 44 per cent of our imports of latex. Curiously, too, Netherland India supplied four-fifths of our imports of leaf tobacco; this is because the Sumatra wrapper has a special place in the American industry.

In 1939 we got one-third of our imports of sisal, essential to less expensive cordages, from Netherland India. We took more than one-fourth of our tea from this archipelago. We got two-thirds of our kopal, for use in varnish; half of our nutmeg; 85 per cent of our mace and three-fourths of our gambier, in the Netherland India trade.

The loss of any of this trade would hardly wreck the American economy or expose us to invasion, but it would make a great difference in the way our economy is organized and in American standards of living and of comfort.

SELLERS ALSO BUY

Thus far we have considered our relation to the South China Sea area only from the point of view of what we bring from it. This is only half of the picture. Our interest is profit as well as strategy, and there is every reason to believe that this corner of Asia will become increasingly important as an outlet for American goods.

This increase of exports to the East has in fact already begun. Netherland Indian purchases from the United States have jumped sharply, and in the Philippine trade our balance is actually favorable at the present time. There are several reasons for believing that this development will continue and become increasingly important.

Factors in the increase of our exports to the East include the two wars. The Japanese attack upon China resulted in a curtailment of some of Japan's normal peacetime exports, and this trade fell to the United States, particularly that of cotton textiles and light manufactures.

The second war, the European, with its disruption of normal channels of commerce with western Europe, has thrown some important markets to the United States. Some of these sales, indeed, have been of war materials; Netherland India has been an important buyer of American military airplanes.

The confusion in western Europe tends to shift trade to the other hemisphere. Some of this is undoubtedly temporary; but it is probable that some of the temporary gains will be consolidated. It seems extremely unlikely, for example, that normal commercial intercourse will be re-established between Netherland India and the Netherlands for some years to come. The most obvious result of the destruction of the mother country is the corresponding increase in importance of its major colonial possession. This is likely to be reflected in increased purchases from new sources of supply. First among them is the United States.

As would be expected, the exports of the United States to Netherland India are almost entirely fabricated or processed goods; it is not a market for raw materials.

Apart from what has happened in Europe, industrial development is increasing and standards of living are rising in Netherland India, opening the field for the products of American manufacturing. In 1939, for example, we shipped more than two million dollars' worth of automobiles to Netherland India—roughly half of her imports. We shipped another two million dollars' worth of steel mill manufactures—one-eighth of the Netherland India imports. We shipped almost a million dollars' worth of tobacco and the manufactures of tobacco. Of fabricated naval stores, gums, and resins, we shipped goods valued at almost half a million dollars. We are the sole suppliers in this field. We sent out six and one-half million dollars' worth of industrial machinery; a million dollars' worth of electric machinery; almost a million dollars' worth of manufactured paper; half a million dollars' worth of chemical specialties and six million dollars' worth of aircraft.

It was because of the growing need for products of this character that United States exports to Netherland India were rising steadily long before the war started in Europe. From less than four million dollars in 1914, this export trade of the United States rose to more than twenty million by 1918. By 1939 this had risen through a series of fluctuations to more than thirty-five million.

The factors that have brought about this rise in Netherland

Indian imports from the United States are also operating in Malaya and French Indo-China.

The rising standard of living there makes itself felt not only in an increased demand for processed luxury goods, as in the Philippines, but also in the demand for some heavy industrial products, such as automobiles. The mother countries have, in some cases, built the roads. The cars that roll on them, mass-produced for a price market, but sturdy enough to meet all competition, are the product of American factories. They are sweeping the Far Eastern field, as every trade report testifies.

It is not suggested that there is likely to be, in the near future, anything like an even balance between American exports and imports to and from this part of the world, with the exception of the Philippines. It is suggested, however, that the potential market in this area is of very great importance to a considerable group of American commodities, and that, since we are dependent on this particular part of the world for an extremely valuable group of raw materials, we may also enjoy a growing market for our own goods that should shortly amount to a quarter of a billion dollars annually.

The Value of an Outpost

The importance of America's position lies not only in the net value of this buying market but also in our accessibility through it to other important commercial outlets. Our economic position in the Philippines, for example, has often been spoken of as valuable because it is a trading post from which we can reach the still undeveloped market of China and, in doing so, make use of an Asiatic clearing house.

The value of this foothold is much disputed. Certainly much of our trade with Asia can be carried on directly from the American continent. It is debatable how far our trade position would suffer with countries other than the Philippines if we withdrew politically from the Asiatic scene.

Our position in the rest of Asia could be made even more important by correlation of our trade efforts. Several possibilities suggest themselves.

Here is an example. Southern and southwestern China are very important producers of hides. Southern Philippines is one of the world's most important producers of cutch, an essential in tanning. Philippine economy needs new and stable industries and crafts, and there is good and reasonably skillful labor available. It should be sound planning to make use of the conjunction of these two important raw materials to build up an excellent tanning industry in the Philippines, close to a logical market outlet—the Malays are just beginning to wear leather shoes.

The proper use of an outpost, however, may be not only economic, but political as well. Our accessibility to Eastern markets depends not only upon price, but also upon prestige. The channels of trade are dependent in part upon the channels of political influence. This is obviously the case when political influence can shut down trade.

"Face" is part of this selling position. We have gained "face" in China, and it can be of immense economic importance to us. Actual political strength is another factor. Manifestly we cannot sell in a Far Eastern market if an unfriendly power orders us out of it, as in the case of Manchukuo, and if we have not the ability or the willingness to make our presence in the market felt.

In short, our political position is a very important chip in the economic poker game. It enables us to deal with problems of supply and demand on the basis of agreement and not on the basis of surrender to someone else's monopoly.

This is true not only of production, but of commerce as well. Any hostile control of the South China Sea would dominate some of Asia's major ship lanes. The South China Sea is not only the outlet for the products of the countries that surround it. It is a highway of world trade. Just as the Philippines lie athwart the ship lanes into Hong Kong, Manila, Saigon, and Singapore, so Netherland India has control of four great straits. Those straits are the channels for much of the trade with the Americas and Australia, and, if Singapore is included, for much of the European trade of eastern Asia.

It requires no stretch of the imagination to see what would happen to these routes of international commerce if the South China Sea were turned into a Japanese lake. What is at present a position of immense political and economic strength to the whole of the Western world would be turned immediately into a position of tragic commercial weakness by the withdrawal of the United States.

Our stake in southeastern Asia is, accordingly, larger than our own strategic dependence and our own possible profits. We help hold together the entire economic pattern of the South China Sea area. Under the status quo ante, we shared that stake with Britain, France, and the Netherlands.

For that reason, in looking to our own future we should examine the productive economy of the entire area of the South China Sea.

CHAPTER II

OUR STAKE IN
THE SOUTH CHINA SEA—2

Economic Geography

THE circle that we drew on the map is of primary importance to us because of products that we derive from the countries within it. We have observed how some of them, such as rubber and tin, are closely tied up with our standards of living.

Figures in the statistical table of South China Sea exports can be readily translated into items of our own comfort. From that region we get quinine to ward off colds, fight chills and fever in the Ohio Valley, or beat the mosquitoes to dig a Panama Canal. We want soap that will lather in hard water, and we get it from South China Sea coconut oil. Tungsten for our electric-light bulbs, pepper on our tables, cinnamon and sago in our kitchens, ramie in our banknotes and gas mantles, even the derris root in the flea powder that we put on our dogs, all come from the countries bordering the South China Sea. The antimony in the type metal that printed this book was probably mined somewhere southwest of Canton. The kapok in the nearest pillow and the shellac on the nearest table came to the United States, in all probability, in ships from the South China Sea.

The normal productive output of that area for world trade is about a billion and a half dollars annually. Much of it is in products that make our lives comfortable. That output might best be observed at its shipping source in the six great harbors of the South China Sea.

HONG KONG

At the northern edge of the circle on the map is Hong Kong. This rocky little island is one of the strategic outposts of the British Empire, military as well as economic.

Six million tons of shipping normally clear Hong Kong harbor every year. A railroad augmenting the sluggish river channel up to Canton terminates in the Kowloon Leased Territory on the mainland, and through Hong Kong the prodigious riches of the South China hinterland are drained. The ships that bring automobiles, tin plate, steel rails, and electric armatures into Hong Kong carry away to the rest of the world the products of all South China.

Tungsten, perhaps first of all. We got acquainted with it thirty years ago as the trade name for an improved electric-light filament. We know it better now as an essential ingredient in high-speed steels. South China contains about 40 per cent of the world's known deposit of the mineral wolframite, from which tungsten is derived. Through Hong Kong it passes to the steel mills of the world.

Antimony next. Some we get from Mexico. We got more of it from South China before the Japanese moved in. The babbitt-metal bearings in our machines and automobiles, type metal, and even a common medicine, tartar emetic, come from the antimony mines of South China.

Up to 1936 more than half of the world's antimony was mined in South China and cleared over the Hong Kong and Kowloon docks. The Japanese invasion has reduced this supply for export by more than one-half, but the United States still gets its major supplies from this area. Of the thousand tons that we imported in 1939, more than half came from Hong Kong.

Tung oil too is close to our everyday life; when we want to put a coat of quick-drying varnish or enamel on the kitchen chairs, we use tung oil from the trees of China, shipped over the wharves of Hong Kong.

A hundred years ago we went into South China for tea, silk, and ceramics, and they still come up over the Hong Kong docks. Not items of control, of course, in the world market for these products, but part of a substantial trade that moves millions of dollars' worth of merchandise back and forth across the Pacific every year.

There is a flourishing live-stock industry back in southwest

China. There are pig bristles for American hairbrushes; the superior bristles of lean Chinese pigs form a substantial export that has helped to pay for machine guns to fight the Japanese. Ham and eggs are important items in the shipments down across the South China Sea.

And so Hong Kong is more than a naval station, more than a pile of rocks from which to fly the Union Jack; Hong Kong is a great outpost in the trade of the world.

MANILA, "THE PEARL OF THE ORIENT"

Down the South China Sea, on the eastern side, is Manila, major port of the Philippines. A million tons of shipping a year go in and out of the narrow channel that leads into Manila Bay. Pier Seven, the longest covered pier in the world, is the scene of the loading and unloading of two hundred million dollars' worth of merchandise every year, three-fourths of which is United States trade.

Sugar, first of all—850,000 long tons of it every year. Copra and coconut oil for American soap factories—200,000 tons of oil, 150,000 tons of copra in a normal year. Cordage—mile upon mile of manila rope, for tugboats from Boston to Jacksonville. Bales of manila hemp for the binder twine of the wheat fields of the United States and Canada.

Philippine cigars—five cents or two for a nickel. Hundreds upon hundreds of thousands of them every year are rolled up by hand in the factories around Manila. Rich aromatic tobacco of the fields of the Cagayan Valley is wrapped in leaf from Connecticut or Sumatra and smoked from New York to San Francisco.

Mother-of-pearl, taken by divers down in Jolo, supplies the factories that button the shirts of the world. This shell trade to the United States alone has ranged from a half to three-quarters of a million dollars a year.

Embroidery and clothing—millions of dollars' worth of it every year. In 1938 the trade figures were: cotton wearing apparel, $5,-651,000; cotton laces and embroidery, $367,000. More than six million dollars' worth of goods shipped to the United States in one year alone, and not a particularly good year at that. At times in the past, the embroidery trade alone has topped the ten-million-dollar mark.

We might translate these statistics into the thousands of baby dresses, little embroidered bibs, lingerie, and the familiar embroidered voile dresses—a large volume of reasonably priced hand-work for American consumers. A substantial part of the 125,000,000 square yards of cotton cloth that the United States sent to the Philippines in 1938, for example, was returned to us as useful consumer goods.

Every now and then, Philippine Constabulary guards accompany an armored car to Pier Seven, and a trans-Pacific liner takes aboard a shipment, small in bulk, that is kept under lock and key on the voyage. Philippine gold.

Just forty years ago they turned out the bands in Seattle and flashed the news all over the country that a million dollars in gold bars had come down from Alaska in one shipment. In 1939 twenty trans-Pacific ships put in at Seattle or San Francisco, carrying a million dollars each, without even getting into the newspapers. Philippine shipments of gold are now so big and so regular that they have become an economic commonplace.

Manila is one of the most beautiful natural harbors in the world. It is ringed by splendid mountains on the west, and the Bay, twenty-five miles across, washes the great Luzon coastal plain on the north, east, and south. The combined fleets of the whole world could find anchorage in that bay.

Its great importance, however, is as a shipping point. Manila is the outlet to the world for those multiplied acres of sugar, coconuts, and tobacco, those towering mountainsides with their scores of producing gold mines, and their still unbroached reserves of millions of tons of iron, chromite, and manganese.

"Paris of the Far East"

Across the South China Sea is Saigon. Its approach is a half-day trip up the sluggish winding Dong Nei River. While the steamships work their way up to the quaysides, the flat-bottomed barges of the Cambodians and the Annamese push down the river with their great loads of sacked rice. French Indo-China is a major granary of East Asia. It is not the greatest of the rice producers—India, China, and Japan outrank it. But French Indo-China, Burma, and Thailand are the only rice-producing countries that have a steady and reliable surplus for export. The extent of French Indo-China's rice cultivation may be judged from the fact that there are more than 5,000,000 acres of rice on the Mekong Delta alone. Saigon is Asia's insurance against a rice famine. When there is a drought in Japan, or a typhoon in the Philippines, or an insect pest in Java, the merchants of those countries congregate on the wharfside at Saigon and bid for the *elon-elon* of French Indo-China.

The trade of Indo-China with the Western world has been growing steadily for two decades. In 1938, for example, we bought 28 per cent of our rubber from French Indo-China. Tin is being mined and shipped down to Malaya for smelting.

Moreover, French Indo-China has been for some years one of our important sources of rattans. Forty different usable species have already been identified in this colony, and it may eventually become as important to us as Netherland India, now our major source of this product. Gums, resins, and shellacs are also among the products that go into the trade with the United States.

The economy of French Indo-China has been, in the past, more closely tied up with the mother country than that of some of the other colonies of the South China Sea. Under normal conditions about two-thirds of the total trade was with France. The French collapse changed this situation; Japan at once began making efforts to gain a dominant position in the trade of French Indo-China through barter agreements. It is too soon to tell how this will work out.

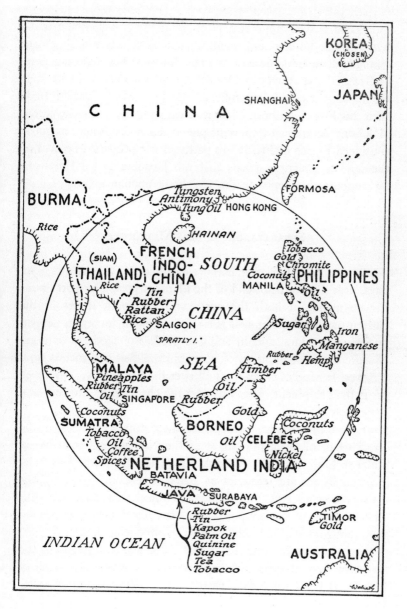

Even prior to the European war, the United States had begun to assume a more important position in the Indo-Chinese trade. The opening up of direct American steamship service into Saigon eliminated some of the cost of trans-shipment through Singapore, and caused the American Department of Commerce in its 1938 report to speak very hopefully of the probable growth of trade with this French outpost. Moreover, with the blockade of Canton, Haiphong became an important port of entry for American goods consigned to free China. It was partly, if not primarily, because of the flow of American goods that the Japanese closed Haiphong by stopping shipments on the Haiphong-Yunnan railway.

SURABAYA, SOUTH SEAS METROPOLIS

The fourth of the great harbors enclosed in our circle is Surabaya, near the northeast end of the island of Java. This port drains the commerce of both the north and the south shores of the eastern part of the island. It is a shipping point for sugar, pepper, and tea from Java, and in addition clears the products of other islands. It takes shipments of peanuts from Bali and metals from Celebes. It handles copra from all over the South Seas. The scope of its trans-shipments gives this port the character and feeling of a little metropolis.

Of first importance, perhaps, in these trans-shipments is the handling of oil from the largest of the Netherland operations in the Far East, the field at Balik Papen on the eastern shore of Borneo. There are refineries at Balik Papen, and some of the tankers load directly. But Surabaya is the control port, and it is therefore one of the key positions of the Royal Dutch-Shell combine that exploits the world's fourth oil-producing area.

Surabaya is an important station for tourists. At one end of the Bali-Java ferry, it offers the best hotel accommodations south of Manila. It is a terminus of the trans-Java railway and gives access to Djokjakarta, the batik of Java, and the mystery of Borobadur.

The position that makes it important to the traveler gives Surabaya some of its importance to the economist. It is a way station on the lines of commerce. It is a clearing house for the strange and rather loosely organized part of Netherland India called the Outer Provinces. It is the approach, not only to beautiful Bali and ponderous Borneo, but also to the islands of Celebes, Timor, Flores, New Guinea and the Moluccas.

BATAVIA, SPICE COUNTER OF THE WORLD

The next great port, Batavia, is at the western end of Java. The great whitewashed port itself, northeast of the city, is a magnificent roadstead of immense facilities. Here Batavia clears the rubber, tea, coffee, spices, and sugar of the enormously productive western and southern shore of the island of Java.

Batavia itself is almost a Netherland city. European architecture has been adapted to the tropics, and there is neatness and order everywhere. Nevertheless, a hundred yards from the cocktail terrace of the best of a half-dozen good hotels is an open canal where a thousand laundry-women do their daily washing.

Back of and around this European city is the immense sprawling city of the Javanese. It is clean and orderly as the Javanese are clean and orderly. It stretches back to the hillsides and emerges finally into the small clearings where each foot of land is cultivated, and on up to the great botanical gardens at Buitenzorg.

Batavia has been important as the terminus of the steamship and air lines between the Netherlands and Netherland India. It is the capital of the great sprawling archipelago. It is the clearing house for the bulk of a trade of more than a half-billion dollars a year. Back of Batavia lie the quinine plantations. Cinchona bark was first discovered in Peru, but it is Java that now turns out the world's supply. Its share at the present time is 99.6 per cent.

On those hills of western Java grow most of the world's pepper trees. We buy more than three million dollars' worth of pepper out of Batavia every year.

Sago is also an item in the daily quotations of Batavia; Java is the world's most important source of supply.

The whole harbor at Batavia is aromatic, because this is the spice pantry of the world. The Javanese cooks on the ships going in and out of Batavia put cinnamon on everything. They hardly need to; the aroma of cinnamon is so strong that even a fried onion tastes of it. The only major spice of the world that does not come primarily from Netherland India is cloves, produced in Zanzibar.

Copra warehouses are everywhere, of course. Batavia is one of the clearing points for the coconut traffic of the South Seas. They ship less from that part of the world than from the Philippines, where the industry is more concentrated, but hundreds of little steamers come in from all the outlying islands with cargoes of dried nut meat that will be shipped across the channel to Singapore for milling.

Up until fifteen years ago the major export product of Batavia was sugar. But the world's market was flooded when the two great low-cost producers—Java and Cuba—were joined by a dozen other sugar-producing areas. So sugar limitation by agreement came into existence, and the Java output was cut to about a million and a half tons a year. Before that, Java had at times surpassed even Cuba as a sugar producer. If the restrictions were taken off now, Java's production could be jumped to three million tons within eighteen months. At one time there was warehoused in Batavia enough sugar to meet the needs of all of the United States, the largest sugar consumer in the world, for more than six months. The famous PO-J sugar cane that was found to be the best producer for the tropics was developed only a few miles southeast of Batavia.

Coffee and tea also cross the wharves at Batavia. Java is one of our synonyms for coffee, and it may very well be, because Java is the third coffee producer in the world. Netherland India's output in 1937, for example, was 217,969,000 pounds. We do not get much Java coffee in the United States. Most of it for years has been going to the European market.

Netherland India is also one of the world's greatest tea producers. It is outranked in exports only by Assam and Ceylon. Its total production is certainly not equal to China's or Japan's, but its export trade in tea is a major factor in the world's markets.

Some of the oil from the workings up on the Sumatra coast is cleared through Batavia. While Sumatra ships some of its oil direct to Singapore, there is no great harbor on the whole great island of Sumatra. Batavia meets this need.

Singapore, at the Asiatic Crossroads

Across the channel is the greatest of the southeastern Asiatic harbors, incredible Singapore. Six thousand ships enter the harbor every year. A normal tonnage clearance is 16,000,000.

This is the greatest crossroads for the commerce of Asia. It is, first of all, the drainage point for the immense colony of British Malaya, whence it derives the bulk of its rubber and tin. Singapore dominates and controls the world market of both these basic products.

But Singapore is more than the port of British Malaya; it is the clearing house for all of the great Far Eastern trade. Netherland India clears more than a third of its products through this British way station. Thailand and Burma ship to Singapore first and thence to the markets of the world.

It is pre-eminently a city of merchants. Four hundred thousand Chinese live in Singapore—in this British city at the tip of the Malay Peninsula. Even the street signs are printed in Chinese. The whole city is a collection of warehouses. It is a gigantic wholesale bazaar.

The roadstead itself is not prepossessing. It has none of the natural beauty of Hong Kong or Manila. Ships lie at anchor, often out in the Strait, and it is not always calm. Thousands of sampans swarm around them. Only one ship in ten ties up to the dock. Barges, scows, and tugs move this body of freight from land to ship. Loading and unloading go on incessantly.

The name Singapore has become to many persons a synonym for

all that is Asiatic, lawless, free from restraint, wicked, and wonderful. Very little of that emotional picture is true, but Singapore has an identity far more important and far more fascinating than that, imposed by its Hollywood halo. Singapore is the city, first and last, of commerce. It is to modern Asia what Venice was to the Renaissance. It is the distributor of safety pins from Connecticut, flashlight bulbs from Osaka, Argentine beef, Kimberley diamonds, and, above all, rubber, tin, copra, and oil. It has the largest refinery plants and the largest storage tanks in eastern Asia. It is the heart of the oil-producing and oil-distributing business east of Arabia and west of California.

When the British decided to build a naval base at Singapore, they must have been thinking about strategic location from the military point of view. They must have been thinking even more of the necessity of guarding and preserving a position in world trade—a post of exchange as important to the South China Sea area as London to the British Isles or New York to the United States.

The interchange of products among these six great ports, and the supply from them to the rest of the world, are factors unifying the areas within the circle we have drawn. In this comparatively remote corner of the world are exercised the outright monopolies of Manila hemp and quinine. There is control of the world's markets in rubber and tin, coconuts, rice, spices, sago, tungsten, and tung oil. Within that circle are produced other major exports to the world: coffee, tea, petroleum, iron, chromium, antimony, manganese, sugar, and even fish.

This is the world's storehouse, a producer of raw materials beyond comparison. Our relation to this storehouse and our access to it must necessarily determine our future in Asia.

ECONOMIC TUG OF WAR

The presence of such riches has made this part of the world the object of an economic tug of war. Our future there, like our past and present, is influenced by the agreements that have been made with other powers and by the concessions that have been offered and given. Since these colonies afford such large producing agencies and such large markets they have naturally been the subject of treaties and counter-treaties, of regulations and agreements in the whole field of world trade.

In the decade between 1920 and 1930, this economic tug of war was partly expressed in the efforts to gain monopolies of certain major products, or, failing that, to allocate production quotas. The first struggle was over oil. The Royal Dutch-Shell combine was not itself large enough to dominate the world market, but it was large enough to prevent anyone else from doing so. This association of British and Netherland petroleum interests became, therefore, a major factor in the understanding between the two mother countries.

In 1924 the first steps were taken to get some stability in the production of sugar. As the result of World War expansion there was a tremendous surplus, and to meet the problem the Chadbourne Plan of limitation was devised. This reduced the output of the two largest sugar producers, Java and Cuba. Javanese sugar was cut to about half of its previous level and remains there. This has necessitated a reorganization of the Javanese economy.

Since the South China Sea area controls the bulk of production of both rubber and tin, it was natural that limitation of output and allocation of quotas should be applied in an effort to sustain price levels.

It is usually believed that the British, shortly after the World War, undertook an outright drive for the complete monopoly of the world's rubber output. They are said to have come within a small fraction of obtaining it. Presumably this ambitious plan was thwarted by the enterprise of certain American consumers who at once undertook to go into the production field. In any case, there were some months of "touch and go" in the rubber situation until an agreement on output was reached and a stabilization effected.

The tin situation is roughly analogous to that of rubber. There has been the necessity of getting a working agreement between the world's largest producer, Malaya, and the world's largest consumer, the United States. This has been done through the establishment of quotas sufficiently restricted to maintain the price of the product, but sufficiently elastic to allow for expansion from time to time to meet the needs of the United States.

The system of quota limitation that has been applied to the Philippines differs in part from these other quota allocations in that it is designed primarily to affect only the relationship between Philippine products and the United States market. Limitations of sugar and coconut oil from the Philippines were actually a part of all the Philippine independence legislation that was drafted in the United States. They were effected, moreover, by the government, acting as a unit in economic policy making, rather than by individual private organizations seeking a method of control of production, as in the case of the rubber, tin, and sugar agreements.

The sugar limitation, as a government-operated policy, fitted, of course, into the privately organized and sponsored Chadbourne Plan, but it was not necessarily part of it, for the reason that the Philippines had not been considered a special entity in relation to this program. The actual limitation of sugar production in the Philippines was taken out of the field of independence legislation by the drafting of the quite separate Jones-Costigan Law that restricted Philippine sales to the United States to about 850,000 long tons annually, and provided for the application of the American system of benefit refunds for non-production.

Limitation of cordage output was also made the subject of separate legislation by the United States, and the Philippine quota of 6,000,000 pounds annually was fixed arbitrarily.

The production of coconut oil was likewise limited, in the independence legislation, to 200,000 long tons annually.

Theoretically, these limitations applied only to the United States market. In practice, Philippine production costs were so high that markets other than the United States were extremely unlikely, and the limitation applied in effect to the world market as well.

MEETING A MARKET CRASH

Some of these agreements preceded the world-wide economic crash of 1929 and 1930. Others, such as the American limitations, grew directly out of it. That general economic recession, however, had its sharpest effect on the economic organization of Netherland India. In 1933 the Netherland Government decided that the problem of declining export markets, and the consequent decline of the favorable balance of trade enjoyed by Netherland India, had to be met by drastic reorganization of domestic structures. As a result there were put into effect the so-called "Crisis Decrees" that took Netherland India out of the field of free marketing and into the field of controlled economy.

These decrees had two large effects. The first was to channel and freeze imports, so as to reduce purchasing; the second was to allocate export quotas through a careful system of registration and regulation of production so that a maximum profit could be made in a world of falling prices. This was primarily a domestic economic policy of the Netherlands for Netherland India, but it had profound political repercussions, as we shall see a little later on.

The next important large-scale influence on the economic tug of war in southeastern Asia was the tremendous growth of Japanese export trade in the twelve years, 1920 to 1932. The Japanese entered the field of large-scale cotton textile exports with a vigor that could not be denied. They were demanding a place in the Far Eastern market and they could undersell anything in sight. In the beginning it was the policy of other countries to keep out Japanese goods, as far as possible, by high tariffs. The British, for example, had a cotton-spinning and -weaving industry in Manchester to protect; in the United States there were exporters in Massachusetts to be considered.

There were, however, some advantages to be gained by some type of concession to Japanese pressure. In the first place, Japan afforded a good export market for some of the raw materials of southeastern Asia. She was willing, for example, to increase her purchases of Javanese sugar, and Javanese sugar was a drug on the market in the darkest days of the depression. In the early thirties Japan was getting 25 per cent of her petroleum products from the Royal Dutch-Shell combine and was eager to increase these purchases to 35 per cent and probably more. Japan was the largest off-shore purchaser of manila hemp, and was putting on pressure to increase purchases of Philippine hardwood, particularly logs. She was also a good customer for Malayan tin and the greatest prospective customer for Philippine iron.

The second factor in favor of some type of agreement with the Japanese was the fact that the Japanese could supply low-cost merchandise to the native populations. In so far as keeping down costs of living was an item in the end-cost of raw materials, and, therefore, an item in the margin of profit, it was good business to let the native workman buy a Japanese shirt for a dime instead of an American shirt for twenty-nine cents or a Lancashire shirt for two shillings. This was true in the whole field of small merchandising.

One school of thought, particularly vocal in the Philippines, held that it was better to pay a dollar for a shirt, and have the dollar to pay for it, than to see the shirt offered for a dime and have only nine cents. With declining export markets, however, these proponents of an even greater degree of local tariff protection lacked the best basis for their argument—that is, having the dollar. It had dropped by this time to sixty-three cents in terms of export trade. Consequently a series of agreements with the Japanese was drawn up and executed.

The most important of the British agreements was not concerned primarily with the Malayan market. It was concerned with the larger Indian market where the Japanese had already been making inroads. An exchange was consummated and a quota for Japanese imports established.

This had its repercussions, however, on Malaya, and necessitated a revision of some of the import strictures that had existed at Singapore.

Netherland India went into a straight quid pro quo agreement under which Japan increased her purchases of Netherland India sugar and obtained larger access to the Netherland India market for cotton textiles and small manufactures.

TENNIS SHOES FOR FIFTEEN CENTS

The Philippines undertook to meet Japanese commercial expansion, first, by a series of higher tariffs. One of the most important items in Japanese export trade with the Philippines in 1930 and 1931 was rubber-soled shoes. The Philippine market was growing enormously and the Japanese were putting down these shoes in Manila to sell at around fifteen cents a pair. They were inferior merchandise. I tried some of them out on Manila tennis courts and the crushed shell surface went through the rubber soles of those Japanese shoes in less than three weeks. The average Filipino out in the country probably did not give them such hard wear.

Charges of dumping were made, and it would seem unlikely that the merchandise could have been produced and shipped at so low a cost and still allow anything for profit. So the Philippines went into action with tariff legislation. A "Merchants Protective Association" (backed by Japanese capital) was immediately formed to lobby against the tariff proposals. It was urged, and not without reason, that the Japanese were meeting a market need. The legislation went through, however, and the rubber shoe dumping ended.

But within three months rubber-soled shoe factories, presumably backed by Japanese capital, and certainly under the management of Japanese technicians, made their appearance in the suburbs of Manila, safely inside the tariff wall.

It was cotton textiles, however, that proved to be the real battleground between Japanese and American interests. The Philippines had been for some years the best off-shore market for American cotton textiles, consuming annually about one hundred million square meters. Part of this was the base material for Philippine embroidery, to be re-shipped to the United States, but most of it was the material with which the Filipino clothed himself.

Very early in the depression the Japanese began to make real inroads into the Philippine market. In one year they reduced American participation in that market from more than 90 per cent to less than 70 per cent. When they had brought the American percentage down to the low sixties, American producers and importers became gravely alarmed. A drastic cotton tariff schedule was drafted in the Philippines and Philippine legislative leaders pledged their assent to it.

In 1934, however, this proposed legislation was dramatically taken out of the Philippine scheme by the conclusion of the "Gentlemen's Agreement" on textiles between the United States and Japan. The Philippines had had no warning whatever that this was coming, and the first reaction in protectionist circles was one of profound resentment.

The position of the American State Department was that nothing could be gained from an attempt arbitrarily to shut the Japanese out of a logical market and that much could be gained in international amity by allowing them a reasonable place.

Under the terms of the agreement, Philippine consumption was estimated at approximately 90 million square meters, and half of this was accorded to Japan. Naturally, as consumption increased, the American importer would profit, the Japanese would at least have access to a large-scale market, and the Philippines would have the advantage of low-cost goods.

The agreement was acceptable to most Philippine leaders, but within a year objection was made that the terms of the agreement were being frequently violated by the Japanese. The agreement covered textiles originating in Japan. Over these the Japanese Government was presumed to have sufficient control to enforce the limitations of the agreement. There is no reason to believe that exports from Japan proper ever entered in substantial violation of the agreement; however, Japanese capital controlled important textile mills in Shanghai, and their merchandise could be admitted as the produce of China. There was, moreover, an extremely suspicious rise in textiles trans-shipped by way of Hong Kong. These textiles came in labeled "Originating in Hong Kong." It was suspected that they were Japanese in origin, but there were no terms of agreement by which they could be stopped, and the Japanese themselves made the plea that their control could be exercised only on exports from Japan proper. Here again there was no ground upon which to challenge their good faith.

The restriction on cotton textiles also had a profound effect on the shipments of rayons to the Philippines. Japanese shipments of this material jumped prodigiously in the first two years of the agreement.

As time went on it became more and more apparent that the "Gentlemen's Agreement" was a very good thing in conception and in theory, but that in practice it needed further attention to a number of details before it could adequately safeguard the interests of the United States and at the same time accord to Japan the market, and only the market, that was originally contemplated.

The course of the China War suddenly made the whole question academic. By channeling her imports into the war materials industries and cutting down on purchases of raw cotton, Japan in 1938 drastically reduced the available export textiles. As a result the Japanese fell far short of their quota under the "Gentlemen's Agreement" and have not filled it since. American textiles have come into a dominant position in the Philippines.

These are incidents in the course of economic adjustments made necessary by the productive power and the buying strength of these outposts of empire. These adjustments reflect an effort to meet the facts of the situation and in some cases to make genuine concessions. They have their foundation in a desire to maintain an economic and political status quo that has proved advantageous. Their operation in the entire productive field and in relation to the economic geography of the South China Sea area is a part of the American stake in southeastern Asia.

CHAPTER III

OUR STAKE IN
THE SOUTH CHINA SEA—3

Our Political Neighbors

J UST as the United States has an economic interest in preserving the productive status quo in the area of the South China Sea, so has it a political interest as well.

The productive unity of these colonies is the counterpart of a political unity, for the South China Sea is bordered by the four major Asiatic outposts of four Western democracies. These outposts have been the frontiers of presumably competing empires, but the profits for all have been sufficient to reduce friction to a minimum. The relations of the mother countries have, for fifty years, been friendly, and this has been reflected in the relations of the colonies to each other.

The stability of the political structures made possible the profitable economic structures, and the friendship of the mother countries was a guarantee of security.

There was an obvious community of interest in the preservation of an empire structure that was profitable to all. That community of interest took on an even sharper significance when the European war put the four Western democratic empires in the same ideological camp. They were naturally aligned in defense of the same political ideal and the same economic program, that is, the maintenance of free government and profitable capitalism. Whether or not this political ideal survives will have the utmost effect upon the maintenance of the political status quo of the colonies.

In the Far Eastern relationship of the colonies of the Western democracies probably the most important single factor has been the fact that none of the mother countries was politically ambitious. The importance of such a situation in keeping the Far Eastern peace can hardly be over-estimated.

Here four great colonial outposts have lain closely contiguous, and yet for more than half a century no one of them has tried to extend its frontiers at the expense of another. Borneo and New Guinea, each geographically a unit, were divided arbitrarily between the British and the Netherlands, and they have afforded a striking demonstration of the validity of even the faintest frontiers when the good will of both parties is assumed. The boundary between the Philippines and North Borneo has at times been under discussion because of the claims of sovereignty of the Sultan of Sulu. Yet this question has never caused more than trifling irritation, and no problem has arisen that could not be solved immediately by amicable discussion.

This lack of political ambition on the part of four great empires created an informal status quo in the whole area within our circle. That status quo had been found profitable and satisfactory to each of the four powers. The pursuits of empire could be followed by each and by all without political infringement on any other.

This peaceful unity existed in spite of somewhat different relations between the various colonies and their mother countries. No two of these colonies could use quite the same language to express the ties that existed between them and the democracies of the West.

LIFE-LINE OF THE NETHERLANDS

Take the case of Netherland India as a first example. I was talking to a Dutch officer down at Batavia several years ago. I asked him particularly about this tie that bound a sprawling archipelago in southeast Asia to a tiny mother country in the northwest of Europe.

"It is very simple," he explained. "That tie is the Netherland life-line. We exist as a first-class political power in western Europe because we are a first-class economic power in southeastern Asia. The Empire has to show a profit because without a profit the mother country would disappear."

This situation created a peculiar intimacy between Netherland India and the Netherlands. The development of wealth in the colonial possession was a matter of investment by about fifteen commercial enterprises in the home country. Some of these were owned directly by the government itself, or by the Crown. The productivity of the colony was, therefore, a matter of immediate concern to these very large family and commercial structures in the Netherlands. The cost of labor on a pepper or rubber planta- tion on the southern shore of Java would be translated immediately into fractions in the quotations on the Stock Exchange in Rotterdam.

At the same time the Netherlands developed an economic philosophy for the colony that was by no means as closely knit as this political-economic tie would indicate. For more than a century it had been held by the Netherlands that the economy of the colony should be essentially a free economy. The colony's goods should not be merely channeled to the home country but should go into the markets of the world as free as possible from restriction. Similarly the imports of the colony should be directed to those channels where purchases could be most advantageously made, in order that a substantial favorable balance of trade for the colony could always be maintained.

This balance of trade was the index of profits in the Netherlands. But it presupposed a complete duality of economy in the colony.

There was one economic standard for native life and one for European life. There was, therefore, little or no incentive to raise the standard of living of the native population, since production and not colonial purchasing power was the index of the success of the relationship of the colony to the mother country.

The function of government was, therefore, politically paternal- istic. It was economically paternalistic only in so far as paternalism would serve the ends of the dual standard. Hence arose the famous characterization of Netherland policy: "Keep their heads empty and their bellies full," which has been thrown up to the Netherlanders as a stigma upon their colonial history.

The implications of that accusation are not quite fair. Their policy has possibly never been as deliberate as that expression would indicate, and while there was great misgovernment for the sake of profits for many years, there has been in the last fifty years a profound amelioration.

This has taken two forms. The first is the guaranteeing of property and land rights to the native population; the alienation of land has been rigidly forbidden. The second is the recognition of the right of the native population to a larger voice in its own affairs. There has grown up, gradually, the Volksrad, a popular native assembly, to which increasing prerogatives have been assigned. It may go over the head of the Governor in petitions to the Crown. It may not legislate except with the Governor's consent, but it can, at the very least, make its voice heard. The new responsibilities that it has faced since early 1940 have given it increasing importance.

FUNCTIONS OF A "PROTECTORATE"

The relationship of the French colony of Indo-China to the French Republic was economically similar to that of the Netherland colony, but quite different politically. French Indo-China showed a profit for the mother country expressed primarily in a favorable balance of trade in the colony. French Indo-China steadily sold much more than it bought, and the bulk of the profit went to France.

In contrast to this close-knit economy the political government of French Indo-China was theoretically a very loose-jointed affair. Actually it has been a rather vigorous piece of colonial administration.

French Indo-China was set up as a system of four protectorates, one colony, and one special territory. The protectorates were exercised over Annam, Tongking, Cambodia, and Laos. The special territory was Kwangchow-wan, a small area around Kwangchow Bay in South China. This was acquired in 1900. The colony was Cochin China, the original foothold of France in the Far East.

French influence in the South China Sea area goes back to 1787. At that time treaties for French assistance were made with local war lords in the Cochin China area. The French extended this nominally military assistance through missionary and commercial activity for the next fifty years.

The native populations were not entirely receptive to Western penetration and by 1858 there had been numerous massacres of Europeans and of Annamese Christians. As a result of these outbreaks France undertook active intervention in 1858 and three years later conducted an extended series of military campaigns under Admiral Charner. As a result of these campaigns the three Eastern Provinces were ceded to France in 1862.

The initial administration of this newly acquired territory was under the Ministry of Marine, and the "Administration of the Admirals" lasted from 1863 to 1879. During that period the three Western Provinces of Cochin China were annexed and a protectorate over Cambodia was assumed. This protectorate was taken over nominally under the formality of a treaty.

Annam, a vassal state of China, was taken over also as a protectorate in 1884 and 1885, and a group of treaties establishing the validity of these protectorates was signed with China in 1895.

In 1891, meanwhile, the entire administration was transferred to the French Ministry of Colonies, and the Governor-General of French Indo-China received the necessary centralized and unified powers of administration for the entire area.

This administration involved a plan for progressive autonomy but kept ultimate authority in the hands of the Governor-General as the representative of the French Ministry. Cochin China, as the original colony, had a high degree of self-rule almost from the beginning. It had its own colonial council, and a deputy in the

French Parliament. The authority of the Governor-General in the provinces, however, was exercised through Residents-General.

The partially elected Council of Government undertook the unification of legislative function for the entire Far Eastern colonial empire. This Superior Council of Indo-China included native members, acted particularly on matters of the budget, and had a permanent mission as a unifying agency, since the council itself might be called first in one district and then another.

The administration of law was, in part, a compromise. An Annamese code was established in 1917 but theoretically French law and French courts were supreme in principle throughout the colony. Native law and native courts, however, continued to function in their respective areas, and the French undertook to leave as much as possible to their jurisdiction whenever French nationals or French interests were not involved.

This, indeed, was characteristic of the whole French administration. The forms of local sovereignty were scrupulously preserved. The French followed the pattern of recognizing in form and in theory the most flamboyant of the native sovereignties. Theoretically the governmental functions of the colony were carried out simply through a friendly protectorate over, and alliance with, the native sovereigns. The sacredness of these imperial personages was preserved and the French were scrupulously careful to pay due respect to their dignity and to call upon their loyalty in the alliance that was formed.

Actually, through the offices of the Governor-General, the French Republic and the French Colonial Office exercised complete authority. There was no representation of the native will as opposed to the French will.

As a result there were many cases of friction between the French and the native rulers or factions. These frictions from time to time necessitated the use of force on the part of the French and there was colonial administration at the point of the bayonet. On the other hand there was a large body of native opinion that supported French rule, and it was possible to maintain close political ties

with the mother country without sending large expeditionary forces
and with the co-operation of the native groups themselves.

How Malaya Is "Ruled"

The ties between British Malaya and Great Britain are again
somewhat different and even more complex. The political organization of British Malaya is without an exact parallel. It has three
parts. There is, first of all, the Straits Settlements, a small but
powerful colony, embracing two great cities and ports, Singapore
and Penang. Then there is the group of Malay States that are
"Federated." Representatives of these States act for their common
good at a common capital and are able to make their wishes known,
as a unit, to the British authorities. There is a larger group of
so-called "Unfederated" States and these preserve the fiction of
independent self-rule under British protection.

Each of these States is governed by its own Sultan or other local
ruler. These local rulers are recognized and honored by the British
government and to them is left the administration of local law,
much of the police function, and minor governmental enterprises.
The British Resident in each case is the real power behind the
local state. Theoretically, his work is done largely in an advisory
capacity, but actually he is the representative of the Crown, carrying out the policies of the Governor and of the Ministry of
Colonies at home.

The relationship of British Malaya to Britain and the Empire
is expressed not so much in these superficial political structures as
in Malaya's gigantic plantation system. The plantation is the real
unit of administration. Conditions are as good or as bad as the
plantation is well or badly administered.

British Malaya is singular, perhaps, in that there is no appreciable
native nationalist movement. It is politically the least self-conscious
of all the British colonies. It is primarily trade-conscious because
the price of tin, the quota for rubber, and the market for pine-

apples are more important to the operations of the country than
the forms of government. British Malaya's relation to the mother
country is expressed therefore rather in terms of trade than in
terms of sovereignty.

THE PHILIPPINES: DEMOCRACY IN EMBRYO

The political structure of the Philippines is unique in Asia. The
Philippines are at the opposite extreme from the other colonies,
in that autonomy, to the greatest possible degree, has been encouraged from the outset. The result is that the Filipino is probably
more politically self-conscious than any other Asiatic, not exclud-
ing even the Japanese.

The American policy has been extremely paternalistic, both
politically and economically. This has had its effect on the standards of living all over the Philippines and on the development of a
political potential that makes self-government possible. The United
States had deliberately restricted the exercise of its sovereignty
even before independence legislation was contemplated, and as a
result the ties between the Philippines and the mother country
may be said to be largely voluntary on both sides.

This democracy in embryo is so important a part of the whole
relation of the United States to Asia that it will be discussed in
detail later.

FAR EASTERN STABILITY

In spite of the apparent diversity of political organization there
has grown up a surprising unity of outlook in this area, because it
has enjoyed what is now so gravely threatened, that is, stability.

This is of great importance, not merely to the mother empires,
but to the colonies themselves. Their growing political self-
consciousness has been possible because for more than forty years
they have been protected from any drastic changes in sovereignty

and from any involvement in political expansion of predatory neighbors. They have been able to discuss their ability to govern themselves because they have not had to be concerned with the problem of defending themselves. Their hope for increasing liberty, just as our hope for increasing profit, is bound up with the preservation of political stability in this area.

The United States has an important part in preserving that stability; the European war has made our strength the most important factor in it. The preservation of stability is a part of our stake in southeastern Asia.

In maintaining stability we are defending not only the Malays, for whom we have assumed much responsibility, but also the empire structures that are threatened in Europe. Our withdrawal from the Asiatic scene would subject those friendly governments to double pressure and would immediately bring about the most drastic changes in the South China Sea area. The British position in all of Asia would be changed immediately. Our withdrawal from the southeastern Asiatic scene would compel the British retirement from the entire China coast and the abandonment of the British Empire outposts at Shanghai and Hong Kong.

The French position would be hopelessly compromised and there would be no possibility for Indo-China other than immediate annexation by Japan.

The Netherland position would be irreparably damaged, because the very intimation of American withdrawal would give the green light to aggression. Aggression would be possible not only in the political but in the physical sense. The presentation of the Philippines to Japan means opening to the Japanese a land bridge from Formosa to Borneo and thence to the remainder of Netherland India.

Our political stake in the South China Sea involves the future of all the Western democratic empires. We are in a position to assist them on the Asiatic frontier, or to strike them a death blow, depending upon the degree to which we realize the importance of our Asiatic policy.

CHAPTER IV

THREATS TO THE STATUS QUO—I

The Question of Empire

WE HAVE observed that the United States has a very considerable stake in the preservation of the status quo in southeastern Asia. It is not to be supposed that we would contemplate abandoning our position without some cogent reasons. Similarly we cannot discuss the possible defense of this area without an understanding of the threats to its stability.

The first threat to our position in the South China Sea does not come from Tokyo or Berlin. It comes from Washington, Philadelphia, Chicago, and the thousand and one small American towns in which opinion is crystallized and the basis laid for American policy. We face the danger, not of a disastrous naval engagement, but of a conviction that we should retire from our Asiatic position before a shot is fired. The first threat to our status as an empire with an important holding in Asia is the American objection to empire itself.

We assumed the functions of an economic empire, in respect to Asia, in the slow processes of building up a Pacific trade, primarily with China, and defending our equality in commercial rights. We became a political empire in Asia back-handedly, as the result of the Spanish-American War and our acquisition of the Philippines in the settlement of a conflict whose focus had been the Caribbean and not the Pacific.

The objections to empire were first of all sentimental, and it is probable that in the sum total of American opinion those sentimental considerations still play a larger part than do the military and economic arguments that were evolved somewhat later.

The first phase of this sentimental objection to an American "empire" is a heritage from the campaign oratory of William Jennings Bryan. In the semantic sense he is probably the first prominent American to make "empire" a bad word. He spoke with the colorful inaccuracy of the demagogue, and his listeners were not concerned primarily with economic foreign policy, when he made "empire" synonymous with predatory attacks upon helpless peoples and types of government and types of mind entirely incompatible with democracy.

The specific clash at the time was whether or not the United States, as the result of the Spanish-American War, should extend its sovereignty over certain islands in the Caribbean and the Pacific that had been dramatically misgoverned by Spain. Since the Republican party was committed to the assumption of American sovereignty over these islands, it was natural that Mr. Bryan should tag such a course of action as "imperialist" and as part of a conspiracy of the political opposition against free government.

Indication that Mr. Bryan's position was opportunist, rather than the fruit of any deep conviction, is the fact that he could preach the wickedness of "imperialistic" domination over subject peoples while deriving the bulk of his political support from the deep South, where domination over the Negro was taken as a matter of course. It is hard, now, to get excited about Mr. Bryan's concern over the down-trodden Filipino when it is remembered how substantially he counted on the votes of Louisiana, Alabama, and Georgia.

Mr. Bryan succeeded, however, in convincing many Americans that there was something wrong with empire as such. The word took on all the unpleasant associations that could be evoked for it. It was made the antithesis of democracy and therefore anathema to the democratic-minded American. That conception still persists in many minds. I have observed it, personally, in the attitude of members of the Congress of the United States when they came to the Philippines to see what had been done by American administration. They held emphatically that the United States could be an empire only against its will, and that it would release itself from that unfortunate political classification at the first opportunity.

This sentimental objection, now rather old on the American scene, has been supplemented in the last decade by another sentimental use of "imperialist" as a bad word. This is the fruit of influences arising largely from the Russian revolution and the Soviet experiment. In this school of sentiment "imperialist" is made synonymous with "capitalist" or "monopolist" and therefore something to be condemned.

A conspicuous use of "imperialist" in this way was the Communist "party line" classification of the European war as "just another imperialist war," with its implication that both sides were wrong and that it should be a matter of indifference to Americans which was the victor. This position was so transparently aimed at the British Empire and so obviously designed to inhibit American aid to the Allies that its propaganda value was weakened.

On the other hand the classification of all war as "imperialist" and therefore inherently wrong put a large number of honest and puzzled pacifists in the "anti-imperialist" camp. Their presumption was simply, "All empires cause wars; wars are wrong; therefore empires are wrong." Many persons who honestly take that position might be chagrined to discover that their sincere desire for peace had unconsciously been used to fit the Stalinist aims.

The growth of this anti-empire sentiment has been furthered, moreover, by the widespread assumption on the part of many so-called "liberals" in politics and economics that capitalism was doomed in any case. This assumption has been regarded in some circles as the first step in "enlightened" thinking, and anyone who professed any doubt as to the imminent disappearance of capitalism from the economic scene was written off as a hopelessly ill-informed reactionary. If to that assumption is added the acceptance of the thesis that empire and capitalism are synonymous, the disappearance of empire is accepted as a matter of course.

Still further weight has been added to the "anti-imperialist" sentiment by a closely allied school of thinking and feeling that concentrates its attack on the profit motive. There are many persons who have come to feel that there is something inherently wrong in making a profit. Empires obviously exist on the profit-making basis. Therefore there is something inherently wrong with empires.

The importance of these ideas and sentiments and their wide-spread acceptance should not be under-estimated. In 1939 and early 1940, for example, I talked to about fifty high school groups in and around New York and found in most cases that students who concerned themselves at all with political problems (and most of them did) took all of these anti-imperialist premises for granted. They felt, indeed, that the identification of empires with a doomed capitalist system, with predatory wars, and with unlawful profits, was so obvious that it did not need proof. Some of these students were clearly quoting the "party line." Others, however, seemed honestly to be reflecting the economics and politics that they had learned in the classroom. That there could be such a thing as a "good" empire had never been considered. It was a contradiction in terms.

Now, in so far as the maintenance of the American position in Asia is the continuance of the structure and function of empire, it faces a threat from this widespread sentiment. It is upon that basis that many Americans readily assert that we had no business in Asia in the first place and the sooner we get out the better.

SHORTENING THE DEFENSE LINE

The next major objection to our Asiatic position is somewhat less sentimental and more carefully defined. This is the objection based upon considerations of national defense. Our military and naval officers have not been in entire agreement on the wisdom of American retirement from the Far East, but they are agreed that Pacific defense would be simplified by the establishment of the Alaska-Hawaii-Panama line rather than attempting to include the Philippine salient. From a strictly strategic point of view we would be stronger if the defense line were shortened.

This factor has been complicated in the last year by the increased emphasis upon hemisphere, and especially South American, defense. The possibility of the disappearance of the British navy as our first line in the Atlantic has caused a closer examination of our entire naval position and the belief in some quarters that hemisphere defense is the logical limit of our capacity. We are already committed to the two-ocean navy, but it is felt by many persons that our forces can be most effectively employed if all of them are kept on this side of the Pacific.

The validity of this argument against our Asiatic empire does not depend, however, upon strictly military grounds. It rests on the larger issue of whether or not our Asiatic position is worth defending. The strategists do not suggest that our Asiatic outpost cannot be defended. They merely point out that a less extended line could be defended more easily and more cheaply. If they feel that the outpost is not worth the cost of its defense, and many of them do feel that, they naturally counsel retirement to a stronger line. If, on the other hand, they feel that the outpost is too valuable to lose, they suggest that it should be strengthened and held and transformed from a position of weakness to a position of strength.

In sympathy with this latter point of view is the group of strategists who hold that if a Pacific war is inevitable it will be better to fight it on the other side of the Pacific than on this.

The military objection to a relatively difficult defense problem is thus allied to the next major objection to our empire position. That objection is that the cost of empire defense is greater than the profits to be derived. This is an economic objection, and a civilian one, as differentiated from the purely strategic or military problem. Obviously the maintenance of an empire means the building up and continuing of a military and naval establishment more expensive than would be necessary for strictly continental defense. It means a greater hazard of war and the likelihood of more costly wars.

From this fact it is urged that the whole public must bear the

costs of this military establishment while the profits from the empire accrue to a relatively few persons. The close connection of
this line of reasoning to the objection to empire on the ground
that it is "capitalist" and "monopolist" is apparent, but the ground
for it is sounder than the mere sentimental objection that we noted
first.

Obviously it is valid or invalid to the degree that the profits accruing from the empire can be translated into improved standards
of living for the whole public in the mother country. In some cases
the accruing advantages have been so apparent as to be beyond
dispute. The entire living standard of the pre-invasion Netherlands, for example, was identified with empire profits, in spite of
the fact that the profits themselves accrued to a relatively few
companies.

In the United States the benefits that the whole public derives
from our empire position are also part of our living standard. They
embrace the access to raw materials that we have already noted,
and the increase in domestic purchasing power through profits that
accrue to companies and individuals.

In any case a valid objection at this point must be not so much
objection to the empire structure as objection to the domestic
structure that either concentrates or distributes the profits.

The larger objection, that no empire can be profitable because
of its excessive defense cost, often overlooks the fact that domestic
defense cost would be inevitable in any case and that the bill
chargeable to the empire position is not the total cost but merely
the difference between a domestic defense establishment and the
larger empire defense organization. In the present case of the
United States the inclusion of hemisphere defense in our domestic
establishment has already made that basic establishment so large
that the difference required for the defense of an empire position
is almost negligible. Once we admit that a two-ocean navy is required for even our domestic, or hemispheric, needs we have gone
three-fourths of the way, at least, toward empire defense.

Still another objection to the empire position comes from producing groups in this country that are in competition with imported or empire products. We shall have occasion to examine some of those groups in detail when we discuss the basis for Philippine independence legislation. At the moment it can be observed that domestic sugar producers, for example, would naturally object to our retention of colonies in which sugar could be produced at a lower cost. Similar objection has been made to duty-free colonial trade in manufactured cordage and in manufactured coconut oil, since these are competitive, on a lower price scale, with domestic industries.

On the other hand, manufacturing enterprises that wish to use colonial raw materials, such as our soap factories, and manufacturing enterprises that need a colonial outlet for their goods, wish to have the colonial position maintained. There is, therefore, no single policy representative of the interests of all groups. We have continued to carry on our empire function in a series of compromises among conflicting domestic interests. Manifestly those interests that are best organized and most vocal are likely to have the most weight in policy making.

The necessity for such compromises is increased by the inclusiveness of the domestic American scene and by the fact that there is not, as yet, a typically "American" mind. So many racial stocks are represented in the United States, so many backgrounds of traditional mental habits, so many preoccupations with local interests and local problems, that it is not easy to hit upon or to follow a policy that is representative of the wishes or the ideas of all. The American character, derived largely from pioneer stock that came to the United States under the compulsion of some type of revolt and in the search for some type of liberty, is reasonably predictable and reasonably uniform. The American mind is much more diverse and has not yet achieved a degree of unity that would allow the classification of "typical."

Wanted: an Empire Mind

Especially is it true that there is not in any large part of our population what is often called the "empire mind." In spite of some conflicting regional or economic interests there is a degree of unity within the continental United States. That unity of concept is not extended to embrace our off-shore possessions, our foreign trade, our shipping, or the interests of our nationals who are doing business beyond the northern half of this hemisphere.

But even so, this failure of the "empire mind" has some curious inconsistencies. Hawaii and Alaska, for example, are quite casually accepted as part of the geographical and political entity "The United States." Puerto Rico, the Virgin Islands, and the Philippines are not so accepted by many persons.

To the person who has the "empire mind" it is impossible to distinguish the interests of any one part of the sovereignty of the United States from any other. Wealth that accrues in or to a possession accrues to the United States. It is no more conceivable that the United States can divorce itself from the interests and responsibilities of the Philippines than from the interests and responsibilities of the state of California or the state of Texas, since all are parts of "The United States."

There is much truth in the statement, often made in a humorous way, that there is no patriot as patriotic as the self-exile. The men who live in the Philippines, who operate our merchant shipping, who carry our trade far back into West China, who drill for oil back of Palembang, are usually intensely patriotic. This patriotism is not a nostalgia for some Middle Western village. It is a respect for, a confidence in, and dependence upon, the far-reaching sovereignty of the United States. That ardor is not always shared and not always understood by many persons whose point of vantage is not remote. Patriotism in an Ohio town or on an Iowa farm may be quite properly associated with the defense of the domestic soil and with that defense only. Patriotism in South Borneo, Harbin, Madagascar, and Buenos Aires is more likely to be associated with the defense of Americans and their interests, wherever the flag flies. The American who earns his living outside the United States accepts the American "empire."

The "average" American somewhere in the interior of the continental United States may feel quite differently. He may feel that this government is an empire inconveniently and against its will, and that it can quietly lop off any embarrassing outposts and again quite promptly become a continental democracy. He may ask why any American lives should be risked, any American money spent, or any American concern displayed, for a position in world affairs that is foreign to his instincts and his sphere of knowledge. What this "average" American thinks may have a profound influence on what his representative in Washington thinks, and as a result the lack of an "empire mind" may make it extremely difficult to formulate policy for an empire, and may, in the end, constitute one of the gravest threats to the empire structure itself.

The first of these great threats to our Far Eastern empire position, therefore, is a combination of sentiment, military caution, anxiety over the cost of empire defense, economic objection to empire organization, self-interest on the part of pressure groups, and sincere inability to encompass the "empire mind." When those are combined or allied they make a formidable array of objections to the maintenance of the Far Eastern status quo. They constitute a grave threat to our position, a threat arising within the United States.

In Defense of Empire

Those who defend our American empire are not without strong grounds upon which to reply to these objections.

The first of these is the fact that we are not self-sufficient, as has already been observed. We can make ourselves more nearly so, especially for defense, but there are still some vital needs. As far as our standard of living and our mode of living are concerned, we are even more greatly dependent upon the continued access to raw materials that is determined by our empire position. Presumably we could still live as a restricted continental democracy, but we could not live as well as we do now. The European experiments with autarchy may have their military proponents. They do not recommend themselves to persons who really prefer butter to guns or desire to have both. In the sense that the "butter" represents comforts of life—a relatively high degree of luxury goods in relation to necessity goods, cheap and widely enjoyed transportation and communication, a diet that includes coffee, tea, sugar, chocolate, bananas, and spices—the United States is the greatest "butter" consumer in the world. And that "butter" depends in part upon our position as an American empire.

The obtaining of raw materials through an empire structure, however, raises an objection that is often made on moral grounds. It is asserted that empire is used for exploitation of cheap labor and for the depletion of resources that should accrue to the colony and not to the piratical monopolies of a mother country. The generalization involved in this argument is hasty. There have undoubtedly been cases where cheap labor has been exploited and native resources drained. They are not necessarily empire procedure, however. Indeed, the actual procurement of raw materials has, in many cases, meant the development of native wealth rather than its drainage. The major oil companies, for example, have frequently been attacked as depleting colonial resources to the disadvantage of native populations. Yet it has usually been the case that oil did not exist as a source of native wealth until its production was developed by the introduction of outside capital and outside technical skill. The "exploitation" of native mineral deposits is strikingly similar. In the Philippines, prior to "empire" exploitation, there were less than 500 Filipinos gainfully employed in mining. Today there are more than 50,000. The payrolls of 240 mining companies are a contribution of empire "exploitation" to the domestic standard of living.

The question of native standards of living, however, is closely associated with the next important ground for the defense of our empire position: the need for access to profitable markets.

Our own manufacturers and exporters naturally wish the widest field in which to dispose of their goods. The interchange of finished products for raw materials affords such a field. It becomes most profitable, moreover, when the exporter can sell his goods in a market whose standard of living is rising. Increased needs in a non-industrial colony mean increased profits for the industrialized mother country.

The recognition of this fact has been the basis for much of present "enlightened" colonial policy. It has been advantageous to the mother country to increase the purchasing power of the dependency. The most striking illustration of this is our Philippine dependency, which has advanced to the position of our fifth off-shore customer; but it has also been the basis for the relations, within the British Empire, between the United Kingdom and such dependencies as Canada, South Africa, and Australia. Any improvement in Indian standards of living, moreover, has had an important relation to the textile export trade. It has been good business as well as good morals to raise the colonial standard of living and get a good customer rather than to depress it and get cheaper raw materials.

The procurement of materials and the maintenance of access to markets has led to another colonial economic role. Capital and skill are being used to develop some native industrial operations related to the home economic structure. Thus empire becomes more than a mere outlet for surplus capital to be invested in raw materials; it becomes an intimate part of a growing operation in the production and use of wealth. The production of centrifugal sugar, the milling of coconuts, the reduction of metals, the canning of fish and pineapples, and the manufacture of embroideries, mother-of-pearl goods, and some kinds of furniture, are examples of this type of operation.

Presumably over a long period of time an empire would be economically self-defeating if one of its major functions were the complete industrialization of the colonial areas. That would presuppose their economic independence. That phase, however, is still far in the future, and in the meantime the gradual building up of the industrial structure can be profitable to both colony and mother country. Industrialization itself forms a major market, as American exports of machinery, electrical equipment, and transport amply testify.

The United States, organized for the production of surpluses for export, has naturally the strongest possible reasons for a continued interest in and defense of its major markets. Our empire position supplies some of those markets directly. It provides access to others through the corollary of our defense of freedom of trade.

It has been the American position that United States nationals should enjoy the right to enter into world commerce upon the basis of abiding by recognized treaty commitments and of keeping the law. We have likewise taken the position that our commerce should be free from strictures on the high seas and that it should enjoy equality of opportunity with that of other powers in commercial relations with independent states. That position has been shared by the British Empire. The authority behind that position has been the combined British and American navies. Our naval strength has, in that way, been a part of our function as an economic empire.

The abandonment of our empire position would mean the retreat also from our position in defense of freedom of trade, since we would be admitting that we cannot or will not depend upon our forces to sustain this declared right of freedom of intercourse. We have declared that such a retreat cannot be considered in respect to Western Hemisphere trade. Yet we contemplate such a retreat from the vastly more important and more profitable Asiatic trade. Thus while we might "realistically" take the position that certain elements of our trade were not worth their defense at certain points, we should be, in effect, accepting the position that freedom itself in our trade structure was not worth defending. Those who support the American empire believe that we cannot, at this stage in world affairs, afford to make such an admission.

This is a different situation from the classic antithesis of "imperialism vs. free trade." Presumably, under previously existing conditions, imperialism might be unnecessary, since free access could be had to all desired market areas. But the use of political power to close trade channels has made it necessary in some areas to maintain the empire position politically, precisely so that the economic freedom of trade could be maintained. Our refusal to accept a Japanese hegemony in all of East Asia, for example, is founded upon our political position in the region where Japanese control is projected. If we abandon the political position, we lose the basis upon which to contest the trade hegemony, and so through a retreat from "imperialism" we actually retreat from the free trade position that we could nominally enjoy. Many Americans feel that we should not repudiate our expressed determination to keep major channels of trade, such as those in southeastern Asia, open to world commerce. It will be recalled that this was the basis for the objection by Secretary of State Cordell Hull to the Japanese closing of the Burma road.

A New "White Man's Burden"

But if we have a relatively vague obligation to this principle of freedom in trade, we have a very definite obligation to the freedom of colonial peoples who are dependent upon us. A part of the function of a "good" empire is the protection of its subject peoples from predatory neighbors.

Thus far we have spoken of our empire chiefly from the point of view of the benefits that accrue to the mother country or its individual citizens. This is only half the picture. Actually the empire structure has resulted in very important benefits to the governed groups.

We have already noted the rise in the standard of living as the direct result of the development of new sources of wealth attended by increased employment. In addition, colonial standards of living rise directly through the impact of another civilization. This is most strikingly illustrated, perhaps, in the field of public health.

Even the most ardent Indian nationalist will readily admit that health conditions in his country have been enormously improved by the operations of the empire. Our American experience is even more convincing than the British, because we have had a smaller field in which to work and fewer obstacles in the form of religious or superstitious taboos.

The increase in the Philippine population, for one thing, is a testimony to the benevolence of our "empire." In the three hundred years of Spanish rule prior to the American occupation the population of the archipelago had gradually grown from 3,000,000 to 6,000,000. In one generation of the American empire it doubled again. In less than forty years it almost tripled. Immigration during that period was negligible. It is doubtful if it reached, legal and illegal, as much as 150,000. The gains were among the native population.

This was brought about by the increase in the birth rate, raised somewhat by improved economic conditions, but largely by the decrease in the death rate. The Philippine expectancy of life and the survival rate (that is, preponderance of births over deaths) jumped from the Middle Ages to the twentieth century in scarcely more than a dozen years. Two factors were of great importance. The first was the conquest of epidemic contagious disease. Prior to the appearance of the American empire on the scene, whenever yearly deaths from cholera were only a few thousand, masses were said in gratitude for the miraculous deliverance of the Islands. After a few years of empire, the appearance of a hundred cases in any one year was reason for someone in the health service to lose his job. Vaccination virtually wiped out smallpox. The combination of inoculation and proper sewage disposal reduced typhoid to a minimum. Rat control did away with bubonic plague. Empire changed the Filipino's opportunity for life, liberty, and the pursuit of happiness.

The second spectacular change in health conditions was the revolutionary conquest of infant mortality. When the first medical census was made in the Walled City in Manila shortly after the

American occupation, the infant mortality, under one year, was 80 per hundred living births. Eighteen years later, in the same district, the rate was 68 per thousand! At the time of the inauguration of the Philippine Commonwealth this had been cut to 56 per thousand.

A change of this sort has an importance in the lives of the people that is greater even than statistics at first indicate. It means that Mrs. Juan de la Cruz, who lived there in the Walled City back in 1902, could expect that four of every five babies that she brought into the world in the course of her fecund life would die before they were a year old. Her daughter or her grand-daughter could expect that any baby born to her had fourteen out of fifteen chances of survival. The course of the American empire has changed the life of Mrs. Juan de la Cruz and her children, and changed it for the better.

If it is urged that this is putting the case for empire on too restricted a basis, it should be remembered that life and death are important factors in any standard of values, and that in this case they reflect a general improvement in living conditions that has raised the Philippine standard to a point reported in 1931 by the then Governor-General Dwight F. Davis to be 300 per cent above that of any neighboring Asiatic country.

This means, of course, that the improvement in the other Asiatic outposts of the Western democracies has not been so rapid nor so great as that in the Philippines; but that there has been such an improvement no one has denied.

It is also beyond dispute that the present threat to these colonies is the threat of a sharply lowered standard of living under a much less benevolent regime. Under any circumstances it means a drastic recession and a loss of some of the most important gains.

A vital function of the present empire structure, therefore, is the protection of weak peoples against depredation and the continuation of a sovereignty that is benevolent.

When this defense of empire is made, it is not infrequently met with the accusation of "hypocrisy," since a humanitarian motive is adduced for a course of action that is obviously profitable. There is no reason why the two motives need to be mutually exclusive. There is nothing inherently wrong in enjoying a profitable position, per se, and the fact that it has a defensible moral basis in addition should make it stronger instead of weaker.

The crux of the defense of empire lies in the recognition that an empire can be good or bad as it is administered, but that it is neither good nor bad simply because it is an empire. There are good arguments for and against our empire position, but we will have gone a step toward better understanding of the basis for our policy if we recognize them as specific arguments on the wisdom or unwisdom of a course of action, and not as dogmas in politics and economics.

There is a threat to our future in Asia in the possible failure to recognize this difference, and in the consequent sentiment against "empire" in the United States.

CHAPTER V

THREATS TO THE STATUS QUO—2

Native Nationalism

IF ANYONE had been discussing the threats to the political status quo in the area of the South China Sea in 1935 he might have put the possibility of native uprisings as the first danger. The Netherland India Volksrad had petitioned for autonomy or complete independence, over the head of the Governor, as a protest against the Crisis Decrees. The autonomous Philippine Commonwealth had been inaugurated in part, at least, in response to a local demand for independence. Not all of the bad feeling engendered by the Annamese outbreak of 1930 in French Indo-China had been dissipated. There was a Fascist revolt in Siam. Britain was using every means of persuasion to keep Indian agitators out of Malaya, and at the same time had granted a separate political status to Burma. The remark sometimes made, that the Western Powers were sitting on a volcano, might have had some justification.

In 1940 the march of aggression has changed that condition more effectively than could have any group of concessions by the mother countries. The possibility that an independent status might be a change for the better has disappeared. The first concern of the native patriot has become self-preservation rather than separation from empire.

The extent of self-conscious nationalism in these various countries is so varied, however, that each should be examined separately. First of all let us consider French Indo-China.

The last serious domestic threat in French Indo-China occurred in 1930. This was a military rebellion among the Annamese. It was put down by force, and undoubtedly some bad feeling was left as a legacy.

The actual threat to the French colonial structure has been lessened, however, by the fact that there has been no unified native nationalist movement. Grievances for the most part have been localized and in most cases might just as well have been directed against the native rulers as against their French overlords.

On the other hand, the French provided themselves with an element of strength by organizing native military forces. The Annamese make good soldiers, and the French used a thousand of them, for example, for patrol duty up in Shanghai. This native army made a civilian nationalist movement unlikely unless it could take the form of a military revolt among the troops themselves. Any other threat to the sovereign structure could be met easily by a show of force.

The French problem, therefore, was to maintain the loyalty of the army. This was done by the development of strong cadres of non-commissioned officers whose loyalty to the French was unquestioned. The French colonial administrators were usually military men who knew how to command respect and loyalty. They were well-trained and infrequently changed. They appear to have been correct in believing that any domestic threat would be a highly localized one, and that it could be met by a local application of force.

The collapse of the French, however, has put a new aspect on this situation. It was suggested immediately by the newspaper correspondents on the scene that the Japanese demand for the right to send numerous "inspectors" into French Indo-China to control shipments on the Haiphong-Yunnan railway, was a transparent scheme to get as many Japanese agents into the country as possible to foment discord among the native population. Undoubtedly the Japanese have already made sweeping promises to whatever native leaders could be persuaded. Tokyo, and only Tokyo, has already reported that there is a widespread demand for Indo-Chinese independence. Naturally this "independence," like the "independence" of Manchukuo, will be enthusiastically fostered by the Japanese. That such a movement represents any genuine local urge toward autonomy is extremely unlikely. If French Indo-China were genuinely to seek a separation from France it would be natural for at least the northern part of the country to seek incorporation in the Chinese Republic. These states at one time gave allegiance to China and there is a strong Chinese intermixture in the dominant Malay blood. The Konoye government dangled the "return" of these states to a Japanese-dominated China, as a bait for peace, before the Chinese Republic. The Chinese have not risen to it. Chiang Kai-shek announced, from the day of the French collapse, that China wished to defend the status quo of French Indo-China. The "return" to China or a spurious "independence" may be the eventual fruit of Japanese pressure in Indo-China. Neither would be the fruit of true native nationalism.

NATIONALISM IN MALAYA

Down in British Malaya (to continue our progress around our circle counter-clockwise) the situation is unique in that there is no self-conscious, native, Malay nationalist movement. The interests of the colony are so intimately bound up with the interests of the Empire that the idea of separation is probably far remote from the Malayan mind.

This has been influenced by the fact that the loyalty of the native rulers is a political tradition. Many of them undoubtedly feel themselves to be personal representatives of the Crown. Impressive gifts have been made by some of the sultanates to imperial defense, and there is no warrant for supposing that these have been made primarily with an eye to the honors list. The British have honored these native rulers; it has been good administration and sound friendship to do so. The administrators in Malaya have felt for some years that there their problem was economic rather than political. The well-being of the population depended upon the success of the plantations and mines and smelters. This in turn depended on the market price of rubber, pineapples, and tin. If the colony was prosperous, discontent could be regarded as negligible.

There was, however, a localized political problem because of the importation of Indians and Burmese for work in Malaya. In contrast to the Malayans, they were intensely self-conscious politically. They were alert for any injustice and trained in effectively protesting against it.

In consequence there has been a large expenditure of administrative skill in recent years in seeing to it that there is no unemployment among the Indians and the Burmese in Malaya, and that their grievances are reduced to a minimum. This has been the basis for quota admission of Indian labor in Malaya.

This Malayan situation raises the large question of the possible effect that Indian nationalism can have upon native populations of other Asiatic countries. Some writers and speakers have declared that Indian nationalism is a gigantic upsurge that will carry a half-dozen other native populations with it, and, particularly, that if the British Empire structure is broken on the Indian front, it will crack on every other.

The whole vexed question of Indian nationalism is beyond the scope of this book as it is beyond the author's full observation. The study of other nationalist movements, farther east, leads me to believe, however, that the Indian influence may be overestimated. The British obviously believe that it is a danger in Malaya, since they have taken steps to meet it. There have been some Indian evangelists in French Indo-China, but there is no reason to believe that they have enjoyed a wide following. Indian nationalist influence in Netherland India is likely to be inhibited as long as its leadership in India is Hindu and its opposition Moslem, since Netherland India is overwhelmingly Mohammedan. Philippine nationalism has posed problems so different from the Indian that there has been little community of interest.

It is quite likely that so important a political change as the establishment of an independent India would have wide repercussions. But at the moment precise predictions as to what those repercussions would be, and what countries would be affected, and how, must remain largely speculation. Under present conditions it is not rash to say that the influence of Indian nationalism does not constitute a major domestic threat to the political structures and the status quo of the area of the South China Sea.

CHANGES IN NETHERLAND RULE

In Netherland India the domestic threat to administrative continuity has gone through a number of changes. In the period of rigorous and not entirely benign administration there was always the possibility of revolt. There were dozens of uprisings against Netherland sovereignty. Most of these arose from local grievances and in most cases the procedure was to put down the revolt first and to ameliorate the grievances afterwards. Since 1880, however, the Netherland rule has been increasingly benevolent. There has been an attempt to extend a degree of popular representation and to adjust administration to the needs of the native population.

This attempt is complicated by two factors. The first is the element of religious influence in Netherland India. Roughly fifty million out of the sixty-six million persons in Netherland India are Mohammedans. It has been necessary, therefore, for the Netherland government to tread softly. Pilgrimages to Mecca and Medina have actually been encouraged. The Netherlands administration has been conspicuously careful to avoid any suggestion of cause for a holy war.

The second major political influence is the body of Eurasians. The Netherlands has adopted a liberal attitude toward intermarriage and has accorded to any person with even a part of Dutch blood the rights of European citizenship. The most important of these rights, from the standpoint of political progress, has been access to education. It was natural, therefore, that the leadership in native political self-consciousness should be supplied by this Eurasian group.

The political instrument of these Eurasians was the Young Indian League. It represented the expression of the desire of the people for a larger autonomy but it was not separatist. An American official told me that the phrase used to characterize this group prior to 1933 was, "More Dutch than the Dutch."

The Crisis Decrees, however, put a different aspect on Netherland Indian nationalism. It was felt by many, not only Eurasians, but outsiders too, that the effect of these decrees was to depress the domestic standard of living and incidentally to drive back into the lower bracket of the dual economy the Eurasian who had emerged from it. It was an attack upon their living conditions, and so necessarily it affected their loyalty.

The result was an unprecedented move. The Young Indian League swept the Volksrad, and petitioned the Queen of the Netherlands, over the head of the Governor, for complete autonomy, or better still, independence, within ten years. This movement, it should be observed, was carried out by the same persons who had been "more Dutch than the Dutch." Therefore, there is some justification for the Netherland position that it did not represent a spontaneous nationalist movement or a real desire for independence, but was rather a sharp and effective protest against the particular economic methods that had been employed.

The adverse economic conditions from 1933 to 1940 sharpened this protest. It was not lessened, moreover, when heavier taxes were levied for national defense in Netherland India, and when the home country made it plain that an increasing part of that defense cost would have to be borne by the colony itself. There were sporadic outbursts. There was the comic-opera mutiny on the famous runaway cruiser, the *Seven Provinces.*

It is entirely probable that if there had not been a European war in 1939, and if the Netherlands had not been overrun by Germany in 1940, there would have been an organized nationalist movement in Netherland India with which the home country might have been obliged to deal by granting a far larger degree of autonomy than had even been imagined. The fortunes of war have, however, changed that picture. They have shifted the center of gravity of the whole Netherland Empire from The Hague to Batavia. For the time being the stability and the continuity of that empire depend in a large measure upon the continuity and stability of southeastern Asia. Naturally under those conditions Javanese nationalism has disappeared, for the simple reason that Javanese nationalism has suddenly become Netherland Empire nationalism.

It is unwise to make any sort of predictions as to the effect that such a major shift will have on the Netherland Empire's political structures. It is safe to predict that for at least the next few years Javanese autonomy will be the problem of Netherland autonomy, and that the survival of the Empire itself will be almost exclusively a matter of the survival of the southeastern Asiatic status quo.

Outpacing the Filipino

Finally we come to the Philippines. Here the threat to existing political structure is not only real but well organized. It derives its prime motive from pressure brought by the United States. Far from undertaking to curb native nationalism the United States has systematically outpaced it. It is no longer a political secret that as early as 1904 the United States helped to organize the independence movement in the Philippines to offset the Federalist Party that desired to make the Philippine Archipelago the next state in the Union. The native nationalist movement in the Philippines enjoys at least the lip service of ninety-nine out of every hundred inhabitants of the island. This situation is so extraordinary that it must be reserved for extended future discussion.

These are the major internal threats to changes in the political structures of the four great outposts of the Western democracies. None of them has presented a problem that could not be solved by wise administration and by co-operation with the local populations. In cases such as the Philippines and Netherland India the very strength of these nationalist movements can be made a gigantic asset to the empire strength of the mother country. This has already taken place in Netherland India, and it can take place in the Philippines with a little more than minor changes in phraseology. The mother countries, therefore, have been justified in the belief that, as far as their relations with the native populations were concerned, the status quo could be preserved. It is this belief that has justified their feeling that the major threat to these posts of empire came from without and not from within.

Meanwhile the course of European aggression and the rise of the Japanese "Greater East Asia" movement have made most of these questions academic. Imminent outside danger has brought the conviction in all of these countries that stability must be preserved, and with it the belief that the interests of the native populations and the mother countries were more identified than inimical.

As long as the mother countries seemed to be secure against any possible threat, it was relatively easy for the local nationalist to plead his cause. He could assert that the economic benefits of the empire structure could be retained while the political benefits of complete independence were enjoyed. There existed the possibility of two separate interests and the right of protest against the sacrifice of one to the other.

That situation has changed. The same aggression that threatens the empire structure threatens both the economic advantages and the political independence of these colonies. The Malay is in the position of being obliged to defend the solidarity of these mother countries in order to preserve his own identity and his own relative freedom. The Malayan or Philippine nationalist might readily have asserted at one time that it would be more desirable to be a citizen of a free republic than a subject of the British Empire or of the United States. That alternative can no longer be presented. His problem is now whether it is more desirable to be a subject of a Western democracy or of Japan. It would require temerity, indeed, to suggest that under those conditions the loss of Western protection would be a change for the better.

CHAPTER VI

THREATS TO THE STATUS QUO—3

The March of Aggression

THERE remains the greatest threat to the stability of the area of the South China Sea. That is the menace of outside aggression.

Obviously the stability of this area is threatened, like almost every other part of the world, by the possibility of a German victory in Europe. In the late summer of 1940 the British were still holding off the power that threatened their island. The disappearance of the British navy would necessarily mean the removal of the major safeguard to colonial stability. It would mean, moreover, that the disposition of the French, British, and Netherland colonies would be made largely at the pleasure of the Wilhelmstrasse.

Disposition has not thus far been made of the French and Netherland colonies, months after the mother countries have been overrun. One reason is the continued existence of the British navy, which would nullify any German decision. The second reason is the continued presence of the United States as a factor in the disposition of Far Eastern colonies with which Germany must reckon. The third is the fact that Germany and Japan have apparently not yet reached an amicable basis for the division of the spoils.

If the British navy disappears there will presumably be an arrangement between Germany and Japan whereby spheres of influence will be marked off. In such an event it is possible that the United States could be squeezed out of Asia by joint German-Japanese pressure, provided, of course, that Russia continued to be friendly with Germany and quiescent toward Japan.

But while these repercussions of the conflict in Europe continue to be speculative, the menace and movement of Japanese expansion is a present factor that can be observed and analyzed.

The Japanese policy is being shaped in such a way that it will continue to move, if possible, toward a dominant position in eastern Asia regardless of the outcome of the European struggle. While the declaration of a Greater East Asia, under Japanese control, is presumably based on the assumption that a German victory in Europe is inevitable, the Konoye Government did not hasten to attach itself publicly to the German cause for better or worse. Naturally a German victory would provide a situation from which the Japanese could profit, but this can be correctly ascribed to Japanese opportunism rather than to genuine mutuality of interest.

Long before the events in Europe accelerated the Japanese timetable, the program for the southward march had taken shape. The European situation made it possible to announce purposes that had previously been concealed.

The threat to French Indo-China, for example, became obvious immediately upon the collapse of France. Actually this threat could have been observed several years before France went into the war. It had become increasingly apparent in the year before European hostilities opened.

The most important single move against the security of French Indo-China, prior to the French collapse, was the Japanese occupation of the island of Hainan in February, 1939.

This large island, lying between the Gulf of Tongking and the South China Sea, commands about half of the coast of Indo-China. It is next door to Hanoi, the capital, and commands the port of Haiphong, which is the access of northern Indo-China to the outside world and the terminus of the French-owned railway into South and Southwest China.

It has additional strategic importance because it lies across the ship lanes from Hong Kong to Singapore, and because it covers the access to the French leased territory of Kwangchow-wan on the northern shores of the Gulf of Tongking.

Hainan was technically part of China, not Indo-China. Its

strategic importance, however, was so clearly recognized that as early as 1907 France and Japan concluded a treaty in which it was agreed that the status of the island should not be changed.

The Japanese occupation was a violation of this treaty, and the French launched a prompt protest. The Japanese replied that the occupation was solely a military move designed to stop the smuggling of arms into South China. This reply could be construed to mean that the occupation was intended to be only temporary, and the French, already watching the storm cloud in Europe, were obliged to be content with that.

Outside observers were extremely skeptical of the temporary character of the occupation, particularly since the Japanese immediately began the construction of large-scale fortifications. Hainan became their air base for South China operations and a part of their fleet was concentrated there as a constant threat to Indo-China.

The necessity for blockading the Chinese Government and cutting off its major supply routes, the most important of which went through northern Indo-China, was given by the Japanese as the reason for all of their operations. From the Oriental point of view this put a good face on what was obviously a bald act of aggression tempered exactly to the ability of the French to resist it.

When the first demands for the closure of the Haiphong-Yunnan railway were made, the French acceded to the extent of assuring Japan that munitions would not be shipped to China over this railway. The French did not, however, include in their definition of munitions the supply of gasoline, motor vehicles, and medicines going into China, chiefly from the United States. When the Japanese were able to push the closure beyond the point of French assurances, they undertook a complete stoppage of all traffic. One branch of the railway had been repeatedly bombed on the Chinese side and, presumably, a successful Japanese invasion of South China could have cut off these supplies within the limits of China without impinging upon the integrity of French Indo-China at all.

The fact that the Japanese took a more drastic course was undoubtedly significant. The correspondent of the New York

Times in Tokyo said that the Japanese "would get into and stay in Indo-China under any pretext."

Coupled with the pressure against France was pressure brought to bear against Britain, on this same ostensible basis of closing communications with China. There were two possible routes by which China could get supplies through British hands. One was through the Crown Colony of Hong Kong and the other through British Burma, from which the Chinese had constructed a motor road into South China.

Hong Kong had been susceptible to blockade from the beginning, and the Japanese saw in that threat the means of forcing the British to close the Burma road. The degree to which that pressure could be brought was entirely a matter of how much naval strength Britain appeared to be able to leave in the Far East. The pace of the Japanese demands was determined almost entirely by the amount of resistance offered them.

The Threat to British Malaya

An actual physical threat to British Malaya, with its key defense position at Singapore, was not apparent in the earlier stages of the Japanese maneuvering. The Japanese declaration of policy in respect to all of southeastern Asia (their "Monroe Doctrine" or "Greater East Asia" policy) would be presumed to take in British Malaya, just as much as French Indo-China. Japanese spokesmen, however, hesitated to push this point, precisely as they hesitated to call the Philippines by name as long as the United States fleet was in the Pacific.

While the frontal threat to British Malaya, therefore, had not appeared to be urgent, there was another threat to the British position that had been for some time a matter of grave concern. The cutting of British shipping lanes has already been noted.

There is another possibility that has caused some gray hairs in Singapore and Whitehall. There is a rumor, and it refuses to be downed, that the Japanese have projected and even surveyed a canal across the Malay Peninsula. Presumably this has been done in connivance with the Thailand Government. Naturally, the announcement on June 12, 1940, that Japan had ratified a new mutual assistance treaty with Thailand, did not help to allay this rumor.

Both the military and commercial significance of such a canal would be enormous. In Japanese hands it would literally isolate Singapore and give the Japanese a short cut to both Burma and India. It would change the entire picture of Britain's domination of the major Asiatic sea lanes and put that domination in the hands of Japan. It would divide the Malay States. It would split off the Straits Settlements from Burma. It would put Japan in a position of dominating Thailand as surely as Britain has dominated Egypt.

It can be presumed, moreover, that such a canal would be made a military base. To one who knows the Japanese mentality, there is no possibility, indeed, of any other presumption. The tin smelters of Pulo Brani and the port and naval base at Singapore would be within a few minutes' cruising range of Japanese bombers. Such a trans-Isthmian canal could reduce Singapore to a fifth-rate city.

There can be no doubt whatever that the British and French had this in mind when they announced their treaty with Thailand at the same time as the Japanese. As a matter of fact, the British have been nervous about increasing Japanese influence in Thailand for a number of years.

Up to about 1906, British influence was prominent in this small kingdom. That was followed in turn by the rise in American influence, and concerning this the British had no reason for alarm. In the last ten years, however, both have been succeeded by the rising star of Japanese influence. Japanese advisers to the Thailand Government have replaced their Occidental prototypes. Young Siamese are going to Japanese agricultural colleges. Japanese instruments are being used to survey Thailand's new roads. And perhaps most important of all, Japanese shipyards have built, and Japanese officers have trained, Thailand's new shiny and self-conscious navy.

The Western Powers feel that this is an obvious foothold for Japanese expansion. The threat to the Western world is obvious.

MENACE TO THE PHILIPPINES

What about the Philippines? What about Japanese expansion there?

The commercial expansion has been going on since the days of the World War, the Japanese following the accepted methods. They colonized in Davao and made that province the biggest hemp-producing province in the Islands. They connived with Philippine dummy corporations to secure land leases on hemp, coconut, and timber property. In some cases they brought down Bogobo women from the hills and went through the formality of marriage, registered property in their "wives'" names, and then chased their convenient spouses back to their camp fires among the wild tribes. The latest estimate, after repeated investigations by the Philippine Department of Agriculture, was that half of the land leases in the Province of Davao were held by Japan and that half of these, in turn, were held illegally.

Some years later came the Japanese expansion in the retail trade of the Philippines. It was significant and it is still important.

How far this commercial expansion is a prelude to political expansion is, of course, an open question. The foothold is already there. Japan, moreover, already has the Mandated Islands that flank the Philippines on the east. There was therefore a good deal of suggestion of the pincer movement last year when the Japanese moved down on the west and laid claim to Spratly Island, far in the south of the South China Sea and just outside the hazy borderline of the Philippine frontier. The island was of no conceivable commercial importance and it could only be imagined that its occupation constituted another move in an attempt to cut off the Philippines by driving salients to the east and to the west.

It is the fixed belief of almost all Americans, and the recently

expressed belief of a great many Filipinos, that the Philippine
Archipelago will drop into Japan's political lap like a ripe apple
the moment American sovereignty is removed. Since the Japanese
themselves have called the Philippines "a barrier to Hong Kong
and a bridge to Borneo," the threat to the whole of southeastern
Asia implicit in this projected expansion is apparent to all four
powers concerned. The actual threat to the Philippines is presumably still in the future. Philippine independence, in 1946, is
the obvious zero hour for the start of this phase of the Japanese
offensive.

NETHERLAND INDIA'S STATUS QUO

In the meantime, it is likely that Netherland India, like Indo-
China, will be increasingly a focus of Japanese pressure.

The conquest of the Netherlands by Germany immediately
precipitated the question of the status of this largest part of the
Netherland colonial empire. There had been rumors ever since the
beginning of the war that in the event of hostilities the Netherlands would ask either Great Britain or the United States, prefer-
ably the latter, to assume the protection of Netherland India for
the duration of the war. These reports were specifically denied in
the Netherlands, in Netherland India, in London, and in
Washington.

Immediately upon the heels of the German invasion of the
Netherlands, however, the Japanese Government undertook to
forestall any such possible protection by an immediate declaration
of its commitment to the preservation of the status quo in Netherland India. This followed a brief newspaper campaign in Japan,
in which the vital interest of Japan in the South China Sea was
emphasized more than ever before.

Within less than forty-eight hours the United States Government
made a reply to Japan's statement. The United States concurred
entirely in the Japanese declaration for the preservation of the
status quo. But Mr. Hull's declaration put the entire matter on a

very different plane. Instead of pleading special interest, as Japan had done, the United States reminded the Japanese Government that Japan, the Netherlands, Great Britain, and the United States were signatories to a four-power treaty, consummated in 1922, specifically pledging support to this status quo. That basis was emphasized, no doubt, because of the fact that the Japanese had insisted since the beginning of the Manchurian campaign that their Far Eastern operations were based on national interest rather than upon treaty commitment. The United States, on the other hand, has repeatedly stressed its treaty position. The retort to Japan, therefore, while an ostensible agreement, was an emphasis on the least comfortable side of the picture from the Japanese point of view.

Two schools of thought immediately made their appearance in respect to the Japanese declaration. The first was that it was "eyewash." One group of persons believed that the Japanese would take advantage of the European situation to disrupt the status quo in Netherland India at the earliest opportunity.

The other point of view, expressed incidentally by the *New York Times* correspondents in both Tokyo and Shanghai, was that the Japanese meant literally what they said. They pointed out that Japan had a very great interest in preserving this status quo because that meant keeping Netherland India under the sovereignty and protection of a relatively weak country with a small navy, instead of allowing it to pass, at least temporarily, under the protection of a very strong country with a very strong navy. Obviously, if the Japanese wished to bring pressure for further economic advantages or political concessions they could do so with greater safety if the non-interference of other powers was assured.

THE BLANK CHECK TO JAPAN

Several complicating factors, however, began to make their appearance very early. First of all, the German Government made a formal declaration that it was not interested in the political status of Netherland India. It was apparent to anyone that the Germans, without a navy, could hardly take any other position. The Japanese nationalist group, however, and particularly that part of it that had insisted upon a German-Japanese alliance, immediately interpreted this German declaration as a grant of carte blanche to the Japanese. The nationalist newspaper *Kokumin* called the German declaration "a blank power of attorney" to Japan.

Under this interpretation the Japanese would be acting virtually as Germany's deputy in any advances they cared to make on Netherland India. The Japanese Government was, therefore, reminded that at no time had the German Government instructed Japan to act on its behalf in the Far East.

Yet the Japanese Government did so act. The Netherland Minister was called up in Tokyo and asked for a report on the treatment of German nationals in Netherland India. The delicacy of the situation is indicated by the fact that the Minister, General J. C. Pabst, instead of telling the Japanese that it was none of their business, responded that he would give the matter his immediate attention and make a personal report.

In the presentation of Japan's case to the world, however, an almost exactly opposite position was taken. The Japanese let it be known that they might be forced to adopt strong measures, not on behalf of the Axis, but for the purpose of forestalling it. It was suggested that the disruption of the Western democracies could very easily lead to a division of their colonies by the victorious powers as spoils of war. This, the Japanese insisted, they were most anxious to forestall. This was a comfortable moral position to take, and one presumably that would meet the natural objections of the United States to further Japanese aggression in the Far East. It was complicated, nevertheless, by the rising tide of the nationalist movement in Japan, the demand for a single party, and the policy of taking whatever could be taken while the taking was good.

This point of view was forcibly stated by the then Japanese War Minister, General Shunroku Hata, and throughout the days of midsummer, 1940, the Cabinet of Admiral Yonai was able to hold off this pressure only by preserving the balance between the belligerent War Office and the more sober Foreign Office, which was still trying to preserve the fiction of pacific intentions. It was upon the issue of its failure to take a more aggressive policy that this Cabinet eventually fell.

Maintaining a nominally pacific course of action has been a delicate and difficult operation because there has been the constant possibility that a specific incident might arise that would give all the necessary ammunition to the expansionist party. Several such incidents involved Netherland India, for example, and began to undermine the original Japanese position that the status quo must be preserved.

For instance, on the twelfth of June, 1940, the correspondent of *Nichi Nichi* at Surabaya reported that the British had landed 2,000 troops in northern Java. It was immediately pointed out that this was a violation of the non-intervention of which Britain had previously given assurance. *Nichi Nichi's* report was promptly denied by the Netherland Legation and the British Embassy but the damage had already been done. Publication was all that was necessary, whether reports were true or false.

A similar incident was the reported firing on a Japanese fishing boat by a Netherland Indian airplane at about the same time. The incursion of these Japanese "fishing boats" into the territorial waters of other powers in the Far East is an old story. Some of them probably are fishing boats and, if they are, they are certainly poaching and ought to be picked up. On the other hand, quite a number of these "fishing boats" are equipped with high-powered engines, fathometers, and camera laboratories. There is certainly no reason why they should be cruising in anyone's territorial waters.

So long as the status quo in Netherland India is maintained by a relatively weak power, a succession of incidents and their use as a means of bringing pressure can be expected.

In the beginning, the Japanese push toward Netherland India

was based largely on the necessity of preserving the supply of essential war materials. Just as the pressure on France and Britain was ostensibly entirely a matter of blockading Generalissimo Chiang Kai-shek, so pressure on Netherland India was represented as only a matter of preserving a flow of materials for the war against him. The Japanese insisted that they would be obliged to maintain their access to these Netherland Indian supplies and could not tolerate their diversion even to the Allies. Any diversion, it was declared, would have to be construed as a hostile act against the Japanese Empire.

The Japanese, in short, were not prepared to admit that there could be such a thing as legitimate self-interest on the part of any other power. The press even went so far as to apply this same reasoning to the United States and suggested that any American embargo on war materials in the interest of American national defense was an unfriendly act toward Japan.

As the Far Eastern campaign gained momentum, however, there was progressively less emphasis on these individual cases and more and more emphasis upon Japan's policy and program as a whole. By midsummer, 1940, the Japanese were able to declare, first through the then Foreign Minister, Hachiro Arita, and subsequently through the new Konoye government, that the so-called "stabilization" of the whole Far Eastern area was a Japanese function. This statement did not go as far as the Japanese militarists desired, but it did go quite far enough to show that the threat to the political structures of southeastern Asia was no longer a matter of suspicion and conjecture. It was a declared Japanese policy.

The only problem left was the problem of timing. The synchronization of previous steps in Japanese aggression with complications in the Western world had become more and more obvious.

Not merely was each move of aggression in the West matched by an aggressive move in the East; not merely do the Japanese militarists want to get on the totalitarian bandwagon. The important fact is that any weakening of the stability of the Western

Powers, and consequently any lessening of their ability to defend their political Far Eastern structures by force, is the signal for a further step in a Japanese policy that had been put into operation long before the first shot was fired on the Western Front.

The stability of those powers has been so threatened by this time that the Japanese feel that their intentions need no longer be concealed. The "Imperial Way" is on the make in Asia.

Manifestly, the one country that is able to meet this threat at the present time is the United States. From the point of view of the Western world, therefore, the American holding in the South China Sea is the one real stabilizing factor. Naturally this involves an element of danger to the United States. It is a position in which international involvement is always possible and even likely. For that reason our entire relationship to the South China Sea area must receive the most searching scrutiny in order that our policy may be made to conform to our essential national interests.

The crux of our relations with the Far East is our political position in the Philippines. We can make the choice there between standing our ground in Asia or retiring from the scene. Accordingly we will do well to examine closely our Philippine venture.

CHAPTER VII

OUR PHILIPPINE VENTURE—I

AFTER an experiment of approximately forty years in the establishment of an Asiatic democracy, the United States at the moment is concerned over the unpleasant and questionable business of trying to find a suitable formula for hauling down the flag. It has been decided that Philippine independence is to be consummated in 1946, but there is still a large amount of backing and filling on both sides of the Pacific in regard to the terms under which this project will be carried out.

No doubt many Americans believe that Philippine independence is a settled issue and a closed book, and that all that is necessary is to let nature and the Tydings-McDuffie Law take their respective courses. There seems to be, indeed, an American tendency to regard Philippine independence as something to which we are irrevocably committed. Many Americans seem to be convinced that however unwise, unsafe, unfair, un-American, and just plain stupid the policy that has been adopted may be upon second thought, there is nothing that can be done about it.

This is, of course, a mistake. There is still in existence a committee for further recommendations on the legislation. The Philippine program has been modified by several subsequent legislative commitments since it was first enacted. Its economic basis has already been changed, and there is a provision in the law for a further all-over conference to take place not later than 1944, to take up once more the basic economic issues involved, and to try to find out if there is some way in which the Filipinos can be "liberated" without simultaneously destroying them.

The Philippine question, far from being settled, is just beginning to be studied. The operation of the law and certain political changes in eastern Asia have already convinced some of the Filipinos themselves that there is no Santa Claus. At the same time, some of the American sponsors of this legislation have already begun to admit that they acted hastily and that they regret it.

While, as has been repeatedly pointed out, it is extremely unlikely that the United States will change its course of action in respect to the Philippines without some expression first from the Filipinos themselves, it is also true that some American legislators are beginning to have sensitive consciences over the extent to which they leaped without looking. The American public is beginning to recover, in part, from the combination of altruism and panic that made the Philippine bill possible in the first place. Thus, while Filipino politicians and newspaper columnists (and quondam presidential aspirants) may debate whether or not there should be a Philippine "re-examination," that re-examination is in fact already beginning to take place, and will continue increasingly until the Philippine deadline—July 4, 1946.

A Self-Contradictory Policy

The peculiar position in which the United States and the Philippines have been placed in regard to the Islands' independence is largely the result of the fact that American policy in the Philippines has been a gigantic self-contradiction almost from the beginning. While the United States has undertaken a big job in political tutoring and has made every effort to see to it that the Filipinos are ready, politically, for self-government, it has at the same time adopted and carried out an economic policy toward the Archipelago that has made economic independence impossible. We have, in a word, informed the Filipinos that it was their right to be "free," and at the same time have made that "freedom" inevitably a synonym for suicide.

Mineral Deposits
now under development
in the
PHILIPPINES

A great many Filipino boys (and girls) got their first lessons in English on the knees of American soldiers back around 1899. By 1902 a contingent of enthusiastic and devoted school teachers had arrived in the Philippines and had begun what was to be an impressively winning fight against illiteracy. They took with them, however, not only *McGuffey's Reader*, but the speeches of Patrick Henry, the Declaration of Independence, and the Preamble to the Constitution of the United States. These became recognized textbooks. The Filipino, in short, was instructed from the outset in the necessity and dignity of self-government.

This instruction fell upon fertile soil. The Filipinos had been monumentally misruled by Spain for 300 years. The tyrannical combination of absentee landlordism, an entrenched church as a proprietor, and unsympathetic government officials, plus the muskets of a heavy-handed Civil Guard, had given the Filipinos ample reason for revolt. The American occupation was therefore a natural first step in liberation, and when it was coupled with consistent American preachment about the beauties of liberty, it was not unnatural that the American pulpiteers should have been taken at their face value.

A relatively high degree of autonomy was supposed to be established as rapidly as the Philippines could assimilate it. Actually, progress in political structure went several jumps ahead of even the remarkable progress that the Filipinos made. This was demonstrated in part by the attempt during the administration of Francis Burton Harrison (1913-1919) to Filipinize the government services at the expense of trained executives already in office. The motive undoubtedly was laudable, but the results in some cases were unfortunate. Cholera and rinderpest, previously under control, reappeared. The Philippine National Bank was looted. And for the first time under American administration the peso was at a big disadvantage.

The chaos in which that administration left the Philippines was cleaned up by General Leonard Wood, but he was obliged to do it at the expense of friendship with the Filipinos. The spanked child may, years later, admit that he was in need of discipline, but that does not prevent him from resenting the chastisement at the time of its application. It was not until General Wood left office that there was a possibility of healing the breaches that had been created and re-establishing fundamentally good relationships between the American and Filipino factions in government.

With the succession of Governors-General Stimson, Davis, Theodore Roosevelt, Jr., and Murphy, co-operation replaced clash. In most cases a reasonably firm policy was sustained but it was marked by a higher degree of sympathy and understanding. Political tutelage of the Filipinos was making rapid strides.

Throughout this period, of course, literacy all over the Archipelago was coming up. As early as 1920 more than a million Filipino children throughout the Islands went to school voluntarily. There was, moreover, steady practice in political institutions. Every town, every club, every cockpit, had its elected officers. The Filipinos took to democracy like ducks to water.

This type of training, coupled with the Filipinos' natural aptitude for some phases of political organization, gave the Islands an immense start towards self-government.

The question is often asked: Are the Filipinos capable of governing themselves? The answer must positively be in the affirmative. They might not devise and run a government that would be suitable or desirable for Wisconsin or for Switzerland, but they can and do operate a government that is what they want and that satisfies, thus far, their idea of autonomy. The question is not whether the Filipinos are capable of governing in the abstract, but whether or not they are capable of governing themselves. Actually there are political operations in the Philippines that could give pointers to Tammany Hall.

CREATING AN ECONOMIC DEPENDENCY

Now while this training in self-government was going on, and while the United States was enthusiastically preparing the Filipinos for all the fruits of "liberty," an economic policy had been adopted that bound the Philippines each year tighter and tighter to the United States.

By 1913 all tariff restrictions had been removed, and the products of the Islands were admitted freely to American markets. The passage of the Underwood Tariff Act in that year constituted the first big upswing in Philippine economy. It was followed by the World War, which put premium prices on sugar and coconut oil, increased the demands for Philippine hardwood and tobacco, brought new and large capital investments, modified transportation and shipping, and once and for all brought the Philippine Archipelago out of the bush leagues.

The effect of the American tariff policy, however, was to channel Philippine exports into the American market. Prior to 1913 less than half of the exports of the Philippines went to the United States. Since 1925 the amount has never been less than three-fourths. In 1932 and 1933 the percentage was more than 86. Even since the American quotas have been established, and under the Commonwealth status American purchases from the Philippines restricted, the Philippines still send almost 80 per cent of their total exports to the United States. Philippine purchases from this country have been similarly channeled and have risen steadily from less than 20 per cent in 1905, to approximately 70 per cent in 1940.

The effect of the war boom was to make the Philippines conscious of money crops instead of sustaining crops. As a result of these two factors the whole economic structure of the Islands became ultimately dependent on four or five major crops produced for sale in the free markets of the United States. Most important of these was sugar, and it still represents about half of the total value of Philippine exports, in spite of restrictive legislation by the United States. Second was copra and coconut oil. Third was manila hemp, and fourth was Philippine tobacco and cigars.

It will be observed that these crops, as such, do not make a particularly good diet. Rice, of course, was the one great sustaining crop of the Islands. Yet even today the Philippines are not really self-sufficient in rice. Any slightly unfavorable variation in weather makes importation of this basic staple necessary. Vegetables are scarce and of poor quality. The majority of the good meat consumed has to be imported. The Filipinos, living on rice and fish in the middle of one of the best fishing grounds in the world, buy canned fish as a major import and have a nationally organized corporation for the purpose of buying rice in French Indo-China.

The reason for this dislocation, naturally, was that there was plenty of money to be made in export crops. There was money to buy rice and fish as long as the country could sell a million tons of centrifugal sugar and export six million pounds of cordage every year.

Furthermore, the high prices that these products brought in the free American market naturally brought about a sharp rise in the standard of living. No other country in Asia has ever had anything that compares with that rise. When the Americans went to the Philippines, the average daily wage was five cents. The latest bit of social legislation fixed the minimum daily wage at sixty cents. That may seem low to Americans, but sixty cents will buy enough rice and fish to feed a family of five for a week. When Dwight F. Davis made his observation tour of neighboring countries in 1931, he reported that the standard of living in the Philippines was 300 per cent higher than that in any neighboring Asiatic country.

The development of these money crops, coupled with the phenomenal increase in population brought about by improved sanitation and better economic conditions, made a relatively high proportion of the population directly dependent upon these export products for their very existence. It was estimated in April 1940 that 4,000,000 Filipinos are at the present time dependent upon the coconut industry alone. Two million derive their immediate livelihood from the production of sugar, and it is believed that another 4,000,000 are directly dependent upon this crop. Actually then, ten out of every sixteen persons in the Philippines live and flourish at the present time because of two major crops that cannot be eaten locally, but can be sold in the United States. For this

reason economic dependence upon the United States becomes a
matter of life and death to the Archipelago. And this dependence
is an American creation.

In the case of the major export products, moreover, no really
satisfactory world market, apart from the American market, is open
to the Filipinos. The world's sugar market, for example, has suffered from a surplus for twenty years. There is a good copra and
copra meal market in Europe, but the bulk of the product goes
into soap making, and the United States is the biggest soap maker
and soap user in the world. The manila hemp situation, from the
strict market point of view, is not so bad. Japan is a large purchaser, and cordage can be sold to almost any maritime country.
As a matter of fact, however, the development of steel cable at
the top of the industry and the development of sisal fibers at the
bottom have so severely reduced the use of manila hemp that the
industry has for some years steadily declined in its relative
importance in Philippine trade.

The additional fact that the American market is free gives
Philippine goods a price edge against taxed competitors that com-
pensates in part for the length of the trans-Pacific haul and often
for higher costs of production. For this reason levels can be sustained for Philippine goods, competing in a tax-free market, that
would be consistently at a disadvantage if that market were taxed.

A Problem in Centralization

The dependence of the Philippines on the free American market
is accentuated also by the type of governmental structure that has
grown up in the Philippines. There is a relatively high degree of
centralization. The Insular government, corresponding to our
Federal government, collects the bulk of the taxes and makes the
bulk of the expenditures. Local taxation is astonishingly low, and
in many cases the Philippine Provinces, corresponding roughly to
our States, do not even pretend to be self-supporting. The major

sources of revenue are the Insular income tax, customs duties, and land taxes. The first two of these are collected solely by the Insular government.

The effect of this policy has been to concentrate not only collections but all appropriations in the central government. As a result, the major public services all over the Islands are directly dependent upon the financial stability of the Insular government.

There is no little red schoolhouse in the Philippines supported by the township. There is an imposing concrete structure built out of Insular appropriations, authorized in a pork barrel in the Philippine Assembly. Even the city of Manila makes no pretense of being able to support its own school system, but is dependent year after year on emergency grants from the central government. Similarly, there are few city or provincial hospitals; virtually none that could run independent of the Insular appropriations for public health. Roads, likewise, are not a township or provincial function, but are built by the Insular government. Bridges have been constructed for years through a revolving fund administered, not in the local districts, but in the capital. Wharves and harbors are an Insular, not a local, function. Plant-pest control, animal industry, vaccination, hotel building, tourist trade, rice-farm relief—all of these are carried out by the money that the Insular government collects and dispenses.

There has been a hue and cry for so-called provincial autonomy in the Philippines, but it is always an agitation for political autonomy, not economic. As a matter of fact, the Insular government has repeatedly made it a practice to remit provincial taxes and to suspend the penalties for non-payment. Such remission and suspension was actually operating in more than half of the Philippine Provinces at the very time that the Philippine independence bill was being debated in Washington.

So long as the Insular government has plenty of money to spend, this system is probably not disadvantageous. It makes possible a centralization of control, and probably the use of better-trained personnel than might be obtained locally. On the other hand, it makes the whole Philippine economy extraordinarily vulnerable. Because little Juan de la Cruz, way out in the Provinces, is dependent upon appropriations from Manila for his schoolhouse, his toothbrush, his road through the *barrio* (and, for that matter, his daily dish of rice and the electric current that runs his radio), he will be quick to feel any dislocation in the economy at the top.

It may be hard for an American to understand this. Obviously, in the United States we can run on an unbalanced Federal budget for years without closing the second and third grades in the primary schools out in New Albany, Indiana. In the Philippines, on the other hand, a dislocation of the Insular budget produces an automatic school crisis that may be felt in every hamlet on 500 islands.

A course of action for the Philippines that will reduce the revenues of the Insular government by approximately two-thirds is, therefore, more than a matter of book-keeping. It is a matter of essential public services for the vast bulk of the population. For this reason when the Filipino begins to wonder what is going to happen to his sugar, coconut oil, cordage, and tobacco after 1946, he is wondering what will happen to him personally. And he has a right to wonder.

Thus the United States is committed to a Philippine policy for which the Filipinos have been very well prepared from the point of view of ideas, and very ill prepared from the point of view of their pocketbooks.

How to Dynamite "Preparation"

This process of economic mis-preparation has been in no way counteracted or checked by Philippine independence legislation, but on the contrary has actually been accelerated. The Filipinos are now less able to understand the shock of separation from the United States than they were five years ago. Actually, while they are doing lip service to the program of "preparation," there is every reason to believe that they will be even less well prepared five years hence. The reason for this is also a matter of American policy.

Even at the present time, while the United States is theoretically subjecting the Philippines to a group of economic strictures that will force a sounder economy, it has dynamited any hope of sound economic planning in the Philippines by pouring into the Insular government a gigantic slush fund from the refunds of excise and processing taxes imposed on coconut oil and sugar, collected in the United States and returned to the Philippine Government. At the precise time when it is imperative for the Filipinos to accommodate their whole structure of government to an income of not more than one-half of their present normal expectations, the United States has added a third to their national income through a lump-sum subsidy.

This is, in effect, a denial of the whole theory of economic preparation. That theory has been implicit in all the Philippine independence bills. Senator Vandenberg of Michigan was one of the first persons to give this proposal concrete form. As early as 1930 he proposed a Philippine independence plan to extend over a period of twenty years, during which time American tariffs would be progressively imposed on Philippine goods, and Philippine exports thus adjusted to a diminishing market. It was also a part of his plan that the Filipinos themselves should decide biennially whether or not they were willing to accept the additional burdens. This was a real economic-preparation plan with a series of plebiscites to determine the state of mind of the Filipino people when they should have begun to face the real facts of economic independence.

By the time the Hare-Hawes-Cutting Bill was passed in 1932, the Vandenberg idea had had some considerable pushing about. The period of "preparation" was reduced to ten years, and the gradually imposed American tariffs cut to only 5 per cent a year within the last five years of the ten-year period. Likewise, the plebiscite element was transferred from the middle or the end of the experiment to the beginning. Thus the Filipinos were obliged to make an economic decision without having had any experience to justify such a decision.

These features were taken over almost entirely in the Tydings-McDuffie Bill, which became the eventual Philippine independence law. The plebiscite by this time had become a vote on the Philippine Constitution, and the entirely theoretical desire for independence, and had little or no relationship to economic preparation for independence or the adaptation of Filipino judgment to it.

Now the limitations of even this bill have been held to be too severe, and the imposition of the export taxes has been lightened in part by the substitution of a quota system for the period 1941–1946. However, what export taxes are imposed under this more favorable modification will be put into a special fund to liquidate certain bonded indebtedness of the Philippines in the United States.

The preparatory committee on Philippine-American relations has, moreover, with the approval of President Roosevelt, suggested that the entire period of economic separation be further spread out so that the full force of American tariffs will not be felt in the Philippines until 1961. But in the meantime the same contradiction between politics and economics has been carried on, since it is not proposed to change the political provisions of the law.

In other words, the policy still is to grant Philippine political independence first and worry about Philippine economy afterward.

In the meantime, the possibility of real readjustment to a lower economic scale has been pushed entirely out of the picture by the return to the Philippines of these tax collections by the United States.

In normal pre-Commonwealth times the working income of the Philippines was about $35,000,000 annually. President Quezon, through increased taxation and vitalized collection, was able to step this up to around $45,000,000. But on top of that, the United States has been sluicing into the Philippines between $15,000,000 and $20,000,000 annually in the form of this remarkable subsidy to be expended "for the preparation of the country for independence."

Under the terms of an amendment passed by Congress in 1939 the expenditures of this money must be kept in a separate budget and must be applied to the general purpose of preparing the country for an independent economic existence. The Philippine Assembly in the spring of 1940 had its first wrestle with the independent budget of the coconut-oil fund, but manifestly the latitude given in the general instruction is such that almost any "worthy" enterprise in the Islands can get its hands on some of this money, if Mr. Quezon approves. The initial budget plotted the outlay of the $22,500,000 collected between November, 1938, and June, 1939. About half of it went to a new agricultural bank. Other sizable chunks went to various government promotional corporations. Finally, $5,000,000 of it went into a legislative pork barrel at the rate of $10,000 a head for the Assemblymen, to be expended upon "necessary" public works in their various districts.

Undoubtedly the motives for returning this coconut-oil excise tax to the Philippines were laudable. There were possibly some sensitive consciences about the raw deal involved in the legislation that imposed the tax originally and there was possibly some honest belief that the wise expenditure of a certain amount of money might help to establish institutions that would protect Philippine economy. Moreover, the American consumer had already paid part of the tax in increased prices on soap, oleomargarine, and some other vegetable oil products, and the Philippine producer had paid the rest of it in lowered prices and the disorganization of his industry. The American consuming public could be counted upon not to complain, and the Philippine producer undoubtedly needed some help.

In the long run, however, what the tax legislation actually provided was the liquidation of the Philippine oil-milling industry and the turning over of the tax proceeds of the liquidation in cash to the Philippine Government. This would, of course, be temporarily popular with the government, but could hardly be called a sound preparation for independence from the point of view of the industry.

The original legislation had provided that none of the refund could go back to the producer, but that has been changed now, so long as his "stability" is a part of the general "preparation for independence."

However worthy these motives may have been, it is now obvious that the net result of the policy was to prepare the Philippines for poverty by sending them on a spending spree. We have undertaken to get the Filipino ready for a beer income by supplying a champagne taste. This is another instance in which our economic policy and our political policy have been hopelessly at odds.

The Motives behind Independence

It would seem wise, therefore, to examine the motives that have gone into this legislation, to try to discover why the United States acted as it did when it did, and why the Filipinos were ostensibly willing to accept such action. Quite apart from the probability of foreign invasion, which is the biggest bugbear at the moment, it has long been known by almost everyone, Filipino or American, who has made even a cursory examination of the facts, that Philippine economic independence from the United States is a short cut to a major disaster. Why, then, did the Filipinos ask for this course of action, and why did the United States take it? Let's start with the American motives first.

There was, in the first place, undoubtedly a certain amount of sincere political idealism on the part of many Americans. Some members of our Congress believed quite genuinely and profoundly that the United States should not exercise its rule over any people, anywhere, against that people's will. Such persons accepted the Filipinos' demand for independence at its face value, and felt that, so long as we were a liberal democracy, we could not do otherwise than to accede to it. This, for example, was the point of view for many years of Senator William H. King, who was the father of numerous resolutions on behalf of Philippine independence. International repercussions have since made Senator King repent of his idealism, it appears, but few persons have had the temerity to challenge his forthright sincerity.

It is unfortunately not likely that this was the paramount motive of the Congress that ultimately passed the Philippine independence legislation. It is likely, however, that it was the strongest motive of the public at large. Unquestionably, the uninformed public felt that the best argument for Philippine independence was the fact that the Filipinos had asked for it, and that the one important argument against retaining the Philippines was that we would do so against the Filipinos' will.

There was a second type of apparently sincere political feeling closely allied to this, expressed by some members of Congress. They felt that we were fundamentally a continental democracy, and that the Spanish-American War had trapped us into becoming an empire against our will. Some of this was a hang-over from the campaign speeches of William Jennings Bryan. But there were probably some good honest Democrats who felt that the arguments against "imperialism" that were trumpeted up and down the country in 1900 were actually valid in 1932. Philippine independence, moreover, had from time to time been made a plank of the Democratic platform, and the commitment was strong enough to make some party regulars feel that they could not get away from it.

Another body of sincere opinion which gave much aid and comfort to the proponents of Philippine independence was that of our military experts who believed that the Philippines constituted a strategic weakness in national defense. Neither the army nor the navy was unanimous on this point, and officers' testimony in various congressional hearings covered a wide range of opinion. They were enormously assisted, however, by certain military "experts," civilian or retired, who, in a position of self-nominated and self-recommended responsibility, undertook to advertise that the United States had a costly military weakness that ought to be dispensed with.

The whole problem of Philippine defense will be discussed a little later on, but for the time being it is well enough to note that the whole school of thought, both military and economic, that felt that our western frontier should end at Hawaii, was interested in lopping off what was believed to be a weak, vulnerable, and expensive outpost.

Thus, from the outset, when the Filipinos began talking about independence, they found themselves with some honest, able, and sincere friends in court.

When they got ready to submit an actual proposal early in the 1930's, however, they suddenly found themselves embarrassed with the riches of this support. They had not only a few friends in court; they woke up to discover that their case was in the hands of three or four powerful, rich, well-organized lobbies, which were ready to push Philippine independence through hell and high water. Some of the economic factors that were mentioned in discussing the dependence of the Philippines on the United States had supplied just about the choicest collection of axes that have ever been ground in the Congress of the United States.

THE GRINDING OF THE AXES

In the first place there was sugar. Philippine sugar production had gone up to more than a million tons a year. It came into the United States duty-free. There were powerful elements that were more than willing to keep it out. One group was the American beet-sugar farmers. Their dog-in-the-manger attitude was a little bit puzzling to some of the Filipinos. The United States was consuming six million tons of sugar a year, and the beet farmers couldn't hope to produce a quarter of that. But their interests, they felt, were jeopardized by the possibility of the expansion of Philippine production. (The Filipinos, as a matter of fact, had very unwisely decided against a voluntary limitation of sugar planting that would have disarmed much of the objection to their major crop.) The sugar farmers, however, were only part of the lobby. Even more important were the sugar bankers. It was estimated at one time that the loans of two of the major New York banks to Cuban sugar producers went up as high as nine million dollars. The Cubans were in a different position from the beet farmers. They could expand production indefinitely, and, moreover, because of their plantation methods, they could expand immediately in any given year to fill up any hole in the world market. Cuba had been producing less than a third of capacity for almost fifteen years. The banks were anxious to protect their investment. Keeping a million tons of Philippine sugar out of the United States was one way of insuring that Cuban properties would have to produce at least some of the million tons to take its place.

The beet-sugar farmers had a vigorous ally in another farm group, the dairy farmers. About 25 per cent of the American imports of coconut oil were going into the manufacture of oleomargarine, and after 1930 oleomargarine was declared to be fair game in both local and national economic witch hunts. The dairy farmers wanted to keep out Philippine coconut oil, and one way to do that with a straight face was to grant Philippine independence.

Their logic was puzzling to unbiased economists. The Philippines had been for a number of years the best overseas market for American dairy products. Under normal conditions the Philippine import of canned milk and other dairy goods amounted to more than two million dollars. (In 1929 it was $3,157,000.) The total tariff protection for the dairy farmers on the total coconut-oil output of the Philippines at the current rates would be only about one million dollars. There was, consequently, some skepticism about the shrewdness of these Yankee traders who wanted to give away dollar bills for fifty-cent pieces. "The coconut cow," however, had become an American superstition, and Philippine independence was readily accepted as the bludgeon with which to strike it down.

American cordage companies also had an interest in Philippine independence. Their raw material, abaca, was on the free list; but the finished product, cordage, was rated as a competitor of the manufacturing operations of these companies. When the manufacture of rope became the second most important Philippine industry, the American cordage companies went all out for Philippine independence.

By this time the pack was in full cry. The Farm Bureau was functioning in Washington as the "friend of Philippine freedom," and the Middle West got an upsurge of idealism unparalleled in modern history. Organized labor joined the ranks of the liberators —the objective, of course, was to keep Filipino labor out of California. The Filipinos had worked at lower wage scales, had definitely depressed wages in some industries—truck gardening, for example—and did constitute a minor threat.

There was not one of these groups that lacked ammunition. The Filipinos themselves had supplied it. None of these groups had to take a bad public position; they were the defenders of "liberty." Congress eventually passed the first Filipino independence bill over a Presidential veto and the second one by a vote of more than three to one. There was obviously pressure, and it was obviously not all pressure of public opinion.

There are several curious sidelights on these pressure operations. The most outstanding is the fact that Philippine independence, as ultimately agreed on, did not apply the heat fast enough to the competing Philippine agricultural products. Quick strictures, as well as ultimate extinction, were demanded for the Philippine industries. And so, although the sugar and coconut-oil and cordage industries had been doomed to eventual collapse, the same groups were able to pile on the quotas long in advance of the "liberation" of the Philippines. A quota of 850,000 long tons was put on Philippine sugar, with or without independence. A restriction on cordage was enacted above which no imports, free or duty-paid, would be admitted. The coconut cow was assaulted, not by limitation, but by that fantastic excise tax on all vegetable oils brought into the United States. Philippine tobacco was already paying an internal revenue tax.

The most curious part of these assaults on Philippine economy was the fact that at the last moment somebody's conscience hurt. It had long been the practice of the United States to return to the Philippine Government the internal revenue tax collected in this country on Philippine tobacco products. So, as a *sop* to conscience, the same process was applied to the excise tax on Philippine coconut oil. Theoretical sugar-land limitation had also been put into effect (in spite of the fact that the quota itself would effectively limit planting), and this substantial processing tax was collected and distributed to the Philippines. The effect of this bounty on Philippine economy has already been observed.

THE FRUITS OF PANIC

Another factor was operating at this time that made for smooth sailing for the lobbies. The United States was in more than a depression—it was in a panic. The Congresses of 1932, 1933, and 1934 were panic-stricken assemblies clutching at anything that might prove to be a panacea to offset the disaster that appeared to be overwhelming the nation. For a number of years our balance of trade with the Philippines had been unfavorable by about 15 per cent. Japanese goods were edging American products out of the Philippine market, and it was easy to make a case to the effect that the Philippines were an economic liability. The fact that the Philippines, even at that time, were our eighth customer, and the fact that our unfavorable balance in the Philippines was being translated into a favorable operation through the triangular trade clearance with Japan, were lost sight of. We were buying from the Philippines more than we were selling to them. Consequently, it seemed to many persons that we could improve our position by dropping the purchases even if that meant killing the customer.

Subsequent developments have rectified this situation. The Philippines are now our fifth customer and the balance of trade is in our favor. But back in 1932 and 1933 there were many members of Congress who could not look upon the Islands with anything less than a jaundiced eye. Some of these persons also believed that our military establishment in the Philippines was vastly more expensive than it was. Some of them thought that we actually supported the Insular government through taxation in the United States, and many of them got a vague, confused picture of millions of American dollars being poured into the Philippines with no return in sight. And so Philippine independence found some champions in the name of panic-bred economy.

There was still another emotional factor in operation in the later days of the Philippine independence discussions. It will be remembered that the first independence bill, passed over President Hoover's veto, was subsequently rejected in the Philippines. Within a year Mr. Quezon was back in Washington asking for another bill. There had developed in Congress a very definite take-it-or-leave-it attitude. "You asked for it and here it is," was the attitude of a number of important Congressmen.

As a matter of fact, Millard F. Tydings, who gave his name to the second independence bill, came out to the Philippines after the inauguration of the Commonwealth and put this point of view directly before the Philippine Assembly in one of the bluntest speeches to which I have ever listened.

It might be going a little too far to say that in the personal case of Mr. Tydings, "disgust" was a ruling factor. But certainly there were more than a few members of Congress who were perfectly willing to vote for a Philippine independence bill for the mere purpose of "getting it over with." No better demonstration of this attitude is afforded than the fact that the House of Representatives passed the Tydings-McDuffie Bill, changing the map of Asia, affecting the lives of 16,000,000 persons, dealing with a quarter of a billion dollars' worth of trade every year, and separating the United States from its richest possession, with a final debate that consumed exactly forty minutes!

This element of disgust may or may not have been a very large factor in determining the Philippine legislation. But it has served to crystallize what is now a fixed Congressional point of view. The Congress of the United States apparently feels that it has paid its full debt to the Philippine question and that it is not prepared to spend more time and effort on it of its own initiative. It is therefore partly out of this attitude that the present American position has arisen—that is, that there will be no modification of the Philippine program henceforth unless the urge for it comes overwhelmingly and unequivocally from the Filipinos themselves.

WHAT DO THEY WANT?

In order to form an opinion as to whether or not this urge will be forthcoming, it is necessary to subject the Filipino demand for independence to the same scrutiny that we have given American motives for enacting the legislation. We must find out, if we can, if the Filipinos really want their independence; if they want it badly enough to pay for it; and if they don't, what they do want.

The Philippine demand for independence has been very vocal for the better part of forty years, and the reaction to it has usually been one of either whole-hearted acceptance or whole-hearted denial. One of two positions is usually taken: either that the Filipinos honestly want their independence, or else that they very definitely do not want it, but feel it necessary to make a noise about it. Either one of these blanket generalizations is dangerous.

One of the things that makes an estimate of the Filipinos' petition for independence so difficult to analyze is that it has a basis probably different from that of any other nationalist movement in the world. The Filipino has literally no grievances. That makes a nationalist movement a puzzle right at the outset.

That statement, indeed, should be amended to put the verb in the past tense. The Filipino has had many more grievances since independence legislation began to be drafted than even the most perfervid orator could lay his hands on before that time. Up until 1934 there was no discrimination against any Philippine product.

The rights of citizenship (in the Philippines, not the United States) had been handed to the Filipino before he had a chance to ask for them. Autonomy had been pushed from the beginning. The American rule was incredibly benevolent.

In the days of General Leonard Wood, as has been noted, there were some collisions over the matter of the exercise of authority. There were not then, and there could not have been, any charges of the abuse or exploitation of Filipinos as persons. General Wood "cracked down" on some political combinations, but the poorest Tao in the Islands knew that he had no stancher friend than the American Governor-General.

This is not meant to be a tribute to American benevolence; it is an important political factor in the situation. Filipino leaders have repeatedly expressed themselves on this point. There are no stains that they wish to wipe out; there is no misrule that they wish to correct. They are obliged to find a ground for seeking a severance of their relationships with the United States in some other sphere than protest. Those spheres, therefore, must be examined.

Now, just as there were honest Americans who believed that the idea of a colonial empire was incompatible with our idea of a democracy, so there are honest Filipinos who believe that self-rule in the largest sense is a matter of so great importance that every other consideration must be sacrificed to it. Declarations to this effect have, of course, been the stock-in-trade of all Filipino orators since the days of the American occupation. But their sincerity must be judged by the degree to which the persons making the statement have actually faced the facts and seen what the other considerations are. Some of the Filipinos are willing to do this.

PORTRAIT OF A PATRIOT

The group that has done so is, in my opinion, relatively small. There are men, however, and some of them hold high office in the Philippine Government, who believe that independence means and should mean a complete reorganization of Philippine life.

In this class, for example, I think of a man like Guillermo Gomez as outstanding. He is an economic realist. A former Under-Secretary of Finance and now Collector of Customs, he is regarded as one of the best financiers in the Philippines. He adds to great integrity an alert and sensitive mind.

I asked Mr. Gomez, at the height of the independence agitation, precisely what he thought of the economic possibility of the survival of the Archipelago if it were separated from the United States. He faced the problem more clearly than any other Filipino I had ever met.

"Our greatest danger," he said, "is that we may delude ourselves. We have become accustomed to say that we will face the dangers and disadvantages of this economic separation, without going on to make clear what those disadvantages are. For my part, I believe that they can be faced and that they should be faced, but we should not be blind to the fact that this will mean a change in our whole mode of living.

"We should be willing, first, to face the fact that such a move means a reduction in our national income to a level probably not more than one-fourth of what we enjoy at present. We should be prepared, therefore, to adjust our national living to that scale.

"It would be reckless for us to assume that under those conditions we can imitate American economy or that we can become, in a short time, a highly industrialized nation with a high standard of living.

"What we must be prepared to do is to go back to the idea of handicraft for our manufactures and simplicity in our living. We will have to go back to real living on the soil.

"If we believe deeply that our independence is necessary to us, we should be prepared to organize our whole society on the basis that makes that independence possible.

"For my part I do not think this price is too high. I believe that we should be completely self-governing and that we should be willing to admit that we will start out as a small and poor nation."

There are undoubtedly a number of Filipinos who agree with

this point of view but few of them express it publicly in anything like such concrete terms. Those who do are foreseeing the hazards of their course of action and are willing to take the chances. They are self-reliant and truly independent. They may be wrong, but they are the salt of the earth.

Much larger than this limited, well-informed, and courageous group, is a body of Filipinos who feel a strong urge to take care of their own affairs without any outside suggestion or help, but who have not fully faced the facts involved in such a desire. This group is in part the product of American schooling, and is influenced by a cultivated super-confidence and a natural optimism. They want real freedom of self-expression. They want the idea of equality with the rest of the world, and they feel that they can make their way without too great a modification of their ways of living. On the whole, their emotional point of view is commendable, their aspirations perfectly natural, and their shortcomings only that they have not been willing to face all the facts in the case. They have seen Santa Claus in operation in the past, and find it hard to believe that Santa Claus will go out of existence in 1946. These men are also patriots, deserving of respect for their aspirations and nothing worse than sympathy for their lack of some important information.

On the fringes of this group some other emotional states begin to work. There are some Filipinos, of course, who are actively anti-American. They just naturally don't like Americans and don't want any surveillance from anyone outside the country. This group is, in my opinion, not large, but it happens to have had from time to time some more than usually competent orators, who have managed to produce an occasional demonstration.

The Vexed Question of Race

Underneath some of these opinions, of course, lies the vexed question of race. Some Americans believe that the racial equation is the deciding factor in all Filipino-American relationships. They believe that there is no possibility of an American's divorcing himself from his sense of superiority; and they usually go on to say that the Filipino has a general inferiority complex that makes it impossible for him to get along with a member of another race.

There should be an exercise of more than a little caution at this point. While it would be folly to assert that racial feeling is not an important factor in a problem such as this, it is very easy to overemphasize it. There have been some instances of friction directly attributable to racial incompatibility. There have been some occasions when Americans simply could not understand Filipinos and Filipinos simply could not understand Americans. There have been some very bad cases of American snobbery, and there have been equally unfortunate cases of Filipino arrogance. There have been some social discriminations in high places that have undoubtedly had political repercussions. There have been points of view that have been definitely warped by the color of a man's skin. This has been true of both Americans and Filipinos.

The astonishing thing, however, is that there has been so little racial friction. The average American who goes to the Philippines can, if he wants to, conduct himself, his business, his social affairs, and his pleasures, without ever having a racial problem to confront. The American who is vexed and embarrassed by racial considerations in the Philippines is usually one who has had racial complexes before he ever went there. The Filipinos who have made an earnest effort to understand Americans usually wind up by liking them enormously and getting on with them famously.

Mixed marriages are not usually a success, and the children of mixed marriages are frequently under a very considerable handicap. It is likely, however, that this handicap is social rather than hereditary.

Equality of the two races is nominal and political. (As a matter of fact, the American is at a political disadvantage.) Actually, completely unself-conscious social equality rarely exists and does not exist in the society as a whole. The Europeans and Americans have a tendency to remain within their own groups, and the fact that they do is sometimes misunderstood and sometimes rightfully resented by the Filipinos.

It has been said that the so-called Philippine "Old-Timer" is the prototype of the "Old China Hand" up the coast. This is not altogether true, nor is it quite fair to some of the Old-Timers. It is true that the largest number of the Americans in the Islands spend their lives there without making any effort to learn the native languages; and it is true that some transient groups never talk to any Filipinos except servants and taxi drivers.

On the other hand, there are many Americans who enjoy a large circle of Filipino friends and who find it possible to get along in peace and harmony with persons of a different race. Business offices and institutions have their own peculiar "feel," established in many cases by the personality of the men who set the tone for the organization. In many of these, month after month can roll by without any raising of the question of race. I make this statement confidently because I worked in such an office for seven years.

A matter as important as race will necessarily make itself felt in manifestations that are not always an exact presentation of the problem involved. There are dozens of curious quirks and twists in the dealings that go on between two groups of persons from two different sides of the world. This offers an opportunity for trouble and misunderstanding on both sides.

It must be recognized, therefore, that the urge for independence on the part of many Filipinos may be the result of unfortunate experiences because of race, of a highly developed race consciousness, or of situations induced by the ineptness, ignorance, lack of sensibility, or just ordinary stupidity of the racial groups with which they have come in contact.

The Philippine "Politico"

Most of the elements that we have noticed above probably appear from time to time in greater or less degree in the group in the

Philippines that has been most important in the demand for independence. That group is that of the famous Philippine *politico*. He "runs" the country. Some of these men are patriots; some of them are very intelligent; most of them are shrewd and many of them are successful.

The politically governing class in the Philippines is not pure Malay. There is a strong mixture of Spanish blood, and in some cases a mixture of Chinese blood. (Some sociologists believe that the mixture of Chinese blood is more successful.) The *politico* is the descendant of the *illustrado* of earlier days, and he occupies a very vital part in the whole Philippine scheme. His profession is politics; his avenue to it, usually, the law. The Philippine people have often been called litigious; that is a mistake. There are simply so many lawyers around that they have to do something for a living.

The *politico* went all out for independence a good many years ago. In many cases he was probably thoroughly sincere. In all cases he found that he had a campaign slogan that could not be beat. Independence, of course, could mean anything that the orator wanted it to mean. And the Filipinos are an oratorical people. The *politico* didn't bother to explain; he didn't have to. He was always preaching the gospel of something better, and as long as he preached it vehemently enough, he was certain to be returned to office.

The sincerity of the Filipino *politico* will always be a big question. Some of them undoubtedly believed what they said; others never bothered about whether they ought to believe it or not as long as it got results.

There are, unfortunately, too many cases in which the political leader has said one thing in public and another thing in private. There is probably not an American in the Philippines today, who has been there for more than ten years, who has not had the experience of having dinner with a Filipino politician and having that politician say to him:

"This is off the record, of course. You know we really don't want our independence. But we couldn't get elected if we didn't say so."

Part of this is the famous Oriental trait of wishing to say what one's listener wishes to hear. Part of it is just the plain and fancy double cross.

The reason the charge of insincerity is often brought against the Filipino political leader with such sharpness and conviction is that so few of these men have had the courage to face the facts, and state the facts when they had them. When the vital problem of readjustment to an entirely different economic and political state has been broached, there has been a tendency to pass it off with the sweeping statement, "We know that there are hardships and difficulties to be faced, but we are willing to face them." Very few political orators in the Philippines have ever had the courage to talk about political readjustment in terms of rice and fish and carabao.

HAND-CUT HEAVEN

This, of course, has had its repercussions in the largest group of all in the Philippines—the common man, the *Tao* out in the Provinces, the rice farmer, the day laborer. What does he think about independence? Does he want it?

The answer is a thunderous "Yes." He has no more idea of the foreign trade of the Philippines than he has of differential calculus. But he has an excellent idea of *independencia*. He has been hearing about it for forty years, and he has been hearing about it always as the synonym for the millennium. There are 16,000,000 people in the Philippines, and to at least 15,000,000 of them, if not more, independence does not mean a severance of any important ties to the United States. It means independence from the tax collector, independence from the landlord. It means independence from the Provincial Commander of Constabulary, and thereby from the District Treasurer. It means no more hunger, no more failure of rice crops, no more sick *carabao*. Independence means a fiesta every day and a *lechonada*, with the sacrificial roast piglet, on Tuesdays, Thursdays, and Saturdays.

I have talked to these fellows out in the Provinces who didn't know that independence would mean that the Americans would leave the Islands. They thought that the only difference was that there would be no more taxes to pay, and that everybody would be automatically out of debt from birth to death.

Under those circumstances the common man has been the victim of a lot of misleading oratory. He loves a parade and there is a band around every corner.

There is strong sentiment in the Philippines against independence, but it is not the sentiment of the common man. It is the sentiment of Filipino men in business, of Filipino sugar planters and coconut millers. The common man has had no reason to share their apprehension. He has been told for years that there was nothing to fear. He is convinced that once *independencia* arrives, the new world will be at hand.

This, naturally, has been particularly true of the older generation. Those who lived under Spanish rule have had good reason to believe that any change in government would be a change for the better. They have seen the progress of their country under the American occupation. They have had plenty to eat in comparison with their early years. They have seen definitely that the world is getting better. Now, just beyond the horizon, is this tremendous new day for the Philippines, when all cares and troubles will be washed away. Does the Philippine *Tao* want independence? Of course he does. He'd be crazy if he didn't.

LIBERTY VS. INDEPENDENCE: ROUND ONE

What has happened is that the Filipino, like many of his American cousins, has been allowed to confuse independence with liberty. Newspaper headline writers, who liked the shorter word, have not helped him at this point. "Liberty" and "freedom" have become the psychologically accepted synonyms for "independence," when they are not necessarily the same thing at all. In the Philippine case, indeed, they are inevitably mutually exclusive.

Independence is a technical term in international law. It designates the residual sovereignty in relation to geography. Liberty is a philosophical term. It designates the relation of an individual to the world in which he lives. It is perfectly possible for a nation to have its complete technical independence, while the individuals in that nation live in slavery. The example of Germany need hardly be adduced. On the other hand, it is equally possible, as in the case of Canada or Australia, not to have technical independence but to have the highest degree of liberty for the individual that society has achieved. (We are speaking of peace time, of course.)

In the Philippine case it has been precisely the fact that the Filipinos have not had to cope with the problem of independence that has made it possible for them to achieve their very high degree of liberty.

In the Philippines there is liberty of self-expression. There is liberty in government. There is liberty of movement. There is freedom of speech, of religion. There is, moreover, freedom from overwhelming economic pressure. There is the liberty that is achieved as one's standard of living goes up instead of down. There is the loosening of the shackles of poverty. There is the possibility of a son's having a better opportunity in life than his father. These liberties have been achieved and enjoyed in the Philippines. And these liberties have been possible because of American "rule."

The overwhelming economic pressure of independence would necessarily curtail most of these liberties. In addition, there are persons unkind enough to suggest that political liberties would be sharply curtailed through the presence of a well-organized ruling clique. In any case, it is clear that in the present situation in the Philippines the only prospect of preserving liberty is in finding a substitute for independence.

The Filipinos who are now concerned with the necessity of re-examining their position, are facing the threat to both liberty and independence. They face the destruction of the first through the collapse of their economic system, and the loss of the second through the inevitable invasion by Japan. They face the prospect of losing not only their liberty in the name of independence, but of losing their independence itself in the name of some visionary greater liberty.

Not even the most optimistic of the informed Filipinos can believe that the standard of living could be sustained without American assistance. Many of them, including the President of the Philippine Commonwealth, believe that the integrity of the Islands might easily be sacrificed in the present state of international affairs.

This situation puts the United States in a peculiar position. It knocks the bottom out of the lofty motives that inspired the grant of Philippine independence. For those who are really sincere in wishing the Filipinos well, it is one thing to say, "We hope you'll make a go of it, and we'll help you," and quite another thing to say, "God help you, we're throwing you to the wolves."

And yet that is precisely the position in which the United States has been placed. There is no longer any possibility of misapprehension as to what would happen to an independent Philippines. Even the most sanguine are now convinced that it would disappear in very short order. The whole crux of the problem of the future of the Philippines, therefore, has shifted from the lofty plane of allowing a people to achieve liberty, to a determination to give them independence in spite of their own interests.

This throws the spotlight, much more sharply than it has been thrown before, on American motives. The problem now is not whether the Filipinos shall have their independence from the United States, but whether this country, willy-nilly, will see to it that the United States has its independence from the Philippines.

CHAPTER VIII

OUR PHILIPPINE VENTURE—2

IN JULY, 1936, Major General Douglas MacArthur made the cables with a vengeance. He gave a forthright answer to a question that had been asked repeatedly from the time that the Philippine independence question was first broached: "Can the Filipinos defend themselves?"

General MacArthur answered, "Yes."

General MacArthur went much further than that. He had outlined a complete program whereby, he believed, the Philippines could not only be defended, but could be defended at a cost so low as to make it the all-time bargain in munitions and armaments.

He outlined a ten-year program that would require the expenditure of about eight million dollars, and at the end of the ten years, he said, the Philippines would be in an extraordinarily satisfactory position as far as their national defense was concerned.

General MacArthur did not say, as he was freely paraphrased, that the Philippines would be made inpregnable under his program. What he did say was that the defense of the Philippines would be so well organized and so effective that its conquest would not be worth the price, and that, therefore, any major power contemplating an invasion would be deterred by the obvious cost of the operation.

The defense program was based, first of all, upon the training of a citizen army. It was a plan for compulsory military service, handling approximately 40,000 men a year. Each class was to be trained for about six months. At the end of ten years the Philippines would have available a trained army of about 400,000 men.

This was to be supplemented by a small but efficient air corps and by a Philippine navy. This navy was to consist of very small, fast, torpedo boats. It will be recalled that this was shortly after the retirement of the British navy from the Mediterranean, presumably because of the threat of the Italian "mosquito fleet." A mosquito fleet was therefore planned for the Philippines.

It was the thesis of General MacArthur that this type of military establishment was well within the means of the Philippine Government (as it certainly was) and that it would afford virtually the only type of national defense that was practicable under existing conditions.

In elaborating on his program, General MacArthur pointed out that a landing operation at a considerable distance from a home base was a hazardous and expensive proposition. He estimated that the ratio of the striking force would have to be so overwhelmingly great that an enormous expedition would be involved. He did not go into complete tactical details for publication, but it was generally assumed that the logical landing place for such an expedition would have to be either Lingayan Gulf in northwestern Luzon or Batangas Bay in southwestern Luzon. From either of these points there is a reasonable overland approach to Manila. The Philippine citizen army was, therefore, to be trained to make a landing extremely difficult at either of these points, and a march on Manila too costly to be contemplated.

General MacArthur had been called to the Philippines upon his retirement as Chief of Staff of the United States army at the insistence of President Quezon. The story is told (and it is probably apocryphal) that Mr. Quezon called upon General MacArthur in Washington and asked him only one question.

"Can you defend the Philippines?" Mr. Quezon is said to have asked.

"Yes," General MacArthur is said to have replied.

"You have a job," is supposed to have been Mr. Quezon's way of concluding the deal and the conversation.

The story is probably not true in any detail, but it does indicate something of the way in which each of these two men approached the problem. General MacArthur came out to the Philippines in time for the inauguration of the Commonwealth, and immediately set to work putting his plan into operation. A national defense bill embodying most of his provisions was promptly drafted and passed.

The new organization was created, and at this point General MacArthur and his assistants had the advantage of being able to use the Philippine Constabulary as a nucleus. The Constabulary was a national police force organized along military lines, and its roster included some very able officers, both American and Filipino, and some well-trained companies. Its total strength at that time was about 8,000 men. It was the plan to use the Constabulary not only as the nucleus for the army, but also to make it a sort of provost-marshal's department of the army organization, in which capacity it would continue its normal police functions.

Uses for an Army

It was obvious at the outset that General MacArthur's program had a number of advantages quite apart from the question of defending the Philippines. The young Philippine Commonwealth was badly in need of some social discipline, and army training was one way to get it. The enrollment and assembling of 40,000 young men a year from all over the Islands was a move toward national unity, had possibilities as an educational project, and afforded an excellent opportunity to develop a working national self-consciousness.

The Philippine Scouts, a part of the American military establishment for many years, had already demonstrated that the Filipinos were capable of assimilating and profiting by military training and discipline. It was readily foreseen that the addition each year of a sizable body of trained young men to the forces of the country would have a stabilizing effect both on them and on the Commonwealth Government.

There was one other possibility. In the event that, before Philippine independence was consummated, the United States became embroiled in any Asiatic conflict, the presence of a trained Filipino force in the Islands would definitely reduce the number of American troops that would have to be sent to the zone of operations. In short, behind the program, in some minds, was probably the idea that whether the United States or the Philippines undertook to defend the Philippines, it was a good idea to do it in part with Filipinos.

To General MacArthur's statement that the program ought to be a success, and that it ought to secure a reasonable degree of safety to the young government, the reaction was profound. There was an accession of self-confidence and a general feeling that one of the largest obstacles to an independence program had been hurdled.

General MacArthur was, after all, a former Chief of Staff of the United States army. He had had three tours of duty in the Philippines, once as Commander-in-Chief of the Philippine Department. He was regarded as probably America's most brilliant military mind. And he knew his Philippines. If anybody's word on a defense program for the Philippines should carry weight, his was certainly that word.

This program also offered the Filipinos an opportunity to escape from the nebulous proposals of neutralization, in which there had never been very much confidence. Thus a good many of the fears were allayed and a good many of the worries set aside.

General MacArthur had been made a Field Marshal by the grateful Filipinos and had received his baton from the hands of Mrs. Quezon herself at a beautiful dinner at Malacañan Palace. Filipino major generals sprang into life; the ground was broken for a military academy ("the West Point of the Philippines"); a camp site outside of Manila was named in honor of the former Governor-General, Frank Murphy; and all was well.

The first class was called up for registration. The combination of the fact that the population was larger than the estimates (based on the outdated census of 1918), and the fact that there was genuine popular enthusiasm for a military program and little or no opposition to it, made the initial classes larger than had been expected. The defense of the Philippines swung into high gear.

After several years had elapsed, some of this ardor cooled. The program had called for the training of 40,000 men a year. By 1939 this had dropped to 20,000 a year. The ostensible reason was the lack of funds. This, of course, was absurd on the face of it. The Philippine Government was rolling in money. The military appropriations for 1939 were less than a million dollars in a budget of forty-five million. Excessive cost could not possibly have been a factor.

There was apparently beginning to grow in the Philippine Assembly some feeling that parts of the establishment were too expensive. There was an attack, for example, on the salary and emoluments paid to General MacArthur. The emoluments included a splendid suite in a Manila hotel, and the fact that it was air-conditioned may have irritated some of the Assemblymen from the steaming provinces. Appropriations, accordingly, were kept at a low level, and the program was operated on a much more modest basis.

It is also possible that many of the legislators had lost some of their initial confidence. They may have felt that a defenseless Philippines could make a more effective plea for outside assistance than could a Philippines in which there were presumably independent defense forces.

It is extremely likely, moreover, that one of the most immediate reasons for the curtailment of the program was not the lack of money nor any basic unsoundness in the program itself, but rather the fact that no sufficient cadres of trained officers and non-coms were available to handle 40,000 new trainees every year. The physical plant also got into operation rather slowly, and it was necessary to handle only such men as could be taken care of in limited quarters.

Another part of the program had not worked out so well as had been hoped. It was originally planned to equip the soldiers almost entirely with locally manufactured materials. Campaign hats were to be made of local fiber; beds were to be made of bamboo; and cloth spun and woven from abaca was eventually to provide the uniforms. Even the feeding of the army, it was hoped, would be taken care of eventually by some of the self-sustaining government farms, including the prison farms. This part of the program was tied up to the idea of developing local industries and promoting diversified local agriculture. It was unquestionably sound on paper, and would make the Philippine army much less expensive than if its equipment had to be imported. Not all of it worked out as planned. The locally made campaign hats, for example, wouldn't stand the rain.

Confidence in the Philippine defense program was severely shaken by the Japanese invasion of China in the summer of 1937. The progress of that campaign eventually changed the attitude of many of the Filipinos in responsible positions.

THE EBB-TIDE OF CONFIDENCE

By March of 1940 Mr. Quezon himself was ready to disagree with General MacArthur's inspiring confidence, and come out with the statement that the Philippines could not be defended even if every citizen in the Islands were put under arms. The same view was voiced by the American High Commissioner, Francis B. Sayre, on February 15, 1940; and Mr. Sayre went even further than Mr. Quezon. Mr. Sayre suggested that not even the United States, let alone the Filipinos, could defend the Archipelago.

This point of view was no novelty. Those persons in the United States who had felt that the Philippines constituted a strategic weakness had frequently stated that an expedition to the other side of the Pacific for Philippine defense would be extremely hazardous, and that, at best, all the United States could hope for was the terribly costly re-conquest of the Islands after they had fallen into enemy hands.

This point of view had been presented by some military and naval men to Senate and House committees at the time that Philippine independence was being discussed. The Philippines were often referred to as a sore thumb jutting out into the Pacific, and the hazards of distances from bases of operation were carefully mapped.

Mr. Sayre's statement, however, put the defense of the Philippines on a somewhat different basis. Apparently he was not thinking so much about operating defense—that is, actual naval and military battle forces—as he was about fixed positions in the Islands themselves. He referred to the cost of building and maintaining the strongest of these positions, the island of Corregidor at the entrance to Manila Bay, and observed that adequate defense for the Islands would necessitate the building of a large number of other Corregidors at a cost that would be prohibitive even to the United States.

Skepticism in regard to the feasibility of the whole Philippine defense program was likewise no novelty. When General MacArthur first made the statement that for all practical purposes the Philippines could be considered relatively safe from invasion after his citizen army had been trained, there were a good many arched eyebrows both in the Philippines and in the United States. Some persons even recalled that officers of the War Department, actually serving under General MacArthur when he was the Chief of Staff, had testified at committee hearings in Congress that the United States, with its tremendous resources, large navy, working wealth, and trained officers, could not and ought not to undertake to defend the Philippines. It was, therefore, wondered by what magic General MacArthur was going to pull the rabbit out of the hat and do the job on less than ten million dollars.

MacArthur Restates His Case

Three years later General MacArthur repeated and in some respects amplified his position. In Manila, on June 28, 1939, he again issued a formal statement on the problem of Philippine defense. That statement is so important, considering its source, that it should be quoted in full. It follows:

"I have been asked to state publicly my professional opinion as to the possibility of successful defense of the Philippines in case of a foreign invasion by Japan, if independence of the Commonwealth is encompassed in 1946 as now provided by law. There are so many imponderables involved that I would be a fool or a knave to attempt to play the part of an accurate prophet on such a distant and obscure horizon. Certain broad basic facts can be enunciated, however, which lead to possible conjectures.

"Security is a relative term, and the uncertainty as to all factors involved in national combat is so great that only the actual test of war can give the answer. The measure of the relative chances of two nations is not always determined by the actual strength and potentialities of the combatants. It is usually decided by the local strengths which are brought to bear at the decisive point of contact.

"In the case under consideration, the battle would have to be brought to these shores, so that the full strength of the enemy would be relatively vitiated by the vicissitudes of an overseas expedition. If the present national defense plan is earnestly and thoroughly carried out it would be a matter of serious doubt as to whether an enemy could concentrate superior forces at any vital Philippine area. His chances of victory would, therefore, be problematical at best.

"Napoleon Bonaparte once said he never fought unless he felt that he had a 70 per cent chance of victory. His was sage advice. No such percentage of prospective victory would exist in such a struggle. This maximum expeditionary force that could be launched in aggression against these Islands can be more or less accurately estimated, based upon the capacity of the adversary's commercial and naval fleets. The maximum force could be more than matched by the Philippine nation. Intelligent military leadership, therefore, would give a reasonable prospect of successful defense.

"In any event, it would cost the enemy, in my opinion, at least a half million of men as casualties and upwards of five billions of dollars in money to pursue such an adventure with any hope of success. Would it be worth such a staggering cost? There would be constantly the added risk on the part of Japan of foreign intervention. If committed to such an attack the Japanese position would become desperate if such intervention should occur on the part of a nation equipped with a powerful fleet. A Japanese blockade would be practically unfeasible without the tacit agreement of the other nations surrounding the Pacific. It would be foolhardy for Japan to attempt such an overseas campaign until assured beforehand of the neutrality and even acquiescence of other interested powers.

"It has been assumed, in my opinion erroneously, that Japan covets these Islands. Just why has never been satisfactorily explained. Proponents of such a theory fail fully to credit the logic of the Japanese mind. Strategically, possession of these Islands would introduce an element of extraordinary weakness in the Japanese empire. It would split that empire militarily into two parts, separated by a broad stretch of ocean, and between it would lie its present military enemy, China. Every reason that is now advanced as to the indefensibility of the Archipelago by the United States, because of its distance therefrom, would apply in principle to its defense by Japan.

"As a matter of fact, its defense by Japan would be inferentially more complicated because of the invincibility of the hostility of the Filipino to foreign rule and his undoubted refusal to render military service to the Japanese empire. He has rendered and does render loyal service to the United States, but that nation has always co-operated in the goal of independence. He could not fail to become a hostile element in the Japanese empire. Economically, Japan would gain nothing by conquest in these Islands that it could not consummate more advantageously and cheaply by normal commercial and friendly process.

"No rational reason exists why Japan or any other nation should covet the sovereignty of this country. The projected Philippine nation would be a menace to no other nation on earth so long as it is neutral in its internationalism as provided by the Tydings-McDuffie Act, and armed and secure against predatory effort against its integrity. A number of nations would undoubtedly resist its control by some other rival. But as long as it is under the sovereignity of the United States, whose pacific intentions are known and recognized throughout the world, or as long as, under its own flag, it is completely neutral and relatively secure from seizure by others. I can see no reason for dire predictions as to its bloody future and possible destruction."

A Touch of Skepticism

If the statement of 1936 was courageous on the part of General MacArthur and heartening to the Filipinos, it is nothing short of astonishing that this position could have been so vigorously reiterated and amplified in 1939, after the major bastions in China had fallen. Not many persons, I suspect, shared General MacArthur's confidence in regard to the first phase of his statement, and no responsible student of Far Eastern affairs whom I have ever met quite agrees with the second.

The first part of his statement, it will be observed, is largely a repetition of the professional considerations that General MacArthur, as a soldier, set forth in his first declaration. There is, first, the repetition of his thesis that a trained defense force, even if it is small, will act as a sufficient deterrent to safeguard the Islands against invasion.

Obviously, this is a matter of opinion. Opinion varies as one does or does not believe that cost-counting is an essential part of the prelude to any Japanese military move. Many persons, who have watched the invasion of China and now of other countries in the Far East, are not inclined to believe that any such economic prevision has had an important part in making up Japanese policy. Filipinos have observed that Japan was not deterred by the "staggering" cost of invading a country of 450,000,000 persons and of facing an army of 2,500,000 men. They may, therefore, be entitled to wonder if Japan would be so promptly and vigorously deterred by the cost of invading a country of 16,000,000 with an army of less than 400,000.

General MacArthur may be deeply and correctly imbued with the precepts of Napoleon but the evidence has still to be submitted that the Japanese High Command has taken these particular precepts very much to heart. Obviously, losses are figured against possible profits. Even if we accepted General MacArthur's figure of a half-million men and several billion dollars, we might still have:

to face the fact that the Japanese would regard the conquest as
cheap at that price.

Similarly, the argument based on the supposed strategic weakness in the southward thrust may seem to many persons to overlook
one very important element in the case. Strategically, General
MacArthur points out, the conquest of the Philippines would
expose the Japanese flank to the "present enemy in China." But
the whole declared purpose of the Japanese invasion of China is
to see to it that China is not an "enemy" but a vassal. The General's logic would hold only if Japan attempted the conquest of
the Philippines while the China war was still in progress, or after
that war had been concluded without a Japanese victory over the
Chinese enemy. No Japanese has ever admitted this possibility.
Rather Japanese movements in China seem calculated to eliminate
precisely the enemy that General MacArthur depends on to forestall
the Japanese conquest of the Philippines.

There has been a failure, says the General, fully to respect the
logic of the Japanese mind. Apparently that mind was logical
enough to foresee the difficulty that General MacArthur raised and
to undertake to eliminate it before the real southward push started.

These are, of course, largely matters of opinion, and General
MacArthur, naturally, is entitled to his opinion that the Japanese
will be afraid enough of the Filipino citizen army to stay away
from the Islands.

But the second group of judgments in his statement goes beyond
questions of strategy and tactics into the field of international
politics, economics, and philosophy. In this sphere General Mac-
Arthur makes two assertions. He says, first, that in his opinion the
assumption that the Japanese covet the Philippines is erroneous,
and, second, that no rational reason exists why the Japanese or
anyone else should covet the sovereignty of the Islands. At this
point one may hazard taking issue with a great professional soldier
because he is not on his professional ground.

The first of the General's assertions, that it is erroneous to suppose that Japanese southward expansion includes the Philippines,

is strong medicine even for the gullible. The Japanese Foreign Office has repeatedly declared its overwhelming interest in this particular quarter of the globe. It has appointed a special bureau to take care of its interests there; it has sent out the usual ambassadors of aggression; and it has climaxed this course of action by declaring an Asiatic Monroe Doctrine. If the Japanese do not covet the Philippines, their entire policy, both military and political, has not only been a series of meaningless contortions, but has been systematically misrepresented, not by outside alarmists, but by the Japanese themselves.

CONCERNING "RATIONAL REASONS"

The second statement, that no rational reason exists why Japan or any other nation should covet the Philippines, goes much farther than the first. Those rational reasons are so overwhelming that it is hard to see how they could have been overlooked.

No nation in the world has ever needed gold exports more than Japan needs them at the present time. This year's gold production in the Philippines would more than double the Japanese output. That, possibly, is one rational reason.

The Japanese require a very large volume of raw materials, and they want raw materials that can be obtained without the politically inconvenient interference of export restrictions or the economically inconvenient necessity of buying. Those raw materials exist in the Philippines. Manifestly they would be far more accessible to the Japanese under Japanese sovereignty than they are under foreign control. There is a second rational reason.

The Japanese require large off-shore markets. They have been embarrassed in the search for those markets by the imposition of tariffs or quotas on their goods. Such tariffs and quotas now exist in the Philippines against Japanese goods. Obviously they would be eliminated by Japanese sovereignty, and the Japanese would have an accessible and growing market. There is another rational reason.

The Japanese have stated repeatedly in the last six months that it is their manifest destiny to control the political and economic affairs of eastern Asia. If any objection is made to such control, the objection can be overcome by running up the Japanese flag. That has already taken place in some quarter of a million square miles on the mainland. General MacArthur has indicated that the Filipinos might be hostile to foreign domination. If that is true, one of the strongest rational reasons why the Japanese would require sovereignty over the Philippines would be to have control over that hostility.

But this statement goes much further than mere confidence in Japan's pacific intentions. It says also that no rational reason exists why any other nation should covet the sovereignty of the Philippines. Frankly, I believe that any economic-minded person would find such a declaration inconceivable. It is tantamount to stating that the Philippine Archipelago is worthless. That, of course, is an astonishing fallacy. The Philippines are incredibly rich, with enormous resources, developed agricultural wealth, great mineral reserves, a splendid population. They lie at the crossroads of great lines of international trade. They form a gigantic control point, with great harbors and excellent communications.

The wealth of this great Archipelago is just beginning to be realized and developed. To state, therefore, that no rational reason exists why any nation should covet sovereignty over such a treasure-house and over such a future, is to fly in the face of rationality itself. They would be a magnificently rich prize for any nation.

It is, indeed, one of the most startling phenomena of the world's political scene that the United States is probably the only country in the world that would even dream of relinquishing possession of such a valuable territory, once sovereignty had been established. General MacArthur urges that we do not fully do credit to the logic of the Japanese mind. If the Japanese are even remotely logical it is hard to accept the belief that they do not covet sovereignty of an Archipelago that would double their national wealth, crystallize their position in Far Eastern Asia, set them across all the paths of Asiatic trade, and provide the geographic continuity of the Japanese empire from the Arctic Circle to the Equator.

ARMED AGAINST WHAT?

From the point of view of strict logic-chopping there might possibly be another objection brought at this point. If neither Japan nor, as General MacArthur says, any other nation covets the Philippines, it might possibly be asked why the General was asked to defend them in the first place. If no rational reason exists why their sovereignty should be challenged, why spend money on protecting their sovereignty? On the face of it General MacArthur is spending good time and good money to forestall a danger that he himself says does not exist.

But that is pushing the point too far. His meaning is, of course, that the value of the Archipelago is not sufficiently large to warrant a very costly operation, but that probably if it were entirely undefended some accident might be expected to happen. Obviously, this gets out of the question of defense and into the question of how valuable the stakes are. General MacArthur's position is that the essential values can be acquired by normal and peaceful means. He says, in fact, "Japan would gain nothing by conquest in these Islands that it could not consummate more advantageously and cheaply by normal commercial and friendly process."

Obviously, there are two words here that need defining. One is "normal" and the other is "friendly." Certainly, economically, Japan would gain nothing by conquest that could not be gained by abnormal penetration coupled with the application of a sufficient threat of force to bring the Philippines into the Japanese economic orbit.

Similarly, the point of the word "friendly" depends on its definition. The Japanese in China have already shown what they mean by this word. They have protested their "friendliness" from the first bombing, and they are even now in the process of acquiring what they term a "friendly" China. They mean, obviously, a China willing to take dictation from Tokyo.

At this point General MacArthur faces the larger realities in the Philippine situation. It is certainly correct to assume that the Japanese would not undertake the military invasion of the Philippines if they could get all that they wanted by non-military means. If the Filipinos are willing to bow to Japanese penetration, they can undoubtedly be spared a military invasion. It is obvious that they can be spared only at the price of economic and political surrender in advance.

Several years ago the distinguished head of one of the habitual Japanese good-will missions to Manila took a group of us newspapermen out to a good geisha-sukiyaki dinner. The usual protestations of undying friendship were made. After the dinner three of us American correspondents got rid of the stool-pigeons and took this "envoy of friendship" up to my house. After about an hour and a half of "careful mellowing," we asked him for a statement of the real Japanese attitude toward possible changes of sovereignty in the Philippines. By that time he was delightfully frank, with a total loss of his official inhibitions. He replied:

"My friend, Japan not give one damn whose flag fly over beautiful Islands, so long Japan own and operate Islands."

There is the problem of the defense of the Philippines in a nutshell. If the Filipinos are willing to be owned and operated by the Japanese, they can fly the flag of independence to their hearts' content. So when General MacArthur says that the Japanese could gain what they want by "friendly" processes, he is perfectly correct if the Filipinos are willing to accept the Japanese definition of friendliness. The United States might just possibly decide that this definition ought to be modified.

It certainly is to be presumed that the Japanese would not send a military expedition to the Philippines if they could get everything they wanted without the bother of even fueling their cruisers. The real Japanese threat to the Philippines has never been simply a military invasion of the island of Luzon. The real threat is economic and political penetration by means of which the Philippines would drop into the lap of Japan, without the necessity for firing a shot, as soon as the United States retired.

ADVANCE GUARD OF INVASION

The advance guard of that invasion is already at work. It consists of hemp-producers in the province of Davao, where there is so strong a nucleus that the Japanese already control more than half the total output of Philippine hemp. It consists also of small merchandisers, admirably supported by export cartels in Japan, and trained by long experience in beating anti-Japanese boycotts.

For example, in 1931, the Chinese began to clamp down on the handling of Japanese goods in the Philippine markets. The Chinese were the major middlemen of the Islands, and this boycott hurt. The obvious Japanese answer to that boycott throughout the Far East was the attack on Shanghai in February of 1932.

But the far more subtle and far-reaching answer to it, in the Philippines, was the phenomenal increase in Japanese merchandising. In the city of Manila the Japanese built a bazaar on literally every main street. In two years' time Japanese control of retail trade in Manila increased from less than 5 per cent to 27 per cent, and the figure was subsequently pushed even higher. The gains were made at the expense of the Chinese retailers. These bazaars did not necessarily make money. All they had to do was keep books and collect their 6 per cent profit from Tokyo.

They dumped rubber-soled shoes on the Philippine market at fifteen cents a pair. (And they all had good United States trademarks on them.) They sold undershirts, the major garment of the Filipino, at less than ten cents apiece. Electric light bulbs could be had for one-third the cost of the American or European product. Japanese textiles by 1934 had more than one-half of the Philippine market, which had been the best off-shore purchaser of American fabricated cotton goods. Towns all over the Philippines had Japanese running photograph establishments. There were Japanese barbers and Japanese filling-station operators scattered from one end of the Archipelago to the other.

Their numbers were relatively small. There are probably not more than about 30,000 Japanese in the Islands at the present time. But they quickly came to occupy an economic position out of all proportion to their numbers.

The retirement of the United States from the field will necessarily make their economic position infinitely stronger. We have already noticed that more than half of the Philippine population is directly dependent upon major export crops that are sold in the American market. The retirement of the United States from the Philippines means the closing of this advantageous market, and, therefore, necessarily the curtailment of the means of life for more than half of the Philippine population.

Now it is not to be supposed that 10,000,000 Filipinos will conveniently sit down and die just to please the American Farm Bureau and the bankers who happen to have sugar investments in Cuba and so want to eliminate the Philippine competitor. It is equally unlikely from present indications that a shift in Philippine producing economy will be made with either sufficient speed or sufficient enthusiasm to put these 10,000,000 persons into the production of sustaining crops.

The fact is that when the American market is withdrawn, the Filipinos will sell what they can, where they can, and as much as they can. The one market that will be open to them is Japan.

JAPAN BECOMES GENEROUS

Two years before the Philippine Commonwealth came into existence, the outspoken Japanese consul-general in Manila publicly informed the Filipinos that they need not fear the loss of the American market for their sugar, since Japan would be very happy to buy, instead, all the cotton that they could produce, up to $30,000,000 a year. All they needed to do was to change from growing sugar to growing cotton, and Japan would do the rest.

Early in 1940 another Japanese consul reassured the Philippines by pointing out that Japan would be quite willing to become a market for a substantial part of the Philippine sugar production. He even suggested a figure of roughly a million tons, and that would amply satisfy present sugar producers. (Since Japan is one of the smallest per capita sugar consumers in the world, there ought to be much skepticism over this figure. Japan supplies her domestic needs from Formosa, and can purchase Java sugar at a lower price than Philippine.)

In any case, it is obvious that as Japan's industrialization accelerates, the demand for raw materials will increase. The Philippines can produce cotton for the Japanese textile industry, and iron, chromite, and manganese for the Japanese metal industries. The withdrawal of the United States means that the Filipinos, having to sell where they can, will sell in the most easily available and advantageous market, and that is Japan.

When Japan has become the outlet for what is left of Philippine productive economy, she will hardly undertake to sustain price levels as benevolently as has the United States. If Japan proposes to pay the piper, it is more than reasonable to assume that Japan will call the tune. In the Philippines this obviously means the dictation of what the Filipinos shall produce and for whom, and how much and in what currency they will be paid for it.

Under those conditions the advent of Japanese economic advisers in the Philippines would be inevitable. Political and even military advisers might follow. The orientation of the Philippines toward Japan's "New Order in East Asia" would be a matter of course. The rest of the story can be imagined.

This is not to suggest that the Filipinos are any more venal than any other Asiatic people, or for that matter, Occidental. Naturally, they would dislike exceedingly to see their country come into the orbit of an expanding power. But when their life depended on it, there would be little or nothing they could do about it.

Moreover, if such a movement were carried out with reasonable finesse, and with the expenditure of much less than the cost of sending even two cruisers into Philippine waters, the Japanese could count on some very substantial friends in the Philippine court.

There has already been much loose talk, and some not so loose, about Japanese "Fifth Column" activities in the Philippines. There are free schools for teaching the Japanese language in Manila. There are Filipinos of some substance who are officers in Japan-Philippine "friendly societies." There are junkets galore both ways.

Some of this activity has been exaggerated, and the accusation of treachery has been too readily brought against some Filipinos. But the movement exists, and even if treachery were discounted altogether, there would undoubtedly be found an influential group of Filipinos who sincerely believe that the only possible future for their country lies in the formation of close ties with Japan. It is easy to see how such persons might be put on the Japanese payroll. When to this group are added those who are concerned primarily with the buttered side of the bread (and they exist in the Philippines exactly as they exist everywhere else), the defense of the Philippines becomes a vastly more complicated problem than the stopping of an expeditionary force somewhere in northern Luzon.

More Than a Soldier's Job

In other words, when President Quezon called on General Mac-Arthur to defend the Philippines, he asked a professional soldier to do a job that required also the services of the most competent statesmen and economists.

For the defense of the Philippines is not merely a matter for machine guns and mosquito fleets. Nor can it be accomplished by wishful thinking about the non-existence of the menace of Japanese aggression. Defense requires an economic and political stability that can resist penetration; that can be accomplished only by sustaining economic ties to the advantageous American market to such a degree that other customers cannot gain consumer's control and so dictate terms.

Defense will necessarily at times require imposing tariffs and import restrictions, and, as the Filipinos have already discovered, limiting immigration.

Already the Japanese have strongly protested against the newly adopted Commonwealth policy of limiting immigration from any foreign country to 500 nationals annually. The Japanese bargained for a thousand, and admitted, for the first time, that their present rate was 2,800. Their protests were carried to Washington, where there was a polite refusal to entertain them. Imagine what would happen to the Philippines if a similar restriction were attempted, and similar Japanese objections made, after the Philippines had become an independent government without the backing of the United States. It is hardly to be imagined that the Filipinos could or would then suggest any such limitation to the Japanese.

Another question of Philippine defense is what form the United States military establishment will take after Philippine independence is consummated. The original independence bills provided that after Philippine independence the United States might retain such military and naval bases in the Philippines as were agreed upon between the two governments. The presumption was that valuable military establishments, such as Corregidor, Fort McKinley, Fort Stotsenburg, and the Post of Manila, would be retained by the Americans. One reason for this supposition was the fact that an independent Philippine Government could not possibly afford to maintain them. In the case of Corregidor, for example, an independent Philippine Government would probably have to put on some type of super-tax to afford even target practice for the big coast-defense guns.

When Mr. Quezon wished to substitute a second Philippine bill for the one that was rejected by the Philippine legislature after having been passed by the United States Congress, he hit upon this military establishment clause as one that could be altered without materially changing the terms of the legislation. Accordingly the new law drops the word "military," leaves in the naval bases, and adds "fueling stations" as the correct gesture to expanding air activity in the Pacific.

This re-phraseology was trumpeted up and down the Philippines as a major concession that Mr. Quezon had wrung from the Americans. Actually, of course, it hardly modifies the defense position except to the disadvantage of the Filipinos, for they will have to maintain whatever of the military bases they can.

The Naval Base Problem

The naval base proposal is a subject of negotiation between the two governments. It is, therefore, a problem not so much for the Filipinos as for the United States. The United States has a good small naval base at Cavite, just across an arm of the bay from Manila, and a good drydock and repair station at Olongapo on Subic Bay to the northwest of Manila on the China Sea.

It is quite possible under the terms of the present law that, for the sake of economy, these establishments might be the ones that the United States chose to retain. They have the advantages of nearness to the capital, good communications, a productive hinterland on which they can draw for necessary labor, and, of course, the advantage of their traditional and established position. In the event that the United States wished to create a very strong naval establishment in the Far East, it is possible that some other locations might be chosen.

Probably the best natural site for a naval base in the entire Archipelago is down at Malampaya Sound on the northwest coast of the island of Palawan. This sound would afford deep-water anchorage for all the navies in the world, and has a narrow and highly defensible mouth. It is well surrounded by hills that would form ideal anti-aircraft stations. There are even suitable islands well off the coast for advanced defense positions.

It has, however, some important drawbacks. For one thing, the island of Palawan is one of the least developed of the entire Philippine group. It is sparsely populated, and there are few roads. More important still, it has one of the highest rates of mosquitoes to the square inch in the entire Far East. Malaria is rampant. Before a naval base could be built at Malampaya, it would be necessary to undertake a cleanup somewhat similar to what was done in the Panama Canal Zone.

Moreover, while Palawan has an advantageous position in that it is the most westerly of the Philippine Islands and therefore commands the southern stretches of the South China Sea, it is also relatively remote from some of the more important centers of population; it is roughly 400 miles from Manila. The waters of the China Sea off the Palawan coast, in addition, are treacherous and inadequately charted. There are innumerable reefs and shoals that would make large-scale maneuvers near the base delicate and difficult.

It is assumed that a base at Malampaya would be so expensive that it would be the only major base in the Philippines. This also might be a handicap, since the growing importance of the large island of Mindanao and the expansion of the Japanese by way of the Mandated Islands might make the necessary point of defense the southeast coast of the Archipelago instead of the southwest. The present Japanese concentration of population is in the province of Davao at the southeastern corner of Mindanao, removed from Palawan by several chains of islands and the Sulu Sea. The largest concentration of Philippine base metals, moreover, is in Surigao, also on the eastern shore of Mindanao across the broadest part of the Archipelago from Palawan.

In any event, if the United States were to build a naval base at Malampaya, it would have to be done right, and made much larger than any existing establishment in the Philippines. This would presuppose a very considerable change in policy on the part of the American Government.

AIR BASES OF THE FUTURE

The air-base proposal contained by implication in the authorization for fueling stations in the Philippines is still in the future. The air arm in the Islands at the present time is not particularly strong, but is being strengthened. An aircraft carrier has been assigned to the Asiatic fleet, and this presumably will supplement or replace entirely the present small squadron of seaplanes. The army has a good flying field just outside of the city of Manila, and a fair auxiliary field at Fort Stotsenburg about seventy-five miles north of the capital. There are more than a hundred civilian landing fields in the Islands, but very few of them even remotely approach first class.

The question of air bases and fueling stations was possibly included in the independence program not so much because of its military significance as because of the obviously forthcoming expansion in trans-Pacific commercial aviation. Pan American Airways has built an excellent way station at Manila, which served as the terminus for the trans-Pacific flights for two years before the service was extended to Hong Kong. The Pan American sea base was opened up at Cavite adjoining the naval station. Its land establishment was set up about six miles east of Manila adjacent to the army post at Fort McKinley. This establishment consisted chiefly of a powerful radio station and a reserve fuel depot.

It is the plan eventually to bring the Pan American landing station into Manila proper when the new municipal airport and seaplane base is completed.

Pan American's service is in part a crossroads operation. The Netherlands has repeatedly suggested that K.L.M., the Netherlands air line, ought to come into Manila in a northward flight from Batavia. Experimental trips have been made for the purpose of charting this service.

Thus far, however, the Filipinos have been extremely reluctant to grant the necessary franchise. They are uneasy about opening up the Islands to foreign aircraft lines, believing that if a franchise were granted to the Netherland company, they would not be in a strong position to resist the demand for a similar franchise when the Japanese undertook to extend their southward aviation routes. Moreover, an airline operation coming up from the south would probably not fly directly into Manila, but would make its initial landing elsewhere in the Philippines, probably as far south as Zamboanga. This might bring a foreign company into competition with the local corporations in the handling of inter-island traffic.

It is to be supposed, however, that the United States will eventually expand its north-south flying service in the Pacific, as well as its east-west operations. Thus far, the program for flights to Australia completes its route by way of Hawaii, American Samoa, Fiji, and Sydney. It is by no means beyond possibility, however, that more traffic and better operating conditions could be found on a Philippines-Australian route that might cover Borneo and the rest of Netherland India in its course.

It is conceivable that the opening of these routes to commercial aviation would make it necessary for the United States to preserve its access to the same or similar landing fields for military purposes. Consequently, a fueling base clause was included in the independence law.

The character of modern warfare serves to emphasize the importance of this part of the defense program. It seems likely now that future plans for military and naval operations will include even more emphasis on available landing fields and hangar space than on drydocks and coast-defense artillery. The United States and the Philippines are fortunate, therefore, in that this provision already exists in the law and can be carried out with no further machinery than the already authorized negotiation.

In the long run, of course, the ability of the United States and the Filipinos to defend the Philippines will rest very largely upon their willingness to defend them. The willingness to defend them, in turn, pre-supposes a change in the attitude and policy of the United States toward its Asiatic position.

If one accepts the thesis that we have in this Archipelago a vulnerable outpost, there follow two possible courses of action. The first is to withdraw from the outpost, abandon it to the enemy, and entrench ourselves behind shorter lines that we believe can be more easily and more cheaply fortified. The second is to arm and strengthen the outpost to such a degree that it can resist attack. In that way it would become a strong salient to attract enemy fire and thus divert it from objectives closer to our continental borders. This is the possibility, in short, of preparing a position from which we can fight a Pacific war on the other side of the Pacific.

There is one other consideration in the problem of Philippine defense that is also contingent upon American policy. The discussions of strategy of Philippine defense have been based almost entirely upon the assumption that the United States, unaided, would undertake to defend the Archipelago by means of a naval and military expedition based on Pearl Harbor, Hawaii, and San Diego. The reason for this assumption, originally, was the theory that the United States must plan all of its defenses on the basis of no alliances with any other power. In a word, we accepted the worst possible situation and planned our campaign accordingly. Later developments have reduced the ability of other Western Powers to join in our operations, but have by no means made them helpless in Asia.

Even so, the economic coherence of the South China Sea area and the very future of the Western governments that must salvage as much as they can in this part of the world make the defense of the area more logically a joint operation than a single responsibility resting upon the United States. This, of course, so greatly changes the whole concept of operations and the basis for them that the defense program becomes not a question merely of defending the Philippines, but a question of defending the South China Sea. This considerably larger problem will be discussed later.

CHAPTER IX

OUR PHILIPPINE VENTURE—3

THE picture of the perils of Philippine independence has been presented to Americans largely from the Filipinos' point of view. If there is good reason why the American flag should not be hauled down in the Philippines, it is assumed that the reason is that the Philippines would otherwise pass quickly into economic collapse and under Japanese rule.

The desire to prevent this is probably a combination of humanitarianism and the dislike of seeing substantial American accomplishments so quickly nullified. On either grounds the appeal to the American mind would be largely to generosity and idealism. We have undertaken the protection of a relatively defenseless people, have schooled them in government, and brought about a remarkable increase in their happiness quotient. We assume a strange role, then, if we take a course of action that precipitates them once more into the misery from which American occupation has temporarily lifted them.

This attitude, however, is based on another assumption. It is taken for granted that it would be greatly to our advantage if we could withdraw honorably from the Philippines, and greatly to our disadvantage if we were obliged to remain. This is a fallacy.

The whole theory of the Philippines as an economic liability is based upon a confusion in terms. The unfavorable balance of trade and the presence of competitive products in the American market have led to the assumption that both of these conditions were permanent and that nothing could be done about them. As a matter of fact, the Japanese export position has already changed the first. On the second we have already taken steps through quota limitations, quite apart from the independence program, to regulate the flow of Philippine goods so as to afford the maximum of needed raw materials and the minimum of competition.

This adaptation could be carried on much more wisely through a program of planned expansion in the Philippines of products that are non-competitive with the United States. As has been pointed out, we are by no means self-sufficient in essential raw materials, and the greatest gaps in our economy are in the field of tropical products. There is no economic reason why a large quantity of these products cannot be secured from the Philippines, where we can continue to enjoy a favorable trade position. We could, at the same time, reduce purchases from some other countries where our export market is not commensurate with imports.

We could, for example, produce to good advantage in the Philippines rubber, tea, coffee, and quinine, and thus become more dependent upon a closely associated government or actual possession, and less dependent upon foreign markets, where we are subject to whims of legislation or penalties of barter. Such a program, however, would take time, and would involve the outlay of capital and a greater degree of co-operation from the local Philippine Government. It would be necessary to put the whole agricultural program on a long-term basis, to take some of the money out of sugar, and to plan the Philippine economy in such a way as to achieve a minimum of irritation to specific groups in the United States.

Naturally that course of action is speculative and for the future. It presumes a planned working out of an almost ideal economic relationship between the two countries. Whether there would be enough far-sighted persons on both sides of the Pacific to make that a success is problematical.

OUR FIFTH CUSTOMER

In the meantime, quite apart from any such rosy dreams of the future, there already exists an economic situation that is enormously to the advantage of the United States. At the present time, when we are searching for further overseas markets, we enjoy in the Philippines a trade that runs to an average of about a quarter of a billion dollars a year, with a balance at present well adjusted.

The Philippines at the present time are our fifth customer. More than a hundred million dollars' worth of American products were sold in the Philippines in 1939, and this was a relatively bad year. The Philippines are our first market for fifty-five export products; our second market for another hundred. They are our first overseas market for cotton fabrics—$12,000,000 worth in 1938. In some other years the figure has been considerably larger than this. This is our greatest off-shore market for cigarettes, our best off-shore market for wheat flour, our best market for mining and quarrying machinery, our best market for prepared dairy products. There are nineteen different items in the American foreign commerce list whose exports to the Philippines exceed a million dollars a year even in a bad year.

The relative importance of this market can possibly be better understood when it is compared with our sales to Central and South America. We all look quite naturally to Brazil as an important outlet for American goods. It is. But it ranks tenth on our export list—$20,000,000 a year below the Philippines. Argentina is an important overseas market, and eleventh on the list—$30,000,000 below the Philippines. Cuba's purchases in 1939 were also $20,000,000 below the Philippine level, and Cuba's rank as a market was ninth. Indeed, not one country in the Western Hemisphere, with the exception of Canada, begins to buy as much from us as the Philippine Archipelago.

This market is additionally important because of the fact that the standard of living in the Philippines is now rising and should continue to rise in the future. Access to the American market, as we have observed, has given the Filipinos purchasing power. At the same time the country is not industrialized (80 per cent of the population is engaged in agriculture in one form or another), and so there is a continuously expanding market for American processed goods.

Life itself is relatively simple in a country whose climate is so benign. Heating, clothing, and housing do not absorb anything like so large a part of the normal income as they do in the temperate zones. Even the food problem is relatively simple. The staple diet of the Filipino is inexpensive. Consequently the people afford luxury purchases, as opposed to necessity purchases, at an unusually low economic level. This helps to create an ideal market for the United States, whose exports are likely to be channeled more and more into the field of processed goods and goods designed for a relatively high standard of living.

At a time when our attention is fixed on the need and desirability of finding more and more outlets for our goods, a market of this size and character is not to be despised. In the field of foreign trade, at least, self-interest as well as altruism would suggest the inadvisability of strangling our Philippine customer.

MINING ENTERS THE PICTURE

The economic value of the Philippine Archipelago has been changed in another important respect in the course of the last decade. This change has been brought about by the discovery and development of gigantic mineral resources.

At the present time the most important of these is gold. In 1927 there were only two large-scale mining operations in the Philippines, and only one of them was paying dividends. In 1940 there are more than 200 mining operations, and twenty of them are paying dividends. Fifteen years ago the annual gold output of the Philippines was about a million dollars; at the present time it is between $35,000,000 and $40,000,000. The importance of this production will be observed in the fact that the Philippines are second only to California among gold producers under the American flag.

There has been no Robert W. Service to sing the saga of mushing into the Benguet hills. There is no spell of Baguio to match the fabled fortunes of the Yukon. But four years ago the Philippines passed Alaska as a gold producer, and have since steadily widened the gap. The Alaskan gold output in 1938, for example, was $28,-000,000; in the same year the Philippines produced $34,000,000. Philippine gold production is now just about the size of that of all South America combined.

But gold mining is only the beginning of the story of mineral wealth in these Islands. In the course of the last five years the base metals have come to occupy an increasingly important position.

At the present time the Philippines are producing and shipping to Japan more than a million tons of iron ore annually. Eight iron mining companies are in operation. The oldest and strongest is paying handsome dividends.

The picture in respect to iron ore, however, became much more spectacular in 1939 when H. Foster Bain, American adviser to the Philippine Government on mining, and former chief of the United States Bureau of Mines, announced the discovery of a new and accessible iron ore field that in potential value surpassed anything previously heard of in that part of the world. This deposit is a reserve of the Philippine Government and will be worked through the National Development Company. It is located in Mindanao in the province of Surigao, and is easily accessible. The ore in sight is estimated at more than a billion tons.

Manganese operations are also being carried on successfully in many parts of the Islands. Japan is the chief market for this product, and development has been steady.

The story of chromium in the Philippines is almost fantastic. In the southeastern part of the island of Luzon, as early as twenty-five years ago, there was known to exist a small deposit (about 120,000 tons) of high-grade chromite ore. This was not successfully worked until about six years ago, when the largest of the mining companies in the Philippines, Benguet Consolidated, undertook to put this ore on the market. The deposit has now been just about worked out at a good profit.

In the meantime, however, much impetus was given to the survey of other parts in the Islands for chromite ore. The United States Government more than twenty years ago had made some reservations of lands that were known to be chromite-bearing. The Philippine Government also held reservations. In 1931 one of the most important of the American reservations was returned to the public land of the Philippines, and private companies immediately began to stake out claims.

Two years later it was announced that there had been discovered in the Philippines the largest known accessible deposit of medium-grade chromite ore in the world. This deposit is in the province of Zambales, and it is very conservatively estimated at 10,000,000 tons. It is in the form of an outcrop, highly accessible, and it could be mined with a steam shovel. It is nineteen miles from a deep-water anchorage—downhill all the way—and a gravity railroad is taking the ore direct from the mountain to wharfside loading bins.

This ore is not so high in chromic oxide content as is standard high-grade chromite ore. The chromic oxide content has been running on the average from 33 to 35 per cent. In its present form, however, it is an ideal refractory. This deposit can probably lay claim to being the world's largest accessible source of high-grade refractory ore.

Moreover, recent chemical and engineering discoveries have developed a process of reduction whereby ore of this grade can be made commercially valuable in both the chemical and metallurgical fields. The application of such a process to this gigantic deposit would give the United States the largest available chromium supply in the world and make us under our own flag self-sufficient in one of the strategic war materials in which a major deficiency exists.

CHROMIUM AND FOREIGN POLICY

The presence of chromium in large quantities in the Philippines has already created some international problems. In 1935 an Italian syndicate approached the Philippine companies asking for quotations on large supplies. The Philippine companies were in American hands, and the Americans promptly referred the matter to the United States State Department.

At that time Italy was in the midst of the Ethiopian campaign, and it was not our policy to supply war materials to belligerents. The State Department responded that American policy had not changed, but that observing it was voluntary. The chromite did not go to Italy.

Some Philippine chromite is going to Japan at the present time, since the American policy of denying war materials to belligerents has not been applied to the Japanese Empire. Where American companies, rather than Filipino, are concerned, they prefer as a matter of policy not to use this market, and have repeatedly asked to enjoy a share in the American reserve-supplies program. But thus far none of this ore has been accumulated by the American Government.

Base metal operations also include extensive mining of lead, zinc, copper, and asbestos. Almost any of these can be indefinitely expanded whenever a market makes the investment of capital seem advisable and reasonably safe.

The Philippines have not yet joined the ranks of major oil producers, but extensive exploration is under way. Oil has already been struck on two islands in different parts of the Archipelago. The first successful drillings were on the island of Cebu; but even better prospects are now seen on the Bondoc Peninsula in southern Luzon.

The development of the oil resources of the Philippines became a matter of negotiation two years ago between the Commonwealth Government and representatives of the Standard Oil Company. An exploration and development program on a royalty basis was worked out, under which the American company was to bring the prospective wealth into production and continue exploration throughout the Islands. After the success of the negotiations had already been announced and the contracts were ready for signature, a hitch developed, and the Commonwealth Government withdrew from the negotiations, over an anti-litigation clause in the projected agreement.

As a matter of fact, the motives for the withdrawal were probably more comprehensive than objection to this one phase of the document. Some members of the Philippine Government were undoubtedly uneasy about the prospect of a large-scale exploration program carried out by a non-Philippine company. Consequently the government itself will make the surveys and undertake to bring oil into production.

Every geologic survey in the Philippines has pointed out that this mountainous Archipelago is highly mineralized from the tip of Aparri in the north to the southern end of Jolo across the channel from Borneo. There has been a wildcat stock boom; cow pastures and golf courses have been promoted as mining enterprises; there have been tales of fact and fancy so inextricably interwoven that good judgment of operations in futures has been extremely difficult. Through all of this, however, the Philippines have steadily, year by year, increased their mineral output. New mines have come into production; old companies that were on the edge of the board have started paying dividends. An entire new factor has thus been added to Philippine economy.

It would be short-sighted indeed to imagine that this development could not be very greatly extended. It is more than safe to hazard the prediction that with a reasonable degree of freedom from outside interference the Philippines could develop an enviably strong economy based on a developed agriculture and an expanding mineral wealth.

The Basis of Taxable Wealth

While the mineral wealth of the Islands is spectacular, it is still in agriculture that the great richness of these Islands reposes. Developed agricultural wealth is not only the basis of the standard of living of the majority of the population, it is also the basis upon which taxation can be imposed and the functions of government carried out.

Agricultural wealth consists of a number of factors, among them fertility of the soil and favorable climatic conditions. Developed agricultural wealth consists in the organization of favorable factors to produce for a market. It consists of channels of transportation, roads, piers, navigable streams, power plants (such as those at the sugar centrals), locomotives, and shipping. All of these factors already exist in the Philippines. Plantations are criss-crossed by excellent paved highways. Hardly a point of present agricultural importance in the whole of the Islands is more than fifty miles from a seacoast.

The present net investment in agriculture in the Philippines is usually estimated at something around a half-billion dollars. When these other factors are considered, it will be obvious that the developed wealth of such an agricultural structure must be many, many times that amount.

Developed agricultural wealth, with an operating system of marketing, means purchasing power, and with purchasing power come the desire for and the ability to use luxury goods and tools. In this sense the agricultural wealth of the Philippines is a great deal more than colonial production under a plantation system that bleeds a dependency white to pour money into a mother country. It is a wealth that has stability based on the fact that its collective benefits have already been distributed to a very large number of individual persons.

In addition to this developed wealth, there is the even larger prospect of great undeveloped agricultural resources. Undeveloped agricultural wealth suggests immediately the prospect for opening up the island of Mindanao.

This is the second island in size in the Philippines. With its 37,000 square miles, it is a little larger than Indiana. It has about a third, or less, of Indiana's population. Parts of the interior have not yet been opened up. Roads across the island are just now in process of being built.

This single island has a variety of climatic and geographical conditions that give it enormous potentialities of production. The upland plains of Bukidnon are similar to Texas, while the lowlands are tropical. It is the best livestock country in the Philippines. It produces more than half of the Philippine hemp. It has coal fields and it has also hundreds of thousands of acres of magnificent virgin forest. A great river, the Cotabato, drains the central part of the island. Even this river valley is hardly explored, much less cultivated. There are lofty mountain chains. In the north these splendid hills enclose Lake Lanao, the largest fresh-water body in the Archipelago. In the south is Mt. Apo, the loftiest peak in the Philippines. Over on the west is the hospitable peninsula of Zamboanga, and at its tip the beautiful city of that name, fabled in song and story for the monkeys that have no tails.

The Philippines have become Mindanao-conscious in recent years. The development of the island has become a major expectation of the economy of the future. Experiments in colonization and transplantation of populations from the congested urban centers farther north have already begun. The development of this island to the level of Luzon could mean a virtual doubling of the wealth of the Philippines, accommodation for at least half again, if not double, their present population, and the opening up of entire new vistas in the wealth of this insular possession of the United States.

Where the "Empire Mind" Comes In

Now of course the conception of wealth in such a possession as a part of the accrued wealth of the United States depends entirely upon the point of view of the individual. The person with the empire mind, as we have noted, cannot divorce himself from the idea that, in so far as the Philippines become richer, the United States becomes richer. A contented population living in a satisfactory arrangement with a "mother country" would in itself be an item of enormous wealth. A growing market in that population for goods supplied from other parts of the United States would be part of the producing and consuming wealth of the entire empire. Access to a supply of materials that could be advantageously produced would again be part of our whole wealth as a nation.

With this concept in mind, it would be impossible to conceive of a rich country like the Philippines as a liability. This broader outlook, however, demands that the ordinary American conceive of the United States as something more than a political and geographic entity that is bounded on the east and west by the continental North American shelf. The Filipino, on the other hand, would have to conceive of his wealth as something that ultimately accrues to his own satisfaction of needs, and his own individual riches, and not as something that is being drawn off for the benefit of another racial group on the other side of the world. In a word, political and emotional conceptions have to fit the wide economic picture in order that this wealth can be greatly developed and properly used for the benefit of both parties concerned.

There is quite another factor in the political and economic scene that is often referred to as part of our wealth in our Philippine dependency. This is our position, in government and trade, in respect to Asia.

Just how far the possession of such an important outpost could or would serve as a stepping-off place to other important Far Eastern markets that are still undeveloped is entirely a matter of opinion. There is no reason why the largest part of America's Far Eastern trade would have to be channeled through the Philippines. In practice, however, the possession of such an outpost should give us an enormous advantage. If we foresee the development of a gigantic Chinese market, for example, the presence of a suitable clearing house within 600 miles of Hong Kong ought to be an important asset.

In the larger sense, however, our trade and the control of its channels are dependent in part upon our political position and our prestige. More and more, trade is coming to be a matter of negotiation, a matter of international friendly relationships, a matter of suitable joint identification of interests and ideology. Goods are not always bought and sold on a price basis only. Political and emotional accessibility to markets may be at times equally important.

It goes without saying that the retirement of the United States from its political position in eastern Asia would result in a tremendous loss of prestige. How far this would be translated into a trade disadvantage cannot be estimated in dollars and cents at this point, but it would eventually be so translated.

There should be considered also the effect on the United States of the ultimate disposition of the wealth that has been created under American sovereignty. If there were the prospect, for example, that this wealth would continue to be developed and utilized in a trade and political program by a government entirely friendly to the United States and interested in preserving the closest possible ties with us, the severance of our political relationships might not have any serious repercussions in the field of trade. For example, the technical independence of Cuba is in itself no very considerable drawback to the closest possible trade relationships between Cuba and the United States. And the adjustment of the Cuban and American economies to the mutual advantage of both countries can be a matter of constant study and friendly negotiation.

In the case of the Philippines, on the other hand, we must contemplate in the severance of political ties the possibility of turning over these economic structures to a government that will not make adjustments necessary to friendly relationships with us. If, after having assisted in the development of this productive wealth in the Philippines, we now take a course of action that turns that wealth into the hands of the Japanese, we invite its use in direct competition with us and to the detriment of our interests. We propose to equip the Japanese with the means that we have developed and then to see those means turned against us.

If this is true in the economic field, it is even more true in the political field. In this sphere the development of the mineral wealth of the Philippines becomes of paramount importance. If there is to be any degree of political competition, competitive naval building, or cross-purposes, between Japan and the United States, we will have put ourselves in the position of supplying the Japanese with precisely the materials that can be used to our greatest disadvantage. If our program of supplying war materials to Japan has been paradoxical in the past, it would certainly be even more so in the future, if we turned over to that government an already highly developed arsenal.

The Japanese are getting iron, manganese and chromium out of the Philippines. Obviously it will be much simpler and cheaper, later on, to take over the output than to buy it in the open market. Similarly, it will be easier to use the output of the Philippine gold mines for necessary foreign purchases than to deplete credit reserves abroad or to maintain the constant struggle to create new ones through the expansion of export trade.

The United States, therefore, has a stake in the Philippine wealth not only because of investment, development, and present favorable position; it has also a stake in the preservation of that wealth in order to keep it out of hostile hands.

BLOWING HOT AND COLD

We have already observed that the Filipinos are uneasy over their future. There has been quite a bit of blowing hot and cold on the subject of independence since that 15th day of November, 1935, when the Filipinos were so enthusiastically hurtled into their Commonwealth Government.

Mr. Quezon has changed his mind several times. At one moment he has suggested that he would be quite receptive to a "re-examination" of the whole Philippine question. At other times he has suggested that the program must go through as drafted, come what may. Obviously Mr. Quezon is caught on the horns of a dilemma. As a good patriot, he cannot very well abandon the patriotic slogan to which he has devoted the whole of his political career. Nor, as a good patriot, can he contemplate with equanimity the prospect of the complete disappearance, even in his own lifetime, of the government to which he has given his talents. Mr. Quezon is obviously worried, and he has a right to be.

The entire drama of Philippine independence has worked out along different lines from those intended by the Filipinos when they discovered how useful a tool the cry for independence was. The plain fact that Philippine independence means the actual loss of American protection and of the American market has not been sufficiently faced by the majority of the Philippine politicians who have urged independence year after year.

Even after it became obvious that an independence bill could and would be hammered through the United States Congress, Mr. Quezon himself did not believe that its provisions would ever be carried out. I sat with a group of six other Americans in Mr. Quezon's house at that time and heard Mr. Quezon say that it was his fixed belief that the American declaration of intent to grant Philippine independence would completely satisfy the Filipinos' emotional urge for self-government.

"The generous gesture," he declared, "is all that is required by our people. Once it has been made, we can proceed to work out a better program to the advantage of both countries. So, gentlemen, you need have no fears."

Mr. Quezon told us, of course, that if we ever published his words he would deny them; and if he ever sees this, he will probably deny that he made the statement. But the other Americans must have felt, as I did, as they sat in that front room in Mr. Quezon's house out there in Pasay, that they were listening to a far-sighted psychologist who knew his own people and who was obliged temporarily to practice a policy of deception in order to provide for the good of his own country.

This impression was strengthened when Mr. Quezon stumped the country in opposition to the Hare-Hawes-Cutting Bill. Cynics said that his objection to it was the fact that he had not had enough share in drafting it and was afraid that too much political prestige would accrue to Sergio Osmeña and Manuel Roxas, who had headed the Filipino delegation in the United States.

Certainly Mr. Quezon's triumphant return to the Philippines a year later with a bill that he was willing to support, and that differed from its predecessor in no really important respect, gave some basis for this belief. At the time, however, those who had heard Mr. Quezon's supposedly confidential declaration of intent, believed that his opposition to the Hare-Hawes-Cutting Bill was a play for time, designed to reject the bill on any convenient grounds in order to put the settlement of the problem on an entirely different basis.

In the course of events Mr. Quezon has become the President of the Commonwealth, and he enjoys it. His leadership is unchallenged, his political prestige at its highest point. Naturally, he cannot afford now to take a larger risk. He has never been more sensitive than now to the currents of opinion among his constituents. He has decided for and against a second term for himself (which involves a Constitutional amendment) at least four times. He has been, on different occasions within six weeks' time, the most ardent *independista* and the most conservative re-examinationist. He is in a tough spot. He and a group of his followers have to find a face-saving formula that will preserve their political prestige and at the same time preserve their country.

Wanted: A Face-Saving Formula

One group in the Philippine Assembly, headed by José Romero, a former Speaker, has already attempted to find this formula. They have proposed some form of permanent dominion status for the Philippines within the limits of the sovereignty and protection of the United States. They have been greatly influenced, of course, by the example of Canada. They face the difficulty that there exists in the American Government no single entity such as the British Crown to which they could give allegiance and at the same time preserve complete autonomy. Their political program, therefore, is in a highly formative state. They can go so far as to suggest that some important ties (including protection) should be preserved between the Philippines and the United States, but they cannot at this point suggest the exact point at which American sovereignty should end and Philippine autonomy begin.

Mr. Quezon in one of his recent changes of heart undertook to set these limitations for them. He suggested that the Filipinos could not possibly accept any government structure that did not include their control over tariffs, immigration, coinage, and currency, and over foreign relations at least to the degree of being able to contract trade treaties with other countries without consulting the United States. These points, of course, are the precise fields in which the small residue of American sovereignty is exercised under the present Commonwealth Government. The United States does, however, have a degree of additional control in the authority of the President of the United States to nullify Philippine legislation or executive acts that, in his judgment, would specifically undermine the credit stability of the Philippine Government. Mr. Quezon did not mention this factor, but it is hardly conceivable that it could be retained if autonomy in the other fields were extended.

Under the present arrangement, also, decisions of the Philippine courts involving constitutionality may be appealed to the Supreme Court of the United States. When the difference in the legal and juridical structures of the two countries is considered, it seems unlikely that this could be retained.

The proposal for an acceptable program of Philippine autonomy, therefore, would seem to resolve itself into a plan under which the Filipinos agreed to some form of nebulous allegiance to the United States, and in return received continued access to the American market and the continued protection of the military and naval establishment of the United States. This is what has been known colloquially as eating one's cake and having it. It is sometimes abbreviated simply to Santa Claus.

The American position in response to this thesis was stated very succinctly about 1925 by General Leonard Wood, when he was Governor-General. He declared that the United States could not accept a responsibility where it did not exercise a corresponding authority. In other words, the United States could not agree to protect the Philippines unless it could have some control over the ability of the Philippines to get the United States into trouble.

This position has been in the back of American minds ever since that time, and is undoubtedly the attitude of a large part of the American Congress. Under present conditions it is felt that if we forego the advantages that we would enjoy by continued occupation of the Philippines, we must necessarily forego also the disadvantage and expense of undertaking their protection. This is so logical on the face of it that it is the hardest nut to crack in the whole Philippine problem.

PRESTIGE AND SOVEREIGNTY

Actually, there has already been a very considerable American retreat from this position. Under the Commonwealth Government, for example, we extend a degree of protection and accord a degree of benefit out of all proportion to the degree of authority that we exercise. At the present time this exercise of sovereignty is quite remote from the Philippine scene. It was dramatized out of all proportion to the actual facts by questions of "face" and precedent. These questions were correctly raised by American authorities in the Philippines because of the importance of "face" and prestige on the Oriental scene. That importance was not recognized in the United States, and it was assumed that a mountain had been made out of a molehill. Actually the preservation of "face" and prestige was of far more importance to American sovereignty than the specific exercise of function at that time carried on by the office of the United States High Commissioner.

The American grant of autonomy has been so generous that it is only in rare and drastic cases that the United States would be in a position to intervene in the functioning of the Philippine Government. It has been obvious that some of the policy that has already been carried out by the Commonwealth Government has not met with the entire approval of careful American administration. The fiscal policy, particularly, was unsound enough to require a Congressional remedy in respect to the expenditure of the coconut oil excise tax refund. It has been the policy of the United States to allow this growing government to work out its own salvation with a minimum of interference.

In no sense, however, can our responsibility be said to have diminished in the meantime. The United States is just as strongly pledged to the continuity of the Commonwealth Government, and to its support by every means in our power, as it was to the defense of the Philippines when it was just another insular possession administered through the United States War Department.

We have already jockeyed ourselves into a position wherein we have accepted large responsibility without exercising corresponding authority. Our great unwillingness to impose government against the consent of the governed has put us in the position of being obliged to defend our altruism. We are carrying on the functions of an empire with the conscience of a non-imperialistic democracy.

It is quite possible that our relationship to the Philippines, the advantages that accrue to us from it, and changes in the international scene, may dictate the necessity of continuing this policy indefinitely. It is all very well to say that the Filipinos may not eat their cake and have it, but self-interest, national defense, the need for foreign markets, and the necessity for preserving an Asiatic position, may make it imperative that the United States not only allow the Filipinos to eat their cake and have it, but that the United States deliberately undertake a policy of providing for the Filipinos a larger and juicier cake.

Our stake in the Philippines is not merely the exercise of sovereignty. If it were, we could have got out with a good face years ago. The Philippines give us an economic and political position in relation to all of the Asiatic world. Our position in the Philippines is to a great extent our future in Asia.

How to Reduce Risks

The problem of the United States, therefore, is to devise a formula under which its Philippine risks can be reduced as far as possible and its Philippine advantages retained. This task would suggest some form of control over Philippine foreign relations. It would suggest, at the very least, the strongest possible advisory capacity in such fields as foreign trade, immigration, credit, currency stability, and political relationships with foreign countries. How far this supervisory function can be carried out without violating the natural aspirations of the Filipino to self-rule is an extremely ticklish problem.

The Filipino faces an almost identical problem, and, like the United States, needs a face-saving formula. His natural and correct urge toward the highest possible degree of self-government ought not to be violated. Regardless of its origins, as long as we believe in our form of government, we must believe in his ambition for self-government.

At the same time, the Filipino needs markets and he needs protection. He can get them both from the United States, and it is extremely doubtful how much of either he can get anywhere else.

The degree to which he can enjoy those advantages will be dependent very largely upon the degree to which he is willing to orient his political and economic future toward American needs and carry out his ambitions for the development of his country within the orbit of the United States. Some formula is therefore needed under which he can preserve the advantages of the present relationship without violating his political conscience, and whereby he can guarantee to the United States an equitable return in profitable mutual association for the services that the United States proposes to render to his country.

Those formulas on both sides have not yet been found. The dominion status proposal is a move toward finding them. It does not enjoy the support as yet of the majority of the Filipinos, but it has enlisted the more far-sighted Filipino business men and some of the more realistic of the politicians. In the long run it may easily meet more opposition in the United States than it meets in the Philippines.

The pressure groups in the United States have not disappeared. They will be as suspicious as ever of any move designed to promote Philippine prosperity at what they believe to be their expense. They will require substantial assurances that any future Philippine arrangement will not be to their disadvantage and that dividends will be in sight.

Similarly, the panic state of mind in this country has not disappeared. There is as yet no confidence, in high places or in low, of assured economic recovery. There arises indeed the suggestion that our whole productive structures have to be modified, the bases of wealth redistributed, and production handled through entirely other channels. As long as that frame of mind persists, any modification in the panic-born divorce from Philippine production will be vigorously resisted. Until there is genuine economic recovery in the United States, it will be impossible for many persons to view our relationship to the Philippines with anything but anxiety.

SECURITY IN THE LONG VIEW

Finally, an arrangement providing for Philippine security must not violate American security. Those honest Americans who feel that our dangerous outpost should be lopped off will have to be convinced that the outpost can be made a position of strength instead of a position of weakness. Americans will have to be convinced that the defense of the Philippines is, in the long run, the defense of the United States.

That conviction does not at the present time obtain in this

country. To find a suitable Philippine formula the United States will have to be convinced that our interests in southeastern Asia do not begin and end in the Philippine Archipelago. We shall have to see the picture of the South China Sea as a whole, and our political position in the Philippines as a part of our economic relations to Kwangtung, Singapore, and Netherland India. We shall be obliged to see our position in relation to other governments that are dealing with the same problem and facing the same dangers that confront us.

This entails a different outlook from what has been evident so far. At the same time, shifting pressures in Asia are bringing these factors closer and closer to the American mind. A year ago Netherland India could not, short of a disastrous earthquake, have made the front page of any metropolitan newspaper. The South China Sea was good for a cable in a typhoon, and at no other time.

But the Japanese are on the move. Their "Imperial Way" is asserting itself. The bastions of democracy are falling to Dai Nippon.

Mr. Hull has pointed out that the United States also has an interest in that part of the world. We have begun to survey our defenses. We are taking account of our strategic materials. Rubber, tin, iron, chromium, and hemp are beginning to be spelled with capital letters. The man in the street is beginning to learn what tungsten is, where it comes from, and what it is for. The hammer blows of aggression have forced us out of our complacency, first in respect to Europe, now in respect to Asia. Isolationism is not directional. If we discover that we cannot cut ourselves off from one part of the world, we are likely to discover that we cannot cut ourselves off from another.

We are facing a possible complete re-orientation of foreign policy. Sooner or later we shall get very tired of pulling in our horns. When that re-orientation is accomplished, we shall have a new intellectual and emotional equation for approaching the problem of the Philippines and the problem of the South China Sea.

The precise form that this re-orientation will take cannot be predicted. It is safe to say, however, that if it is to be a re-orientation for the better, it must be based upon a facing of the facts in the case. It will be imperative that we divorce ourselves from certain outmoded superstitions. We shall be obliged to divorce ourselves from the idea that any commitment once made is irrevocable. There is no reason to believe that we must already have found an inflexible program and that it must be fitted to a changing scene regardless of consequences. Some of the facts in the case were never examined. Some of the facts were examined and ignored. Some of the facts have changed. A re-examination, therefore, should be nothing more nor less than a fact-finding expedition to discover which facts not earlier considered should now enter our consideration of a feasible plan for our future in Asia.

CHAPTER X

OUR LEGAL POSITION IN ASIA

THUS far we have considered the threats to political and economic structures. Our international business implies the safeguarding of legal and contractual structures also. The march of aggression is directed not only against "vested" interests, but against the regime of law and the commitments that have hitherto determined international policy. For full knowledge of what is at stake in Asia, we must therefore examine our position in international law as it affects policy.

It is sometimes supposed that the United States' first legal relation with Asia was the enunciation of the so-called Open Door Policy for China by the then Secretary of State John Hay, in 1899. But our Open Door policy, not only for China, but for the world, dates from about 1789, was re-enunciated in 1793, and has been the basis for all of the scores of commercial conventions signed by the Government of the United States in the course of 150 years.

The Open Door in China was not a new idea. A similar policy was applied sharply to Great Britain in 1842 at the time of the Opium War. It was re-stated a few years later at the time of the Tai Ping Rebellion. The United States, in a word, has never accepted the idea of a "closed door" in China.

The enunciation of this policy by John Hay was, moreover, not directed at China. It was a declaration of our intent to enjoy equality with the rest of the world. The fact that it subsequently became a touchstone for Chinese policy, and a means of defense welcomed by the Chinese themselves, can be ascribed largely to the fact that the Chinese had more confidence in the United

States, and in the fact that we were non-predatory, than they had in some other powers. We objected to the physical partition of China, and once more our good Yankee self-interest coincided, fortunately, with a high moral impulse. Our motives were put in a favorable light by the Chinese.

The commitment of the United States to this position of equality with other powers in China made it impossible, however, for us to tolerate the conception of any special advantage enjoyed by any other power. This concept came to a head in 1916 and 1917 in the celebrated exchange of correspondence between the then Japanese Ambassador, Viscount Ishii, and our Secretary of State, Robert Lansing.

The Japanese at that time suggested that we admit the "paramount" interest of Japan in China and conduct our future relationships accordingly. Mr. Lansing took the position that under our long-standing previous commitments the word "paramount" could not possibly be admitted, and the farthest he would go was the admission that Japan's proximity to China produced a "special" interest based on geography. This was taken by the Chinese to be strong support from the United States to their struggling republic, for Japan's special geographical position was no more than anyone with a map could see. The denial of a "paramount" position, on the other hand, was a clear warning to Japan that the United States proposed to recognize, succor, and sustain the sovereignty of an independent China, and to protect as well its own interests.

This was not necessarily international missionary work. It was an application in the political sphere of our well-established theory of economic interest and economic parity. But it gave great aid and comfort to the struggling young Chinese Government.

Within five years the United States had the opportunity to translate this declaration of principle into a concrete multi-lateral treaty.

THE NINE-POWER PACIFIC TREATY

When the Washington Naval Disarmament Conference was called in 1922, the Chinese were carrying on an undercover but effective boycott of Japanese merchandise. The Japanese had tried to break this boycott but had been unsuccessful. When they were invited to join with other powers in a declaration of intent with respect to China, the boycott was an important stumbling block.

The United States agreed at that time to exert its good offices with the Chinese to have the boycott called off, if, in return, the Japanese Government would join with the United States and the six other powers immediately involved in the Pacific in a clear declaration of intent in respect to the Chinese Government. It was not an easy quid pro quo for the Japanese to swallow, but it was better than a boycott. And so the Nine-Power Pacific Treaty was drafted and signed.

The parties most immediately involved, of course, were Japan, China, and the United States. Other powers that had interests in the Pacific area, however, were by no means unwilling to make a declaration of intention, and when the first hurdle was passed, the signatories came in. In addition to the three powers named, the treaty was signed by the British Empire, France, Italy, the Netherlands, Belgium, and Portugal. They declared that it was their purpose to "adopt a policy designed to stabilize conditions in the Far East, to safeguard the rights and interests of China, and to promote intercourse between China and the other powers upon the basis of equality of opportunity."

Article I of the treaty stated that the contracting powers (this included Japan but excluded China at this point) agreed:

"(1) To respect the sovereignty, the independence, and the territorial and administrative integrity of China;

"(2) To provide the fullest and most unembarrassed opportunity to China to develop and maintain for herself an effective and stable government;

"(3) To use their influence for the purpose of effectually establishing and maintaining the principle of equal opportunity for the commerce and industry of all nations throughout the territory of China;

"(4) To refrain from taking advantage of conditions in China in order to seek special rights or privileges which would abridge the rights of subjects or citizens of friendly states, and from countenancing action inimical to the security of such states."

In subsequent articles the contracting powers disavowed the intention of seeking any special privileges by treaty or other arrangement, any monopolies or preferences to the disadvantage of others, or any spheres of influence.

China, on the other hand, pledged herself not to exercise or permit unfair discrimination of any kind toward the facilities within her country.

The powers also agreed to respect China's rights as a neutral, and China undertook to sustain the obligations of neutrality. The powers, moreover, pledged themselves to frank and free communication whenever the provisions of the treaty should be involved in any controversy, and opened the treaty to the adherence of any other powers who desired to stabilize their relationships with China on this treaty basis.

A Basis for Discussion

The Nine-Power Pacific Treaty so drawn up has become the crux of much of the discussion of American relationships to Asia, for two reasons.

First of all, it embraces very clearly in writing the principles upon which American relationships with China have been based for so long a time. Presumably those relationships and those commitments still continue. The United States at least has made no formal recession from this treaty position.

The mere reading of the treaty, in the second place, should make it clear to anyone except a Japanese that every phrase of every article of the treaty has been vigorously and repeatedly violated by the Japanese Government within the last ten years. It is inconceivable that anyone can suggest that Japan, a signatory to this treaty, has respected the sovereignty, the independence, or the territorial and administrative integrity of China. On the contrary, they have been outrageously violated. It is equally apparent that Japan's pledge to provide the fullest and most unembarrassed opportunity to China to develop and maintain an effective and stable government has long since gone the way of Nazi non-aggression pacts.

Opportunity to develop a stable government in China can hardly be "unembarrassed" while eleven hundred thousand Japanese soldiers are within the confines of the Chinese Republic. The Japanese Government, pledged to maintain equal opportunity for the commerce and industry of all nations in China, has furthermore established a system of currency, of customs claims, of monopolies and controls, whose manifest purpose is to see to it that opportunity exists only for the Japanese.

Finally, the pledge to refrain from seeking special rights or privileges abridging the rights of subjects and citizens of other states is hardly compatible with the closing of the Yangtze River by Japanese gunboats.

The Nine-Power Treaty serves as a keynote for American relations in Asia, for, while the Japanese have reduced it to meaningless words, it still states our position without equivocation.

It should be observed that the Japanese have justified their violation of all of their treaty obligations by the statement that conditions have changed in East Asia, and that therefore the concepts embodied in various treaties are no longer applicable. This particular dodge is not a Japanese invention. It can be found back in the seventeenth century in the writings of a Hollander by the name of Bynkershoek. He advanced the theory that treaties were operative and applicable only so long as the conditions under which they were drafted continued to obtain. That is obviously the gist of the Japanese position three centuries later. In the middle of the last century Otto von Bismarck, with an eye on Schleswig-Holstein,

Austria, and France, and with an embarrassing deskful of treaties, went Bynkershoek one better and declared that treaties could not be conceived of as operative except in so far as it was to the interest of the signatories to keep them so. The present Japanese position takes a leaf from both books.

THE VALIDITY OF OBLIGATIONS

The United States has insisted that treaties, even declarations of principle, are, in a sense, moral contractual obligations, and that, since they are arrived at by agreement, they cannot be dissolved except by similar agreement or by the faithful fulfillment of such provisions as they may contain for their own dissolution. While this point of view may seem to be somewhat idealistic, it actually produces some working operations in our own foreign policy. It was to sustain this theory of international relationships that the United States, when it was ready to abrogate its most recent treaty of commerce and navigation with Japan, gave the required six months' notice stipulated in the treaty, and carried out its obligations to the smallest lower-case letter.

From the legal point of view, this was relatively simple in a bi-lateral treaty such as our 1911 treaty with Japan. On the larger scale, in multi-lateral commitments such as the Nine-Power Pact, which do not carry within themselves the machinery for their legal termination, it is obvious that such a termination could be accomplished only by a degree of international accord sufficient to lay the foundation for some subsequent agreement.

For this reason the Japanese assert that the American position is illogical and that a multi-lateral treaty is necessarily subject to uni-lateral abrogation when it becomes necessary for any signatory to take this action. The United States takes the position that one party cannot legally nullify a contract of many parties. At this point also the Japanese position is in accord with German political philosophy; the American position is dissimilar.

The importance to the United States of the violation of the

Nine-Power Treaty lies in the fact that it constitutes the legal basis for any action that the United States may choose to take in respect to Japan. Within the treaty itself there is no provision beyond that of consultation. It was under this consultative clause that the ill-starred 1937 conference in Brussels was held. Japan did not attend, and there was nothing that the other eight powers could do about it.

Scrutiny of the text of the treaty will reveal that the pledges are given not only to China, but to all the other signatories too. For this reason the United States has legal justification for the ground that her rights and interests under the treaty have been violated. And in this respect the United States has become a partner with China as a victim of Japanese aggression.

THE KELLOGG-BRIAND TREATY

The next major multi-lateral commitment of the United States in respect to East Asia was the Kellogg-Briand Peace Treaty of 1928. Japan is a signatory to this treaty also. The Kellogg-Briand Pact is, to an even greater degree than the Nine-Power Treaty, a declaration of purpose rather than a group of contractual commitments. It is astonishingly brief. The high contracting parties declare in the names of their respective peoples "that they condemn recourse to war for the solution of international controversies and renounce it as an instrument of national policy in their relations with one another." The contracting parties further pledged that in the solution of all disputes or conflicts, "of whatever nature or of whatever origin," they would seek no solution except by pacific means.

It goes without saying that this treaty too has been violated in the recourse to war as the primary instrument of Japanese policy in China. The Japanese have, however, just enough moral sensitivity to this much-publicized commitment to keep them from officially calling the invasion of China a war. It is still the "China affair" or the "China incident" in their official correspondence.

The United States has here again no direct responsibility for the enforcement of treaty provisions. The United States does have, however, a moral responsibility to sustain its declaration of purpose. The Kellogg-Briand commitment has had an interesting translation into practical policy. The idea of American recognition of the fruits of conquest had always been an unpopular one in the United States. Back in the days of the first World War the United States made it quite clear to Japan that this government would not recognize a new status in the province of Shantung brought about by duress. Then in the late fall of 1931 the Japanese invaded Manchuria and established a puppet government, and the United States had to decide what to do about recognition. Secretary of State Henry L. Stimson talked this problem over with President Hoover, and, as he recounts in his book, *The Far Eastern Crisis,* two possible courses of action were plotted out. The first was a repetition of the previous American position, narrowly restricted in its scope to this one particular invasion at this one particular point; the second was the application of this idea of non-recognition to somewhat wider grounds as a general moral basis for American foreign relationships. The second course was adopted.

In the celebrated note of January 7, 1932, Mr. Stimson not only told the governments of Japan and China that the American Government would not admit the legality of any situation that would impair the Nine-Power Treaty, but went on to say that "it [the American Government] does not intend to recognize any situation, treaty, or agreement which may be brought about by means contrary to the covenants and obligations of the Pact of Paris of August 27, 1928, to which treaty both China and Japan, as well as the United States, are parties."

Thus the obligation not to resort to war as an instrument of national policy was translated into a declaration of intent not to recognize the fruits of the conquest that violated this obligation.

There is a slight misunderstanding of what Mr. Stimson said that ought to be cleared up by a textual examination. It has often been declared that Mr. Stimson said, "the United States will never recognize" such fruits of conquest. Mr. Stimson did not go that far.

He said the United States "does not intend to recognize . . ." The distinction is clear, but thus far that intention of the United States does not appear to have been modified very greatly.

Mr. Stimson did not change the basic policy of the United States, but he did give an exceedingly lucid exposition of American obligations under the Pact of Paris, which, from our point of view, is still operative. Mr. Stimson's declaration of intention has not yet been revoked. It certainly does not seem illogical to suggest that the American non-recognition not only of Manchukuo, but of Ethiopia, Albania, Austria, Czechoslovakia, Poland, and the more recent Axis conquests, is founded upon a substantial basis in our declared interpretation of international law and our obligations under it.

The immediate application of this doctrine to the Far Eastern problem is the question of recognizing or not the puppet government set up by the Japanese at Nanking under Wang Ching-wei. Until the United States modifies its clear definition of intent as given by Mr. Stimson, there is little likelihood that the bribe of opening the Yangtze will be accepted.

It might be advantageous to the United States to recognize Mr. Wang, "the renegade Chinese who ran for the presidency of China on the Japanese ticket." But until some more substantial basis is offered, or until the suggestion that we "appease" Japan reaches panic proportions, it is extremely unlikely that the United States will modify a position so sharply declared and nullify its obligations under the Kellogg-Briand Pact.

This phase of our relationships with Asia is governed, as we have seen, by two treaties that, from our point of view, are still in force. Our relationship to Asia is also vitally affected by two treaties that have lapsed.

OUR NAVAL TREATIES

The first of these was the Pacific Naval Pact, embracing the Washington and London naval commitments. This treaty basis for our naval position in respect to Great Britain and Japan in the Pacific was originally drafted in 1922, and abrogated, uni-laterally, by the Japanese in 1936.

This naval "disarmament" commitment was designed primarily to stabilize the ratios between the Japanese, British, and American navies. It put into writing the accepted 5-5-3 formula, and also provided for tonnage limitation on capital ships and for certain specific category limitations of armament. The heavy cruiser, for example, was to be of no more than 10,000 tons and armed with no more than eight-inch guns. Capital ships were limited to 35,000 tons.

What was possibly an even more important part of this compact was the limit upon fortifications in the Pacific. Under the terms of the agreement, these were to be kept at the 1922 level. No new bases were to be acquired, and existing bases were not to be "modernized," in the sense of adding to their military strength.

The Japanese objected to the 5-5-3 ratio, which they felt was incompatible with their dignity as a first-class power. Various means were sought to change this ratio, and the Japanese, indeed, indicated that they would be willing to abide by it in fact, if only it were abandoned in principle. This is obviously another point at which the problem of "face" was important.

The abrogation of this treaty by the Japanese has a vital effect upon American Pacific naval policy. The building of larger battle-ships and the mounting of heavier armament on ships of some other categories are relatively minor. The abrogation of the treaty has put the United States into a position where new bases can be acquired in the Pacific, or old bases fortified, without any violation of international commitments. Thus, while the Japanese have freed themselves to build up to parity if they can, the United States has been freed to undertake whatever new naval policy in the Pacific seems to be desirable.

It should be observed that this modification of our position was brought about against our will and our representations. But mani-festly there is no law against our taking advantage of it now that it has occurred. As a result of this newly acquired freedom, the United States may overhaul its existing shore establishments, materially strengthen Corregidor, and, if necessary, put in a naval base at Guam.

The lapse of this treaty, therefore, has worked both ways; and while it has given us a higher naval mark at which to aim, it has above all given us a free hand in naval policy. Japan started us on the road to the two-ocean navy.

THE TRADE TREATY OF 1911

The second of the lapsed commitments is the Treaty of Commerce and Navigation with Japan, signed in 1911, and lapsed by act of the United States on January 26, 1940. Notice of the lapsing of this treaty was formally presented to the Japanese Ambassador in Washington on July 26, 1939, under the terms of the treaty that allowed for its abrogation upon six months' notice.

This treaty of commerce and navigation was the great-grand-child of our first commercial relationships with Japan, established by the opening of Japanese intercourse with the Western world by Commodore Perry at about the middle of the last century. Following up the consular agreement that Commodore Perry obtained, Townsend Harris, American plenipotentiary, negotiated our first formal convention with Japan in 1857 and 1858. This treaty was modified and expanded at the request of Japan in 1894, and the 1911 treaty was a subsequent revision of this same accord.

Our treaty of commerce and navigation with Japan was a typical American commercial treaty. It established normal modes of intercourse between the two signatories, provided for an establishment of consulates, provided against discriminations, and in general extended to American-Japanese relationships the "most favored nation" treatment. The 1911 treaty was a condensation of the earlier documents and a very considerable improvement upon them.

The lapse of this treaty, brought about by the United States, served several functions. The method of ending the treaty demonstrated that the United States proposed to honor its obligations to the letter, even in terminating them. This was in contrast to the fashion in which Japan had handled some other commitments.

The second function served by the lapse of this treaty was to bring the unsatisfactory state of American-Japanese relations sharply to the attention not only of the Japanese Government, but of the Japanese public.

In the course of the war in China American interests had been frequently violated, American property damaged, and American nationals endangered. More than 600 of these incidents had occurred. They had been made the subject of protest either to Japanese authorities in the field or to the Japanese Government in Tokyo. More than 200 of these protests were on file with the Japanese Government in Japan at the time of the lapse of the treaty. Less than thirty of them had been formally acknowledged; less than a dozen had been acted upon.

In each case the Japanese procedure was to suggest that the facts would be investigated, and then to pigeon-hole the protests. The lapse of the treaty was, therefore, an attempt, in part, to break through this wall of Oriental procrastination and bring to the attention of the Japanese Government the fact that the United States had not abandoned its proclaimed policy of protecting its nationals and their property when those nationals were in lawful pursuit of their occupations in foreign countries.

The third function of the lapse of this treaty bears a curious analogy to Japan's lapse of the naval commitments. It frees the hands of the United States in the political and economic field precisely as Japan's abrogation of the naval treaty freed the hands of the United States in the naval field.

Tokyo Gets Worried

Japanese apprehension over the lapse of this treaty was instantly expressed, and indeed with good cause. The relationships between the two countries were no longer upon the stabilized basis of mutual agreement, but upon what Washington was pleased to call a day-to-day basis. That means, of course, that modification of the economic and political relationships between Japan and the United States can take place without previous warning through legislative enactment or administrative action in the United States.

Here is an example: Back in 1823 the United States enacted legislation authorizing the collection of a 10 per cent tax on all imports into the United States carried in foreign bottoms. The object of this legislation was to afford an indirect subsidy to the young American merchant marine. The application of this law to Japanese commerce (when the Japanese had acquired a merchant marine) was suspended by President Grant through executive proclamation. That suspension has not since been revoked, and for that reason Japanese ships can bring their goods into American harbors without a surtax on the goods.

This exemption does not rest upon either legislative enactment or treaty agreement, and presumably what one President decreed another President can un-decree. So by one stroke of the pen, the present President may simply revoke President Grant's exemption, and Japanese commerce, carried in Japanese ships, will from that time on pay a 10 per cent tax. This is more than the margin of profit on many items.

The treaty gave the Japanese protection in other minor matters, in which now, with the treaty removed, they are vulnerable.

Unquestionably, however, the major issue upon the lapse of this treaty is whether or not the United States will use its freedom to impose embargoes upon shipments of war materials to Japan. A commercial treaty such as that of 1911 made the embargo a violation of contract, but on the day-to-day basis nothing in international law deters us from such a course of action. At the time many persons believed that the treaty was abrogated for the specific purpose of clearing the decks for an embargo, and it was this fear undoubtedly that led the Japanese to exert every possible effort to get a substitute commitment for the one that had disappeared. As time went on, however, it seemed less likely that an embargo would be imposed, and the Japanese campaign to renew the treaty quieted.

Our legal position in respect to Asia rests at present upon declarations of intent even more than upon contractual obligations. We have undertaken to establish a mode of doing business with other people, and we have committed ourselves to certain courses of action. But the Japanese attack upon China has removed the basis for friendly agreement. As a consequence it is not unnatural that the specific contractual obligations, such as those embodied in the naval treaty and the commercial treaty of 1911, should likewise have disappeared.

So long as the United States continues to honor the Nine-Power Treaty and the Pact of Paris, the basis for our actions in the Pacific remains unchanged. But now that we are left without a limitation of naval establishment and have ended our commercial contractual obligations with Japan, we have placed ourselves in a position to create a new practical policy.

In a word, we have not changed our ideas, but we have changed the conditions under which they may be put into operation. The United States has a free hand to evolve, not new theories about Asia, but a new and practical policy.

CHAPTER XI

OUR RELATIONS WITH CHINA

OUR policy in respect to Asia must necessarily be determined to a very considerable degree by the relationship that we sustain, and wish to sustain, toward the largest and most important element in East Asia, the Republic of China. Our future in Asia is a larger problem than our economic and political stake in the South China Sea. It involves our continued good relations with the Chinese.

The United States made its first real acquaintance with the Chinese by way of the clipper ship. In those adventurous days when New England sailors were driving around the Horn, the Canton tea trade was the magnet that drew American enterprise and adventure.

The relationship from the beginning was commercial rather than political. The growing American public was not interested in establishing spheres of influence, and all that was asked was equality in trade. From the days of the Opium War in 1842, the influence of the United States was thrown against the idea of the partition of China. We asked only free and friendly access to the Chinese market.

American business and missionary enterprise assumed a steadily increasing importance in China throughout the last half of the nineteenth century. Sometimes these two phases of American "penetration" went hand in hand. More often they did not. It is not surprising, however, that missionary communities should have become the nucleus for American centers at Peking, Hankow, Suchow, and other important cities, both coastal and interior.

American commercial investment was not made on the same scale, as, for example, that of Great Britain, but some American money went into the building of the first Chinese railways and the establishment of the first nation-wide public services.

Shortly before the turn of the century the relations of the United States with China became more than ever politically important. At that time the pressure of outside powers on a decaying empire was very strong. The United States, through its entrance into the Philippines, had become, politically, an Asiatic power, and therefore its relationship was a matter of the utmost importance. That relationship had previously been expressed through the conventional trade treaties and through mutual declarations of friendship.

In 1899 the United States, as we have observed, met the threat of partition with the enunciation, by Secretary of State John Hay, of the famous Open Door policy for China.

On the face of it, the motive for such a declaration would be said to be a selfish desire on the part of the United States to guarantee continued access on equal terms to this valuable market. Under the circumstances, however, it was a declaration of rights for China even more than for the United States, since it committed the United States to oppose extension of special spheres of influence. This declaration, therefore, not only stabilized the relationships of these powers with each other but gave the Chinese an internationally recognized ground upon which to resist any further concessions to other powers. It was the strongest single step that had been taken to cement the friendship of China with the United States.

Two years later, with the rise of anti-foreign nationalism in China, came the unhappy Boxer Rebellion. The rapidity with which it was put down, by force, established the position of the Western Powers in China, but at the same time some of the attending incidents afforded a new means of improving American-Chinese relationships and of deriving some good out of what had been an exceedingly deplorable incident.

Indemnities were assessed against the Chinese for the damage to foreign properties and the lives of foreign nationals. The United States returned its share of the indemnity to the Chinese Government to be used for the extension of benevolent public services and particularly of education. There was a strong feeling in many American minds that the Boxer indemnity should never have been collected in the first place, and its return served not only to ease the American conscience but to make it plain that we proposed to be friendly in deed as well as in word.

ABRAHAM LINCOLN PARAPHRASED

In 1911 the Chinese Republic was born. It has been repeatedly pointed out that the famous Three Principles of Dr. Sun Yat-sen were a plain paraphrase of the American "government of the people, by the people, for the people." Under those conditions it was natural that American sympathy toward the republic should have been enlisted from the outset.

It should be remembered also that many of the young Chinese intellectuals had received their schooling either in American missionary schools in China or in universities in the United States, or both. To some extent, at least, it is correct to say that much of the impulse that made the establishment of the Chinese Republic possible came from contact with the United States.

During the World War the United States became much more than ever before a real defender of China. The Open Door policy, originally directed to nations of the Western world, was applied to the threat to China from her Japanese neighbor.

This application had two phases. The first, as we have seen, was the refusal by the United States in the Ishii-Lansing conversations to admit Japan's claim of a paramount position in respect to China. This was actually nothing more than a repetition of the Open Door policy. The second phase was the application of American pressure in resistance to Japan's Twenty-one Demands on

China that arose out of the Shantung incident. These demands constituted a grave incursion on Chinese sovereignty, and the United States took the position that Japan should be obliged to retreat from them.

The Washington Disarmament Conference, called in 1921, gave the United States an opportunity to clarify and to crystallize the relationship of foreign powers to China. The Chinese had enthusiastically backed this conference from the beginning and placed their hopes upon the good faith of the United States.

While the avowed purpose of that conference was naval disarmament, it was obliged to assume that some measures would be taken for the stabilization of Asiatic political conditions. Such a stabilization would have to take place before naval disarmament could become a reality. Thus the Nine-Power Pacific Pact emerged.

The good offices of the United States were enjoyed by the Chinese in forming this treaty and securing the recognition of the sovereign independence and integrity of China. The Open Door policy was put into a solemn public compact, and to it was added what had always been the American position, that China was, and would continue to be, a sovereign and independent State.

The Chinese at that time declared, and declared correctly, that the consummation of the Nine-Power Treaty was the greatest diplomatic victory that China had ever won, and they declared that it had been won because of the authority and good will of the United States. Thus the basis for mutual friendly intercourse between the two countries was greatly strengthened.

The Attack on Inequality

With increasing Chinese nationalism and self-confidence, it was natural that the special position of foreign powers in China should come under examination. It was part and parcel of the whole Chinese Republican movement that the treaties that gave a special legal and administrative position to foreign powers in China would have to be revised so as to put China on a basis of true equality with the Western Powers.

This Chinese drive on the "unequal" treaties was full of political dynamite. The foreign powers had long-established concessions in China and some of them had assumed gigantic importance. The International Settlement at Shanghai, for example, was the trading base for the greatest port in eastern Asia, and it made possible the building up on the flat marshes of Whangpoo of an immense commercial metropolis.

There were other extremely valuable concessions. There was the legation quarter at Peiping, guarded by foreign troops. There were valuable foreign concessions at Tientsin where foreign troops were stationed. There was the whole series of treaty ports in which freedom of intercourse was guaranteed and in which outside powers enjoyed very special privileges.

Obviously, the Chinese could not expect to reclaim all of these interests with one overnight movement. It was true that the Japanese had done so, twenty years before, when they abolished all unequal treatment "with one stroke of the pen." But the foreign holdings in Japan and the foreign relationship to Japanese life were infinitesimal in comparison with what had been built up in a couple of centuries in China.

In connection with their holdings in China the foreign powers had established the special jurisdiction of consular courts to treat cases in which their nationals were involved. The basis for these courts was the fact that Chinese law did not correspond even remotely to the law of the Western Powers, and the entire juridical establishment of China was inadequate to deal with causes of the importance and delicacy of those involving foreign nationals.

The justice of this position, under the circumstances, was widely recognized by the Chinese leaders, and they took the stand from the start that consular courts could and should be abolished only when the Chinese had established adequate courts and guaranteed procedure to replace them.

The Chinese position throughout the discussion of extra-territoriality was marked by an extraordinary degree of moderation. Forceful confiscation was not even hinted at by their responsible leaders. It was not suggested that assumption of the function by the Chinese should ever be anything but orderly.

Pressure against the unequal treaties reached its height in 1928 and 1929. There were some incidents, but they were of minor importance. Under this pressure the foreign powers had withdrawn from some special concessions.

There was naturally much bitter opposition to the whole idea of withdrawing. Some Old China Hands, for example, said that such a step was unthinkable and marshaled all the arguments they could find to prove that millions of dollars of wealth would be put at the mercy of predatory savages.

The official position of the United States was very different. The United States, in representations to China, made it plain that this country agreed fully in principle to the abolition of the unequal treaties. It qualified that position only by suggesting that the Chinese be fully able to assume the functions of protection and adequate legal administration when the withdrawal of extra-territorial privileges was consummated.

This point of view did not help the minor friction in the Chinese cities. It did act as a continual stabilizing factor in the formal relationship between the two governments. The United States had, of course, taken the only position that was compatible with its declarations in regard to the government of China. It had repeatedly held that extra-territoriality and consular jurisdiction had come into existence and had continued only because of the necessity of carrying out functions that the Chinese Government was not in a position to assume. Whenever a Chinese Government appeared that could carry out those functions, the bottom would drop out of the whole justification for the unequal treaties.

The Japanese invasion of China has made the issue of extra-territoriality the most minor of matters as far as the Chinese are concerned. The Japanese, of course, and their puppet mouthpiece, Wang Ching-wei, have asserted that one of their major objectives is liberating the Chinese from those commitments and establishing a government that will make no concessions and allow no infraction of its sovereignty. (Except, of course, in favor of the Japanese.)

The Chinese Government, on the other hand, has in the course of this war found the foreign concessions a source of extraordinary strength. In some instances the concessions have safeguarded the wealth of the government and assured a continuity of intercourse with the outside world. So for the time being the Chinese have no intention of pushing the issue.

This, however, is an exigency of war. Under the present circumstances, the Chinese would rather have foreign concessions shared by three or four friendly powers than have those same concessions entirely in the hands of the Japanese.

If and when the Japanese aggressor is removed, it is to be supposed that the United States will make its word good and withdraw from all special positions as rapidly as the Chinese can assume their functions. This will undoubtedly be used by the Chinese to bring pressure upon any other powers in China. The Chinese, accordingly, look to the United States once more, and again rightly, for major moral assistance toward full sovereignty.

It has often been suggested that behind the American impact on China is the story of just another imperial exploitation. The best answer is that the Chinese do not think so, and they ought to know.

WHAT IS "EXPLOITATION"?

What about this commercial exploitation in China? Obviously it means the production of low-cost materials by cheap labor for the purpose of advantageous sale outside of China. There has been plenty of this. The total American investment in such operations in China is usually estimated at something like $100,000,000.

It has a number of ramifications. It involves, for example, the development of tung oil and tungsten in southern China; the purchase of fuel and hides and bristles in northern China; the low-cost purchase of Chinese tea and silk; and the drainage from Chinese communities of products of local handicraft. This exploitation, however, has in no case imperiled Chinese living standards. Those standards were (it is said sorrowfully) so low that they couldn't be forced down. The worst that can be said of this exploitation is that it has taken advantage of a bad situation and made no sufficient attempt to remedy it.

The next phase of commercial impact in China is the distribution of outside products for sale locally. The most important of these is petroleum. The United States has been the most important middleman in taking oil into China. This has been a big and profitable trade.

In more recent years the business of machinery and transport has grown large. The Western Powers—Great Britain first and the United States second—have played a very important role in industrialization. In some cases this has involved local investment, in others straight sale. In any case it was not until the second year of the Chinese-Japanese War that there appeared any large-scale attempts in China to accomplish industrialization without drawing very heavily upon outside materials and outside capital.

The third form of investment in China has been the advancement of loans, for a number of purposes. Railroad loans are perhaps the most important single group. There have also been loans for the purpose of stabilizing Chinese currency; loans for creating Chinese banks; loans for purchasing materials abroad, and, from time to time, outright loans to assist in carrying on the functions of government.

A criticism brought against these loans is the fact that they have been secured through liens on Chinese customs and on Chinese salt-tax collections. This was the best security that China had to offer and it was accepted. The objection to it is that it has put direct functions of government in the hands of outside administration. Chinese maritime customs, for example, have not been administered by the Chinese themselves for a great many years. In this way the loans have been used as means of obtaining a degree of political and financial control that is a serious encroachment upon Chinese sovereignty.

The fact, moreover, that Chinese imports are largely channeled through foreign concessions or treaty ports has given the concessions additional authority and the means of enforcing their position against the Chinese.

This tax and loan structure has made the Chinese Government vulnerable. In northern China, for example, from 1932 on, the Japanese have been able to play ducks and drakes with the Chinese customs, and hence with the basis for Chinese credit, by wholesale smuggling. The Japanese occupation of important salt-producing areas, moreover, has jeopardized those salt-tax revenues not only in their function as security for outside obligations but also as an important source of funds that should accrue to China. Theoretically, those collections are being sequestered and will be applied eventually by Japan to China's obligations to certain Western Powers. In practice no accounting has yet been made of these funds.

That the Chinese have maintained their credit stability through the course of the last twenty revolutionary years, and then even improved it through three years of Japanese invasion, is a miracle in financing. They have had to do it, at times, however, through concessions that a sovereign state should not be obliged to make.

Our future relations with China in this field will undoubtedly be conditioned by the Chinese effort to get a better basis for credit obligations. Steps are already being taken in this direction. Recent loans to China have been secured by futures on shipments of products that the United States requires. This involves no impairment of Chinese sovereignty, assures an external market for Chinese materials, and assists in the development of productive enterprises.

ANOTHER SORT OF INVESTMENT

The type of investments that we have been discussing so far is the sort that can be put into a column of figures. There is another investment of the United States in China that cannot be so easily classified. This is the moral and cultural investment, by thousands of Americans, assisted by many more thousands of Chinese, that has been going on for almost a century.

First of all there are the missionaries. There have been some hard words spoken about them. Some of them, no doubt, have had unfortunate personalities. Some of them have made a good thing out of it. Some have been stiff-necked intruders, unsympathetic toward the institutions with which they came in contact.

These, however, are individual cases and they do not picture truly the impact of American missionary activity in China. As a body, the American missionaries have been honest, able, industrious, and self-sacrificing. Some of them have been short-sighted; many others have compensated for what may be defective vision by an extraordinarily high devotion to the Chinese themselves.

To the confirmed lovers of the Chinese (as many Americans have come to be), there is something very presumptuous in undertaking to teach the Chinese anything, and above all in attempting to modify their whimsical and philosophical approach to life. But among the Americans who have gone to China there are many whose concentration has not been so much upon changing the Chinese as upon saving their lives.

This attitude has been common in the field of medicine. The doctors in China, working against heartbreaking odds, have done a systematically splendid job. In a great many cases, moreover, they have done it without recognition, and often, too, with no offense to the sensibilities of the most sensitive of Chinese. The Chinese have been good to these doctors, and Americans can be proud of them.

In more recent years the general educational machinery has assumed many of the functions that were previously associated with the religious and medical. Its work is seen in the rapid growth of great Chinese educational institutions, and the development of a large number of splendid Chinese universities.

This has been made possible only by the enthusiastic co-operation and even leadership of the Chinese themselves. Many of them in turn stem from American missionary culture. Chinese education, even that in the Western pattern, is passing more and more, as it properly should, into the hands of the Chinese themselves. The work that is being done in that field, however, is in part the fruit of an American investment in the future of China.

It would be short-sighted indeed for Americans to claim a lion's share in the credit for the reawakening of China. The impact of the United States, however, has had a very important influence on that awakening. It has sometimes been expressed in too simple terms: the three Soong sisters are graduates of American colleges and Chiang Kai-shek has adopted the Christian faith. These facts are undoubtedly important but they derive a great deal of their importance from the additional fact that there are hundreds of thousands of Chinese, all over the country, who have felt the contact of a different civilization, and, at least in part, through the Americans who went to China.

NEW VISTAS IN CHINA

This reawakening of China is undoubtedly the greatest political and moral event in the history of Asia in the last century. It is impossible to over-estimate the scope of this movement and its ultimate effect on the intimate living of hundreds of millions of people. It means a new self-respect for China. It opens up countless fields of achievement. It means not only the emergence of China as a great factor in world history; it means the emergence of each individual Chinese citizen into a new world.

Who shall estimate the American investment in this revolution? It is an investment of courage, of vitality, and of hope; an investment of blood and tears; an investment of devotion and of fortitude. Hundreds and hundreds of times it has been an investment of life itself.

What price will you put on the services of Dr. Fearn, who admitted quite casually that she had helped to bring more than six thousand babies into the world in her own hospital?

What price can be put on the vision of the men who broke the ground for Peking Union Medical Center?

What price is possible for the services of the men who surveyed the first railway down through Shansi?

These Americans made real investments in China. What dividends are they likely to bring?

We have become conscious in the last few years of those four hundred million customers. The possibilities of China's economic future, however, stagger even the wildest of imaginations. In no other country in the world is so great a potential wealth so little developed. The surface has never been scratched, and yet it has been a country of fabulous wealth since centuries before Marco Polo made his first journey to Cathay.

The utilization of this wealth means one thing above all else; it means a change in the standard of living of 450,000,000 Chinese. That, in turn, means the increasing demand for processed goods to supply those rising needs.

This need for processed goods will be met in two ways. The first is by direct importation of the goods themselves. The second is by providing the means by which an increasingly large part of those goods will be fabricated in China itself. In both cases, or in either, there will be a gigantic need for outside materials, outside money, and outside skills.

The development of this producing wealth, moreover, embraces huge enterprises in construction. The most obvious, of course, is the building of highways. It is hard to realize that in all of China, from Peiping to Canton or the Burma border, and from Shanghai to the headwaters of the Yangtze or the mountains of Tibet, in an area the size of all of the continental United States, there are not as many miles of paved road as there are in the state of New Jersey.

Some day those roads will be built. There will be a motor highway from Canton to Tibet. There will be quick communication from the mountains of the Yunnan to the Shantung coastal plain. There will be, not miles of road, or hundreds of miles of road, or thousands of miles of road—there will be literally millions of miles of road from one end of China to the other.

Someone will supply the cement and asphalt for those highways; someone will supply the scrapers and the steam rollers and the concrete mixers. And when China is ribboned from top to bottom there will be the inevitable filling stations—and someone will supply the pumps, and the gasoline that goes into them.

On those roads there will roll millions of motor cars and there will be at least four tires to the car. Someone will supply the materials and skill that build those automobiles and those multiplied millions of miles of rubber on which they roll.

The Chinese themselves will supply a lot of them, but they cannot expect, and do not expect, to accomplish this transformation without a vast and increasing contact with an outside world that will make this gigantic task much easier of consummation.

Someone will assist in building the transport of the New China. The future of China and the future of the United States in Asia may very well be determined by whether or not those rubber tires that roll on the Chinese roads are made in Akron or in Osaka.

The United States has not suggested that it should dominate the awakening of China. It has suggested that, if China's needs can be supplied by this country, the United States should be in a position to supply those needs on a basis of equality with other suppliers. The United States believes, in short, that there is already a "New Order in East Asia" and that it is a Chinese order. It has taken the position that the Chinese themselves have the right to determine the degree and the manner of outside assistance that is to be given to their awakening.

From that position there can be no American retreat. Our interest is not only altruistic. It is also profoundly and correctly selfish. We do not believe that our ends have to be served at the expense of China. We do believe that they can be served in co-operation with China. The history of our past relationships bears this out. There is no reason to believe that those relationships should deteriorate.

We are, therefore, formulating an Asiatic policy, not merely to defend a few hundred million dollars' worth of fixed property already there. That, in itself, would not be worth sending a cruiser squadron from San Pedro to Guam. We are, on the other hand, hoping that we will be able to protect an important moral as well as economic stake in the future of China. That stake, we hope, can pay dividends to us and we believe it will pay even greater dividends to the Chinese.

It is good business to be friendly with the Chinese. They are good business men and they are good and loyal friends. Our association in the past, viewed as a whole, has been a singularly happy one.

Our relations with China must obviously be kept on a basis that is satisfactory and profitable to the Chinese. We are fortunate in the fact that such a basis should prove to be immensely satisfactory and enormously profitable to us. The economics of an awakening China dictate a clear mutuality of interest between China and the United States. It is upon this mutuality that our relationship of the future must rest.

CHAPTER XII

OUR RELATIONS WITH JAPAN

OUR future in China will of course be determined in part by our relations with Japan. Through 1940 the "relations" between Washington and Tokyo have been in the condition that the newspapermen describe as "steadily deteriorating." This, however, is no novelty. Dealings between the United States and Japan are not very old, as the international family counts age—actually only some eighty years—but they have been troublesome enough.

The United States "opened up" Japan to communication with the outside world in 1853. There have been many misapprehensions about what happened at that time. It is usually declared, especially by those who have an anti-American case to make, that the United States sailed a squadron into Yokohama harbor, trained its guns on the defenseless Japanese, and informed them that they must be friendly or else. This version does not entirely conform to the facts. In the first place it wasn't Yokohama harbor at all, and in the second place the matter of establishing relationships with the Japanese, far from being a holdup at the point of a gun, was a matter of extremely delicate and protracted negotiation.

The reason for Commodore Perry's visit, incidentally, was not, as many persons suppose, to make American merchandise acceptable to Japan, and vice versa, but actually to protect American nationals and assure them reasonably fair treatment. In the Forties and Fifties there was a considerable amount of American whaling in the North Pacific, and it was inevitable that seamen from American ships should occasionally be wrecked in the Japanese Archipelago, or obliged to call there for supplies and fuel.

What thereupon happened to these American nationals in Japan, while not a complete mystery, was a matter of considerable dissatisfaction. In their attempt to preserve the sanctity of their island home, the Japanese had for centuries refused to tolerate any foreign entry, with the exception of one small Netherland trading post.

What Commodore Perry asked for and got was merely the right to discuss with the Japanese the possibility of making some provision for intercourse with the rest of the world so that ordinary humane treatment could be assured to Americans who accidentally landed in the Japanese Archipelago.

The story of negotiation at the point of a gun has arisen largely from the second visit of Commodore Perry when he returned to Japan after going to the China coast. Almost a year had elapsed and still no sufficient progress had been made toward achieving the ends for which he had originally set forth. Accordingly Commodore Perry pointed out to the Japanese not simply that the United States possessed force of arms sufficient to command respect, but that other maritime powers were engaged on the China coast and that it would be highly advantageous to the Japanese to take a friendly rather than an unfriendly attitude.

The upshot of this second colloquy was the agreement by the Japanese merely to admit and authorize a diplomatic agent of the United States to discuss the problems that had arisen. That was the extent of opening up Japan at the muzzle of a gun. Naturally, our first emissary went on a warship. If he had entered Japanese waters in any other way he would very probably have died in a Japanese jail, and that was a contingency that the United States desired most earnestly to avoid.

The second agent sent by the United States for the discussions to which Japan had agreed proved to be one of our ablest and most tenacious diplomats. He was Townsend Harris, of New York City.

Mr. Harris went to Japan and lived in comparative isolation for almost three years. He was plagued by ill health, suffered continuous threats from dissident Japanese factions, and survived one of the most extraordinary Oriental "run-arounds" in history. Mr. Harris spent months obtaining an interview with the head of the Shogunate, the feudal military lords, in the innocent belief that he was negotiating with the Japanese Emperor.

Moreover, the Japanese had had no experience in ordinary diplomatic procedure, and Mr. Harris was obliged to hold classes in international law among representatives of the Japanese nobility in order that they might know what he was talking about. He faced a great difficulty also in the fact that it was impossible to ascertain the degree to which the persons with whom he negotiated were really responsible. On several occasions he reached an accord with the immediate circle that had been established around him, only to discover that this group had no authority to bind the daimio, the baronial council, or much less the Japanese court itself.

Mr. Harris was an extraordinary man. He rejoiced over the cultivation of parsnips in his garden, analyzed the almost continuous ringing of bells and gongs, endured the rigors of a highly formalized etiquette with every step of which he was unfamiliar. Nevertheless, he clung doggedly to working out an agreement, a clause at a time, between his country and the Japanese Empire.

OUR FIRST TREATY WITH JAPAN

The result of these efforts was our first treaty with Japan, ratified in 1858. It provided for a limited consular representation in Japan and expressed a mutuality of interest in the establishment of normal trade between the two countries.

The attitude of Mr. Harris and the subsequent reception of Japanese representatives in the United States created, eventually, a very favorable reaction toward this country in Japan. The Japanese, for the most part, came to feel that the American case had been sincerely presented and that there was relatively little basis for misunderstanding between the two countries. The trade that developed was profitable to the Japanese almost from the beginning and they followed the suggestion of Mr. Harris that they collect tariffs in order to acquire and support a navy.

Japanese progress, thereafter, was very rapid. Probably no nation in history has been so transformed in so short a space of time. By the end of the last century the United States, recognizing the progress that had been made, was willing to accede to the Japanese demand that all concessions and special privileges be abolished and that extra-territorial functions, such as existed in China, be no longer continued. By that time Japan was rapidly becoming a real world power. The defeat of China in the war of 1895 was almost back-handed, and it set the pace for a further expansion of Japanese ideas and for a more rapid assimilation of the social and military techniques of the Western world.

The American declaration of the Open Door in China, made at the end of the century, was not aimed at Japan, but at the Western Powers. For this reason it was accepted by the Japanese, at that time, as a still further earnest of American good faith.

It was the Russo-Japanese War that marked both Japanese emergence as a power of the first rank and the crystallization of a truly friendly attitude toward the United States. In that struggle American sympathy was overwhelmingly on the side of the Japanese, possibly because of the misconception that the Japanese were the underdogs. The intervention of the American President to provide a settlement of the issues, in the Treaty of Portsmouth, was undoubtedly favorable to Japanese aims.

Some historians have asserted, in fact, that the American action brought about a negotiated peace, with all the advantages accruing to Japan, at the precise moment when the Russians were warming up for a really good fight. This point of view minimizes the importance of the naval battle off Shimonoseki in which the Russian force was disastrously defeated, and presumes that the Japanese army would not have been in a position to consolidate any of its gains on the Asiatic mainland. This interpretation is probably too unfriendly to the Japanese to be accurate, but it is nevertheless true that American intervention was based upon a preponderance of sympathy toward the Japanese cause.

The First "Gentlemen's Agreement"

It was in the glow of the good feeling that developed as a result of these events that President Theodore Roosevelt tackled the most vexed question in American-Japanese relations—the matter of admitting Japanese immigrant labor to the United States. The Japanese had been barred under our Oriental Exclusion Act and they interpreted their exclusion as an affront.

President Roosevelt, through negotiation, undertook to put exclusion on a different basis by concluding the so-called "Gentlemen's Agreement," by which the Japanese enjoyed moral equality. Their government assumed the responsibility of reducing friction with the United States over immigration by voluntarily keeping Japanese laborers out of this country.

It is impossible to escape the conclusion that the American attitude toward Japanese immigration has had a major influence on everything that has taken place in the relationship of the two countries since that time. The "Gentlemen's Agreement" made it possible for the Japanese to save face and also made it possible for the United States to avoid what was regarded as an undesirable influx of low-standard labor.

Some persons in the United States felt, however, that the Japanese were not honoring the agreement. There was smuggling, of course, but the most interesting part of the American agitation against the agreement was its concentration on the so-called Japanese "picture brides." It was repeatedly charged that by marrying Japanese in Japan to the pictures of persons already admitted to the United States, and then applying for their admission as relatives, Tokyo had succeeded in circumventing entirely the purpose and the operation of the "Gentlemen's Agreement." Just how much of this was true is not easy to establish.

This phase of the propaganda was picturesque, but the basis for it was economic. The Japanese were making important headway in the truck-gardening field and in raisin production in California. It was from California that the pressure for legalizing the machinery of Japanese exclusion was brought to bear. The "yellow peril" slogan was dragged out and an anti-Japanese campaign made some headway.

The events that took place on the Asiatic mainland between the outbreak of the World War and 1920 added some other causes of friction. Japan had been invited to take over the German holdings around Tsingtao but this had been followed up by the peremptory Japanese demand for a solid and permanent foothold in Shantung Province. There were the notorious Twenty-one Demands on China on the Asiatic side of the Pacific and Viscount Ishii's demands in Washington for recognition of Japan's "paramount" position in respect to the Asiatic mainland.

The United States, pursuing its steadfast policy in respect to China, resisted both these Japanese positions vigorously. Exactly to the extent that the Japanese felt their demands just and reasonable did they feel that the American position was arbitrary and open to suspicion. The American position, however, won the day and the Japanese emerged from the war with little to show for their having joined the Allied cause. They did receive the mandate over the former German islands in the Pacific north of the Equator, but even the Japanese saw that these islands, as they stood, were an economic liability, while the terms of the mandate were designed to prevent them from becoming a military advantage.

ANOTHER SETBACK TO PRIDE

There was, then, already tension in Japanese-American relationships when the United States took another step in Pacific affairs by calling the Washington Naval Disarmament Conference. Here again the Japanese suffered a setback to pride because of the insistence of both the United States and Britain that in any agreement the Japanese must assume the inferior place in the 5-5-3 naval ratio. The Japanese ultimately accepted this as the best they could get, signed the Nine-Power Treaty under pressure of a Chinese boycott, and went back to Tokyo with a considerable addition to their growing list of grievances against the United States.

And it was right on top of this that the United States Congress passed the Japanese Exclusion Act. It is now usually believed that the final push to this legislation was given by the statement of the Japanese envoy that such an act upon the part of Congress would be fraught "with grave consequences." This statement was apparently interpreted by the Congress as even more than a warning. It was pictured as a threat, if not an outright ultimatum.

Congress "got its back up" in record time and the legislation was stampeded through. The Japanese Ambassador went home to die of a broken heart. He was not aware, it seems, that "grave consequences" had a specific meaning in diplomatic usage in English; and by a slip of the tongue in a foreign language he had precipitated the one thing he was most anxious to avoid.

Japanese-American relations reached a low ebb.

It is important to point out, however, that the official American policy from 1853 up to and after the passage of the Japanese Exclusion Act was one of friendliness to the Japanese as a nation. Whatever may have been the attitude of individual Californians toward individual Japanese lettuce pickers, the government of the United States had repeatedly committed itself to the position that it was the desire of the United States to secure and preserve a strong, independent, and friendly Japan.

The treaties between Japan and the United States had twice been successfully revised to Japanese advantage, and in both cases at the request of the Japanese themselves. The United States at no time undertook to prescribe any restraints on Japanese sovereignty other than those that were arrived at by open and friendly negotiation, such as in the case of naval limitation.

This factor in policy is important because of its bearing on the

Japanese invasion of China. The United States had also taken an equally strong position in support of a free, strong, and independent China, also friendly toward the United States. It was the position of this country that it was perfectly possible for two such independent sovereignties to exist side by side in Asia. It was not until the Japanese made it plain, in the course of the present Chinese-Japanese War, that they did not agree to this possibility, that the relationship between the United States and Japan reached a non-treaty basis.

On the Day-to-Day Basis

That is the present situation between the two countries. Washington calls it a day-to-day basis. In other words, anything can happen. This constitutes a serious gulf, and it now seems to have been caused, not merely by superficial incidents, but by a wide divergence in outlook.

In March of 1940, for example, Yakichiro Suma, spokesman of the Japanese Foreign Office, declared that there were possibly two bases for "present American-Japanese misunderstanding." The first, he said, was the violation of American property rights in China; the second was possibly some moral objection to the infringement of Chinese sovereignty. The first, he said, was recognized by the Japanese as being the one that was really important from the American point of view.

This very clearly stated position shows the inability of even a trained Japanese diplomat, familiar with Americans and dealing with them daily, to understand the importance to the United States of the moral position that has been taken in respect to treaties and treaty violation. The sincerity of our economic interest is not doubted. Our moral good faith is minimized.

In the present tension, the violation of American rights should not be overlooked. The American rights and the American property are there and they have been violated. We have already noticed the more than 200 American protests that are still in Tokyo under the label of unfinished business. Such a situation naturally does not improve the feeling between the two countries.

Of far more importance, however, is this question of the method of doing international business, that Mr. Suma dismissed as being of relative unimportance. The United States is committed, not only in Asia but elsewhere, to the difficult task of trying to defend and strengthen treaty obligations in the face of a growing disregard for such obligations.

The violation of Chinese sovereignty is interpreted by most thoughtful Americans, not merely as an encroachment upon China and not merely in the light of the incidental destruction of American life and property, but as a far-reaching blow to treaty structures that the United States, over a long period of time, has striven painstakingly to erect and defend. In a large sense, therefore, the present breach between the United States and Japan has an important moral foundation as far as this country is concerned.

FIGHTING A HOLY WAR

But it is no less significant that the same moral basis for ill-feeling exists possibly to an even greater degree on the Japanese side. Japanese "patriotism" is by no means a cheap nationalism. It is a mode of living and a profound religion.

The Japanese Emperor is, to 90,000,000 Japanese, a living deity. He is the direct descendant of the Sun. The Emperor's blessing has been repeatedly and publicly given to the campaign in China and to the point of view that Japan must occupy a dominant position in Asia. What we are pleased to call unbridled aggression is, to most of the Japanese, the invincible "Imperial Way."

For this reason the invasion of China and the subsequent attempt to gain Asiatic supremacy are nothing more nor less than a Holy War to the Japanese. The American attempt to interfere with this very clear expression of the Emperor's god-head, his divine will, and Japan's "manifest destiny," is, therefore, from the Japanese point of view, not merely an unfriendly policy, it is plain sacrilege. This may not be the exact view of a relatively few cynical military and political leaders. It is unquestionably the view of the men in the armies and the Japanese public. Under those conditions the emotional breach between the two countries is extremely important and it is not likely to be bridged by minor concessions and soft words.

The most important single fact in the day-to-day policy is that it opens the door to further action by the United States. We have already observed that with the modification of existing treaties the hands of this country are freed to take action in the military or economic field without violating any of the contracts that we are determined to defend.

POSSIBILITY OF AN EMBARGO

The Japanese viewed the American abrogation of the 1911 Treaty not only with resentment but with genuine alarm, since behind that abrogation stood the specter of an American embargo on the shipment of war materials to Japan. Despite the efforts of the United States State Department to dodge that issue, despite the protestations of the Japanese, and despite all the soothing syrup that can be poured over the situation, the question of an embargo is still the most sensitive single point in the present troubled relationship.

Embargo action by the United States has, by late summer, 1940, had two phases. The first is the moral embargo on airplanes and on formulas for producing aviation gasoline, imposed by the consent of American shippers against nations that bomb open cities. The second is the placing of certain commodities, vital to American national defense, on a list for which export license is required. The second phase began modestly with machine tools, but when, on July 25, 1940, the President announced that scrap metal and petroleum had been added, it was popularly assumed that a general embargo on war materials for Japan had been put into effect.

This was not the case. Weeks later, the *New York Times* reported that exporters were still trying to discover what materials could be shipped and what could not. The scrap metal order, for example, covered only first-grade scrap steel, and this classification proved to be very elastic.

Meanwhile Washington assured the Japanese that the action was taken solely in the interest of the conservation of materials necessary for national defense and that no anti-Japanese construction should be given to it. This obvious dodging of the real issue provided a temporary face-saving formula, but it satisfied neither the Japanese nor the proponents of an embargo in the United States. It may have seemed reasonable to most Americans that stocks of war materials should not be allowed to go out of the country at the time of the most intense concentration on American defense. That did not seem reasonable to the Japanese.

From the beginning the Japanese had taken the position that any interruption of the flow of war materials to Japan would be construed as an unfriendly policy. This position was not declared officially, although each step in American defense was immediately questioned. The Japanese press, however, did not mince words in describing the American action as hostile. As early as June 3 (1940) the authoritative newspaper *Asahi* stated bluntly that Japan would lodge a protest or "take other appropriate measures" if the United States Government announced any restrictions on the export of vital raw materials. The Japanese Government considers, *Asahi* said, that American proposals to make raw material exports subject to license go beyond the moral sanctions already applied to some war material exports. Such proposals, *Asahi* declared, must be interpreted as aimed at Japan, Germany, and Italy.

This reaction to American licensing of exports of machine tools, admittedly an insignificant part of Japan's war trade, grew even more bitter as other products were added. That there might be a sincere desire in the United States to conserve certain materials was not admitted as a possibility.

There is, of course, good reason why the Japanese should have been puzzled by the entire American course of action. The gradual easing of this country into a partial embargo position by the dodge of the export license provision was a further confusing step in a policy that had been muddled and paradoxical from the start. It is easy to understand that the Japanese should have hit upon the only clear motive that could be seen in the whole course of the American actions, that is, hostility to Japanese expansion in Asia.

They had, indeed, more than usually good ground for their assumption, because of the conjunction, which may have been quite accidental, of three events that seemed more than coincidental. In the three weeks prior to the adding of scrap metal and oil to the license list, the Japanese state moved toward declared totalitarianism, with the formation of the Konoye Government, and announced a Pan-Asiatic policy. Henry L. Stimson, who had been the chairman of the Committee for Non-Participation in Japanese Aggression, entered the Roosevelt Cabinet as Secretary of War. T. V. Soong visited Washington. There may have been no connection between these events and the action of July 25 listing scrap metal and petroleum, but the Japanese are likely to think there was.

But this American action might have been expected much earlier. When the United States embarked upon a vigorous armament policy early in 1940 there was little emphasis upon the supply of war materials. Congress was preoccupied with naval building and the increase in the striking strength of the United States. And even this phase of re-armament was not thought to necessitate any interruption of our exports to Japan. The embargo resolutions in the Senate were being pigeon-holed at the same time that Congress was being urged to pour the first billions of dollars into a revitalized naval program.

It should not be overlooked that this new consciousness of

defense needs appeared in the Administration and in Congress long before the collapse of France. At that time it seemed exceedingly unlikely that the French Republic would disappear within a few months and that there would be an immediate menace to the British navy. Italy was not even a belligerent, and the Atlantic seemed safe for months, if not years, to come.

There is justification, therefore, for the assumption that the original impetus to naval rebuilding was given by the one navy that could have been, at that time, a menace to the interests of the United States. That navy was the Japanese.

Thus American re-armament was justifiably viewed with suspicion in Japan, while, at the same time, the American proponents of an embargo were mystified by the inconsistency of the American Administration.

The official "hush-hush" policy on the embargo continued, while Congress was urged to bend every effort to increase our naval strength in the Pacific. Some persons were indiscreet enough to suggest that there was more than a little paradox in voting billions of dollars to increase the United States navy, and continuing at the same time to supply the scrap iron with which the Japanese were building the navy against which we were so unwillingly obliged to compete. If all of Asiatic politics is a poker game, some persons felt entitled to ask why we should be digging into our pockets to stay in the game while slipping the Japanese the chips under the table with which to raise the ante.

And if that was true of those first "modest" proposals, how much more is it true now that we have embarked on a ten-billion-dollar program for building a two-ocean navy!

Other factors, of course, have tended to keep the embargo question before the American mind. One is the repeated Chinese appeal for such action. While shipments of American scrap iron continue and talk of embargo is hushed, any justice-loving American feels a personal revulsion when he hears these words of a Chinese spokesman on the radio:

"Our women and children were bombed again today. We know all Americans disapprove of that. We know that your sympathies are whole-heartedly with China. We appreciate that sympathy. We thank you for your generous assistance. We love you for the work you have done on our behalf; but . . . will you stop arming Japan?"

Some sturdy Americans feel, moreover, that there are limits to patience and that our policy of excessive caution must, sooner or later, be abandoned. They believe that the form of our attempt at neutrality in the European War was a moral betrayal of the instincts and sentiments of a large part of our population. They suggest that while we survey with indignation the fruits of aggression we can hardly do less than remove from aggressor nations, as far as is in our power, the materials that make conquest possible.

No Time Like the Present

While the European War has put increasing burdens on American economy and has imposed new problems on American policy and American defense, it has also put the United States in a peculiarly strong position in relation to Japan and Japanese aggression. If the moral impulse in the United States is to be expressed, the present time, however dangerous, offers an unusual opportunity to set the machinery in motion.

The inability of the Japanese to obtain supplies from the countries at war has made Japan increasingly dependent upon the United States for several military necessities. Oil, for example; the Japanese in 1937 were getting only about half of their supplies from the United States, but by the end of 1939 they were getting 85 per cent. The American share of Japanese scrap metal purchases rose from 60 per cent just prior to the hostilities in China, when the Japanese were accumulating their reserves, to 90 per cent by the end of 1939. At the beginning of 1939 Japan was obtaining 90 per cent of her copper from the United States; by the end of 1939 she was getting 99 per cent of it from us. By the first of July, 1940, Japan was placing here the largest scrap iron order of her history.

The importance of American materials to Japanese war manufacture is perhaps best shown by the percentage of such purchases in the total of Japanese buying from the United States. Partly as a result of the Japanese channeling of imports away from the light industries and into the heavy—that is, bluntly, away from peace manufactures into war materials—Japanese purchases of raw cotton, for example, have steadily gone down. In 1938 Japan bought less than half the amount of raw cotton in the United States that she had purchased four years previously. But war materials purchases were steadily rising. In 1939 Japan, under the strictest wartime regulations, which forbid "unnecessary" imports, was our second-best customer with $231,405,000 worth of purchases. Out of every dollar of that $231,405,000 spent in the United States, 73½ cents went directly for war materials.

This was in the face of the so-called moral embargo in the United States. The moral embargo, however, was necessarily restricted to concentrated operations over which the United States could exercise a high degree of control. The moral embargo stopped the shipment of airplanes to Japan. It did not stop the shipment of the metals out of which airplanes are made. It stopped the export of patented processes for the production of high-grade aviation gasoline. It did not stop the export of all classes of petroleum from which the Japanese could produce their own high-grade gasoline with the methods available.

The Japanese never did purchase finished munitions to any great extent in the United States. It was cheaper to buy the raw materials and fabricate the finished products in Japan. As a result, the net amount of the moral embargo in the United States was never as much as 1.5 per cent of the total Japanese purchases.

There has been much talk during the past few months of Japanese trade agreements with South American countries through which replacements of some of these large-scale American purchases will be found. On the face of it this seems feasible. A glance at the amounts involved, however, will burst the bubble. The great Japanese-Argentine trade pact, the most important and successful of these South American negotiations, covers an over-all exchange of products amounting to roughly $6,000,000 a year. The present Japanese-American exchange is roughly $400,000,000. It will take a great many more Japanese emissaries than have been sent out, a far greater working capital than Japan has at her disposal, and a totally different scale of operations in American trade, if Japan is to get even a fraction of her replacement of United States purchases from South America.

The Japanese have repeatedly emphasized the necessity of keeping their access to the raw materials of Netherland India. This is an important source of petroleum. But those petroleum operations are jointly controlled by the British, and it is hardly conceivable, at this time, that Britain will deprive herself of the access to Netherland Indian production simply to accommodate an increased demand from Japan. Unless Britain were willing or forced to forego her supplies of fuel from southeastern Asia, the Japanese could not begin to compensate from that source for the loss of American supplies of petroleum.

The Japanese position, therefore, is highly vulnerable, and this vulnerability, it has been repeatedly suggested in the United States, is the best argument for taking action now, if any action is to be taken.

Time Works Both Ways

On the other hand there is a quite different time argument presented by the opponents of any real embargo on shipments to Japan. That argument is that the Chinese campaign has been far more costly than the Japanese expected it to be, and that the Japanese economy at the present time is far closer to collapse than the Japanese will admit or than many Americans will believe.

Undoubtedly, living costs in Japan have gone up, and taxes have gone up at the same time. The rate of acceptance of Japanese bonds has steadily deteriorated, and, as nearly as can be estimated, approximately two-thirds of Japanese foreign credits have been exhausted. There is no reason to believe that the metal reserve behind the Japanese currency is adequate.

It is suggested, moreover, that the Japanese armies' bogging down in the field throughout all of 1939 should be attributed not so much to Chinese tactics of resistance as to the economic inability of the Japanese to keep forces of that size in the field. In November 1939, it was specifically reported to the *New York Times* that the Japanese naval operations in South China waters were on a twenty-four-hour basis because of the financial inability of the Japanese to carry on any extended campaign.

How much farther the Japanese peasant can draw in his belt is not known in the Western world. Whether Japan has already been bled white, as some persons suggest, is still an open question. All of the official Japanese statements, of course, declare that the economy of the country is sound, that the Chinese campaign will pay large dividends, and that Japan is in a position, economically and militarily, to carry on indefinitely. That is the official version and subject to a good deal of discount.

At the same time the experiences of the United States in the last ten years have shown that theoretical soundness in economy is not an imperative factor in carrying on national life, while the war that Germany has waged is a good demonstration of the fact that every one of our preconceived economic dogmas can be violated and there can still be a strong army in the field.

Persons who believe, then, that a Japanese collapse will free us from our Asiatic responsibilities if we do nothing are probably somewhat optimistic, but they do have ground for the position that the substitution of a three-year war for a three-month campaign in China, as was expected, has not done the Japanese any good. They urge, therefore, that the element of time should argue for our non-interference with the inexorable working out of economic law. They insist that if we will guard ourselves against a Nazi invasion and a fifth column, avoid Asiatic clashes, keep our mouths shut and play our cards close to our shirts, God and the clock and the Chinese will settle with the Japanese without our getting out on a limb.

The timeliness of any forceful American action, therefore, is subject to argumentation on both sides.

Apparently the course of action that had been projected by our policy-making departments of government did not entirely reflect popular feeling. A recent Gallup poll showed that three-fourths of the American public believed that there should be a drastic curtailment of shipments of war materials to Japan. Editorial support for the embargo is widespread. Our policy of making Japan's aggression possible is in no sense a popular one.

Proposals in the legislative branch of our government have reflected this rising tide of opinion. There have been several resolutions submitted in each branch of Congress, proposing an embargo in one form or another. Their substance was covered most clearly in two joint resolutions submitted to the United States Senate in January 1940. These became a focus of attention. One was by Senator Key Pittman, Chairman of the Committee on Foreign Relations, and the other by Senator Lewis B. Schwellenbach of Washington, who has since been elevated to the judiciary. These resolutions appeared to have a greater degree of Congressional support than any other proposals, and at the time they were submitted many persons thought that one of them would be promptly adopted.

The two resolutions, while differing in phraseology, would, either one, have the effect of putting an immediate stop to American war material shipments to Japan. Senator Pittman's resolution enumerated the materials while Senator Schwellenbach simply designated them as any materials designed to carry on a war of aggression. Treaty violation was given, in each, as the basis for action.

The Senate Committee on Foreign Relations accepted these two resolutions in February 1940, and promptly laid them over "for one week" for further study. That week was still going on eight months later. Before very long it was suggested that the State Department would be greatly embarrassed by the adoption of one of these resolutions; the pigeon-hole anesthetic that was administered to them was presumably inspired from that source. It is not to be supposed that such an attitude would have been taken unless there was some good ground for it. The American whose wish has thus been thwarted will want, at the very least, to examine the real pros and cons of the Japanese embargo proposal to find out, not only whether he accedes to it, but also why, for the time being, it was so effectively shelved.

When a War Is Not a War

The absence of administrative action, moreover, was strikingly apparent because of the fact that the United States had had within its own legal machinery a perfectly simple means of applying the embargo from the outset. The unamended American Neutrality Act was on the statute books in July 1937, when the shooting started at Marco Polo Bridge. It would have been absurdly easy to apply its provisions by the mere Presidential declaration that a state of war existed between Japan and China.

Nobody in his senses could possibly deny that such a state of war did exist: there was an organized large-scale military invasion by a recognized government on the one side, and an organized large-scale military resistance by another recognized government on the other. The Japanese have managed officially to squirm within the limits of the Kellogg-Briand Treaty by calling the war in China "an incident" or "the China affair." But when one bombing raid can net a thousand casualties, when upward of three million troops take the field and stay in the field for three years, when two-fifths of the second largest country in the world is overrun by an invading army, and when the sovereignty of that country mobilizes every resource to check that invasion, to keep up the pretense that no war is going on is a tour de force that gets into the field

of opéra bouffe. There must have been some very compelling reason for this amazing American contradiction of elementary good
sense.

The reason lay primarily in the total inadequacy of the American
Neutrality Act to meet any facts in any given case. Its smug presumption that in any case of hostilities both sides were wrong
violated every canon of American decency. In the case of the China
War, its application would have put the Chinese on the same basis
as the Japanese, and would have precluded from the very beginning
any part of the American assistance that three-fourths of the
American people were earnestly eager to extend to the Chinese.

Its application, in addition, would have meant the American
recognition of Japanese belligerent rights in China, and, therefore,
a denial of the American right to protect its nationals and its property in the Chinese Republic. Admitting that there was a war in
China, therefore, meant committing the United States to a policy
that said there was nothing that could be done about it except to
stay as far away from danger as possible, and the United States
was not ready in 1937 to declare its total disinterest in the future
of Asia.

In addition, it has never been a secret that the State Department
felt that the neutrality legislation was badly conceived and worse
executed. As the functioning branch of government charged with
the responsibility of carrying out the relationships of the United
States with all the rest of the world, the Department felt, very correctly, that an attempt by the Congress to legislate in advance any
course of action that must necessarily be taken under all circumstances was a complete misunderstanding of the whole basis for
our State Department.

In other words, the Neutrality Act was not applied to China,
not because there was no war there, but because the Neutrality
Act itself was so incredibly bad.

These, obviously, were the chief arguments for passing over this
first and logical opportunity to apply an embargo on shipments of
war materials to Japan. It should be remembered that in 1937 the

"cash-and-carry" policy had not been adopted, and that the mere suggestion of possible aid to the democracies in the event of a European war was a political heresy. Some of these are still cogent arguments. Under the Neutrality Act, as amended, the cash-and-carry policy would benefit Japan and damage China, since China has no merchant marine. The act was amended with an eye on Europe, not Asia, and still fails to square with any facing of the facts. Its application to Asia has apparently not even been considered. When, in addition, instead of direct embargo action we get the subterfuge of an export license system that may not be applied at all, the man in the street has a right to wonder about the reasons for our excessive caution.

JAPAN WILL STRIKE BACK

First of all, reprisals. It is not to be expected that the Japanese, prosecuting a Holy War and sacrificing their national economy to it, will take such a body blow as a real embargo lying down. General Honma, the occasionally belligerent commander of the Japanese army in North China, who has been busily baiting the British for the last eighteen months, has already said he cannot accept responsibility for what might happen. The civilian government in Tokyo has been slightly more conservative but has made it abundantly clear that the embargo will be regarded as a gross affront. Some type of counter-action may, therefore, be regarded as inevitable. It will be likely to take two forms.

First, there is a possibility of physical reprisals. These would not even have to be directed from Tokyo. The Japanese army in the field is admittedly irresponsible. It has had some excellent practice in starting and paying for anti-foreign demonstrations in China, and subsequently shrugging its shoulders over regrettable incidents and accidents, and blaming the spontaneous "national feeling" of the Chinese for them. The reign of terror in Shanghai was presumed to have been inspired solely by Wang Ching-wei.

Naturally, if an embargo were imposed, the worst of the anti-American outbursts in China would be said to have been conducted by the Chinese. That technique is already familiar.

The United States has in Japan, and in Japanese-occupied China, about 15,000 nationals and a fixed property investment of several hundred million dollars. It is not to be supposed that these persons and this property would come off scatheless at the hands of the Japanese.

Some of this property in China has already been a source of considerable irritation to the Japanese. Socony-Vacuum is not the only American operation that has an establishment in China. There are mission schools, universities, hospitals, publishing houses, and other cultural operations that represent as large a portion of the physical part of the investment as do the commercial properties. Rightly or wrongly, the Japanese regard these missionary and other cultural centers as hot-beds of anti-Japanese agitation.

The Tokyo newspaper *Kokumin* has complained bitterly that, "Every time a brick is knocked off a missionary chapel in China there is an American diplomatic protest in Tokyo." Because of this resentment it is likely that the cultural properties would bear the first brunt of Japanese displeasure. How far this displeasure would go no one can tell. An American friend of mine who has lived in China for twenty years and is also an astute analyst of Japanese attitudes and Japanese behavior told me, "It is my fixed belief that within forty-eight hours after the declaration of an American embargo against Japan, there would not be left standing, in the whole of Japanese-occupied China, one stone above another in any American missionary property."

This is undoubtedly an extreme outlook, but it does represent what some intelligent Americans in China feel to be an imminent danger at the present time.

It is also quite possible that Japanese reprisals against Americans might take an even more picturesque turn than the destruction of buildings. When Nanking was looted, the Japanese troops, out of control, did not hesitate to tie up living Chinese with baling wire, pour gasoline over them, and set them on fire. A little of this treatment applied to some Americans in the Far East by the same irresponsible Japanese army might very easily have some nasty repercussions.

Two considerations would involve us. The first would be the American policy of undertaking to defend the lives and property of nationals wherever they are lawfully occupied throughout the world. The second would be an undoubted wave of indignation in the United States that would demand at the very least some show of force.

The first of these is very often misunderstood. A bright high-school boy, in a discussion group over in Brooklyn, got up and said to me, a few weeks ago, "I certainly see no reason why the United States should ever have to threaten war with anybody just to protect the Standard Oil Company, and most of the students in this school, and I imagine in other schools, agree with me."

If that boy was telling the truth, there is a considerable misapprehension on the part of many Americans concerning the normal obligations involved in our position as a nation. There is far more at stake than the overseas property of one company. The United States has assumed for 150 years that one of the functions of its sovereignty was to protect its nationals throughout the world. Those nationals, whether they work for the Standard Oil Company or the Women's Foreign Missionary Society, are citizens of the United States, lawfully in a foreign country, under the specific provision of American treaties with that country. We have taken the position repeatedly that, so long as our sovereignty exists, the protection that it implies can be invoked.

There can be no receding from this position if we expect to be able to go on living with other countries. We make exception, under present legislation, to this protection, in specifically designated belligerent zones; but China is not such a belligerent zone under our interpretation of the law, and until those areas are designated as belligerent the obligation to protect our citizens continues.

It will be suggested that before any drastic action is taken, our nationals could be and ought to be evacuated from all zones of potential danger. There is no justification in law for such a procedure, and our nationals would be within their rights as citizens to refuse such evacuation. Moreover, many of them are in positions of grave responsibility and grave trust. They would regard evacuation as a definite flight from danger and the seeking of safety at the cost of conscience.

Here is an American doctor, for example, in a big Chinese hospital within the zone of Japanese penetration. He has a thousand patients dependent for their lives on his willingness to stay on the job. He has fifty post-surgical cases in a critical condition; a crowded maternity ward; he is fighting an epidemic of dysentery and running an out-patient clinic; he is handing out a bowl of rice a day to several thousands more in the attempt to fend off starvation. Can we say to such a man, "Your life is more precious to us than the lives of these thousands who are dependent on you, not because they are dependent, but because your death would be so much more embarrassing than theirs"?

The answer we would get is the answer that has already been given by Americans who have insisted on their right to stay on the job, as long as they obey the law, all over the world.

Even if we could evacuate all these Americans, we would then be turning their property over completely to the invader and that problem would not be solved. The loss, of course, would be written off; it would be inconsequential, but the loss of accomplishment which those physical properties represent could not be compensated for in several generations.

In addition, the mere physical operation of evacuating some of our nationals would in some cases involve the use of naval vessels and might necessitate the entering of what are now closed waters. Even the evacuation would be, in a sense, a show of force.

This discussion of possible reprisals should not be narrowed down to any quite so simple question as, "Would an embargo bring about causes for war with Japan?" The case has many ramifications short of that. But it might easily be one inflammatory factor in a number of causes for war.

The point is that the imposition of an embargo on a nation vitally dependent upon us in the conduct of a Holy War is a drastic action in foreign policy. It is in itself only one step short of a hostile military act. Its consequences, therefore, will have to be considered, and we must be prepared to face the fact that those consequences may quite quickly blast us out of the last remnant of our smug security.

With the possibility of drastic Japanese physical reprisals, it is folly to suggest that we can impose an embargo and then sit back in comfortable isolation and let economic law punish the Japanese. It will be impossible to make of the embargo simply a high-minded moral display of our disapproval of Japanese methods. It is an active and vital challenge to those methods and it cannot be taken with any degree of assurance unless we are willing to back it up. Backing it up may mean using the United States navy. Using the United States navy, moreover, would necessarily mean considerably more than running a couple of destroyers up from Cavite to the Gulf of Chihli. It could very easily mean the necessity of transferring a half-dozen capital ships from Hawaii to the Asiatic Fleet.

The Japanese have made it quite plain that there is no possibility of putting on an embargo and then playing "pussyfoot."

This is not meant to be alarmist or jingoist. It is rather an attempt to face the fact clearly that we are discussing a vigorous action in foreign policy; that such an action cannot be taken if we insist that our first and last motto must be "Safety First." Right or wrong, an embargo is dangerous and that fact should be faced at the outset.

The second type of reprisals that might be expected from the Japanese is economic reprisals. We cannot expect to cut off 73 per cent of our exports to Japan and have the remainder of our trade continue under normal conditions and at normal levels. It is extremely likely, indeed, that a complete rupture of trade relationships would be the immediate upshot of an embargo. Now it is perfectly apparent that at the present time this would hurt Japan a lot more than it would hurt us, but it would hurt us, nevertheless. The cost of such a rupture in trade, to the United States, is a part of the next great argument against the imposition of an embargo at the present time.

PAYING FOR HAVING A CONSCIENCE

An embargo would cost money. It would mean, at the outset, the loss of roughly $175,000,000, for war materials alone, in export trade, at the precise time that we are urgently seeking further export outlets. This loss would be particularly acute because of the fact that one of the products shipped to Japan, cotton, is already an American surplus product. Another product, scrap iron, has been a means of making a handsome profit out of an otherwise relatively non-productive American field.

The Japanese economic reprisals to which we have referred would undoubtedly involve a very serious interruption of the Japanese flow of raw silk into the United States, which is one of our major import commodities and a very important raw material.

It will be suggested that American flexibility and American ingenuity would very readily provide the necessary silk substitutes. That these substitutes could and would be found over a period of years goes without saying. In the clothing field rayon can be made to do many of the things that silk does. The recent manufacture of a silk substitute such as nylon in the stocking industry has led many persons to suppose that we could easily and quickly become independent of our raw silk imports. This is not the case.

This matter of nylon affords a good example. It appears to be a very satisfactory product, admirably adapted to silk substitution in the field where it is to be used. It is well organized; in the hands of a strong producing company; well distributed and well advertised. Years of preparatory work and large money investments have gone into progress to this point. But the initial year's output is planned to be one million pairs of stockings. American annual consumption is *six hundred* million pairs of stockings. Not even the most enthusiastic proponents of silk substitutes would believe that substitute operations could take up this gigantic difference without a period of long-time growth and development or without the most drastic economic dislocation.

It is this dislocation, indeed, that would prove the most disadvantageous and expensive part of the economic cost of an embargo. Steamship services, brokerage houses, import and export merchants, operators in foreign trade of all sorts, would be obliged to go out of business and then be obliged to seek some other field of activity to adjust their losses. Our whole present economic situation is not particularly good. We are already wrestling with a group of dislocations, the unemployment problem, the mammoth cost of government and national defense, and the attempt to bolster up our national income. Under those conditions many persons believe it unwise to add to the burdens we are already carrying.

This economic argument against an embargo, therefore, is not merely a question of whether or not a few rich oil companies or a few scrap iron exporters are unwilling to give up their immoral profits. It cannot be so easily localized. It is not a question of merely two or three pressure groups that wish to save their own skins; it is the plain fact that for every citizen in the country an embargo on Japanese goods will cost money. Just as this course of action cannot be taken in perfect smugness and in perfect safety, neither can it be taken on the cheap. It is not only dangerous; it is expensive.

BACKFIRE IN ASIA

There is another large group of considerations that have seemed to urge a high degree of caution on the part of the United States. The effect of an embargo will necessarily have political repercussions in Japan and in Japan's relations with the other powers. Thus a political factor is added to the military and economic ones.

An embargo would affect political structures within Japan itself. It is no longer a secret that within Japan there has been going on for the last twenty years what amounts to an undeclared civil war. An important group of industrialists, business men, and liberals took the position that the future of Japan lay in the preservation of peace, the establishment of vital trade relationships throughout the world, and the growth within Japan itself of representative democratic government. This group is usually called the Constitutionalists.

A dozen years ago it seemed likely that their struggle to control the future policy of the Empire could be won. Under the political leadership of Baron Goh and economic leadership of the large Japanese commercial houses, there was a chance to write into the Japanese structure of government its entire responsibility to the popular political will.

The crux of this struggle was the position of the Ministers of War and Navy in the Japanese Cabinet. While other members of the Cabinet were nominally chosen from political ranks and were normally responsible to the political majority in the Diet, the Ministers of the defense arms were appointees of the Imperial Household and its advisers. In other words, they were appointees of the services themselves and were usually officers on the active list. Because of this fact, the army or the navy was able to break any projected government at the outset by the mere refusal to recommend an officer for service in one of these posts. It was the desire of the Constitutionalists to make the defense Ministries politically responsible to the same degree that the other Ministries were responsible. They came very close to achieving this ambition ten years ago.

The opening up of the Manchurian campaign, however (precipitated, most persons believe, by the army itself against the wishes of the civil government in Tokyo), changed the aspect of this domestic struggle. For the first half of 1940, in the "most liberal" Cabinet that Japan had had in several years, there were actually as many as four civilians. The military services had won the struggle for the control of governmental machinery. The Konoye Government does not even make a pretense of civil responsibility. It is in "full accord" with the army.

The appeal to patriotism, with its religious connotations, has made it increasingly difficult for any Constitutionalist or Liberal to raise his voice. The last remnant of a Liberal Party was officially pushed out of existence early in May. Significant also was the expulsion from the Diet and from his party of Deputy Saito, who undertook merely to ask what dividends were being paid on the Chinese investment and to urge an at least partially itemized army budget.

Japan has moved with increasing speed toward the one-party Fascist system, and this movement has been accelerated by the course of events in Europe.

But while this struggle was going on, there was the constant hope that the loss of any major objectives in the China War would give renewed courage, and a renewed basis for possible appeal, to the Constitutionalists. The United States in its official representations to Japan, and, much more important, in the off-the-record discussions between American and Japanese diplomats, has thrown as much weight as possible behind the Liberal and Constitutionalist elements.

The imposition of an embargo at the present time would have the automatic effect of uniting all Japan behind the Fascist drive and silencing, permanently, all possibility of opposition. The whole course of the China campaign has shown the importance of finding convenient scapegoats upon whom the failure of the Japanese armies in China could be laid. Great Britain has filled this role most conspicuously. With the imposition of an embargo, however, the United States would assume the inevitable place of Public Enemy No. 1 in the Japanese Empire.

Those reactions are confidentially predicted, not merely on the basis of occasional explosions in the Japanese press, but on the simplest sort of observations. All of us, for example, know of families (perhaps in our immediate relationship) who bicker and quarrel among themselves and appear to be living in an atmosphere of incessant friction. But let an outsider offer the slightest criticism of any member of that family, or offer any threat to the security of any one individual in it, and the whole group coheres into a solid unit offering defiance to the intruder. The domestic Japanese scene presents almost the same picture.

The intervention of the United States, by an embargo, into the Japanese family quarrel over representative government could be expected to wipe out all differences and bring about a perfectly united front—one that would not only be determined to pursue aims inimical to us, but would completely kill off the Constitutionalist movement that we have always been eager to support. Presumably the Konoye Government of 1940 represents a newly united Japan. An American embargo would make that presumption an indisputable fact.

In addition, hostility such as this would undo all the work we have done to build up really friendly relations with the Japanese people. Until the events of only the last few years, the general attitude of Americans toward the Japanese was unmistakably friendly, and there is every reason to believe that this attitude was reciprocated.

In several instances public events have provided an opportunity for extraordinary demonstrations of friendship between the two peoples. A number of Japanese gestures have been very well received in the United States, and within the last twenty years on two different occasions the United States has been able to take actions that bore large dividends in friendship. The first of these was the promptness and generosity of the relief that was extended to Japan at the time of the earthquake and fire in Yokohama and Tokyo. The second, much more recent, was the return to Japan of the ashes of one of her most popular diplomats—who died in the United States—aboard an American cruiser with full ceremonial honors.

In addition to these gestures, the large political policy of the United States has repeatedly shown its friendliness toward the

Japanese, and there is a deep-seated desire on the part of many thousands of Americans to maintain amity. The embargo would promptly wipe out all of the advantages that have accrued to both parties from these friendly steps.

Several Ways to Jump

International repercussions of an embargo against Japan might take several forms, even if the most obvious, direct alignment with Germany and Italy, were not adopted. The Japanese, while keeping up the fiction of non-involvement, if they wished, would be able to adjust their course of action on the basis of expediency in the light of developments in Europe. The Japanese interest in Netherland India suggested, long ago, that an embargo by the United States might precipitate the Japanese rush toward the Netherland possession in order to compensate for the shutting off of American supplies. Thus an embargo might at any time have precipitated the very clash in the South China Sea that the United States was anxious to avoid.

Another possibility that was frequently suggested was that the application of an embargo would bring about an immediate understanding between Japan and Russia. In that case the United States would be placed in the embarrassing position of having forced the Japanese into an alliance that we could scarcely welcome.

On the other hand it is unlikely that Japan will countenance a large-scale deal with Russia as long as Russia continues to support the government of China. In addition to this, there is a genuine desire on the part of most Japanese to avoid any commitments to the Soviet Union. Russia is still the greatest threat to Japan, and the majority of Japanese may be expected to oppose any dealings with Russia unless they are forced into them. It is no secret that the Hitler-Stalin compact headed off an imminent alliance of Japan with Germany.

Another reason for suspecting the possibility of a Japanese-

Russian alliance is that the Japanese themselves have made too much of it from time to time. As soon as the American abrogation of the 1911 treaty with Japan was announced, hints of an understanding with Russia began to appear in all the Japanese papers. When it seemed possible that the United States could be wheedled, cajoled, and threatened into undertaking negotiations for a new treaty, when some Japanese newspapers were confidentially announcing that the United States was preparing a nice Christmas present for Tokyo, this discussion of a closer accord with the Soviets rose in a splendid crescendo. By the first of January 1940, it had reached such proportions that the more outspoken Japanese newspapers did not hesitate to unveil the threat, and say rather broadly, "If the United States does not speedily restore the normal basis of trade with Japan, we will be forced to conclude an alliance with the Soviets."

This was obviously nothing more than a little delicate blackmail, and when it failed to work, and the American Treaty lapsed on January 26, the argument about a Russian alliance began to die down. It is not without significance that from the middle of December to the middle of January the Japanese newspapers frequently announced that steady progress was being made by the negotiators of a trade agreement then in session in Moscow. Even as late as the first of February, it was denied that the negotiations had broken down; and it was not until foreign newspapers announced the departure of the Japanese mission that Tokyo even admitted any obstacles.

The presence of the Soviets in the Far Eastern picture, however, suggests another interesting possibility that might arise from the imposition of an embargo, and one that would put the United States in a very extraordinary position. Some astute military officers believe that Japan's dependence on the United States is so great that an imposition of an embargo would bring about a speedy and disastrous collapse of all the Japanese military establishment. They believe that not only would the Chinese venture be stopped, but that Japan also would be reduced to a position, perhaps more economic than military, in which she could not rely upon her ability to defend herself.

If such a sweeping collapse, precipitated by the embargo, took place, it is conceivable that the Soviets might choose such a moment to regain some of the ground that has been lost to Japan in eastern Asia since 1904.

If that were the case, the United States, having brought Japan to such a position, might be called upon to make representations to Russia on behalf of the Japanese. It will be remembered that the United States is committed to the policy of support for a strong and independent Japan. The United States, therefore, might be in a position of feeling the obligation to assist in extricating the Japanese from a situation that we ourselves had created.

This, of course, is highly speculative. But the mere fact that such speculation is possible indicates the degree to which an embargo might disturb the status quo. In other words, if we put on an embargo we are starting something, and it is not easy under present conditions to see where it would stop.

Of paramount importance, however, has been the constant threat that any action against Japan would be interpreted as our final effort to protect British interests in Asia. The Japanese would assume that we had joined the British cause, and would, therefore, plead that it was our action that had forced their open alignment with Germany and Italy.

As long as the Japanese kept up the fiction of "independent" action in Asia, it was obviously dangerous for the United States to force the open declaration of the European-Asiatic unity of aggression. If we had opposed that aggression, boldly, at one point, there was always the possibility that such opposition might take us straight into a European war by means of the Asiatic door.

All of these possibilities must have weighed upon the minds of those who have directed our policy in Asia. It was, in part, because the Japanese course of action could not be consistently predicted that it was considered unwise to unleash an interplay of political factors over which we could not hope to exercise control.

The case against the embargo, therefore, may be summed up as a case for caution. The embargo means a change from a static and defensive position to a dynamic and offensive position that may be self-defeating. It will certainly be costly. It will certainly be dangerous and its end results are unpredictable. For that reason persons who feel the weight of responsibility in the making of policy have naturally been very hesitant to commit themselves.

THE CASE FOR THE EMBARGO

On the other hand, the demand for such action continued to grow in the United States and there proved to be cogent arguments for a real embargo, no less than arguments against it.

The first of these springs from paradox. Especially at a time when the United States is concentrating on defense, it seems incredible folly to continue to arm a potential enemy. Even France and Britain, in their most short-sighted days, never went so far as we have gone in the building up of one of the very powers that makes our increased defense imperative.

But there are other paradoxes no less striking. The United States has been giving important material aid to the government of China, and at the same time has been supplying to Japan the materials to bomb that government out of existence. This is more than a mere infraction of logic. It is a direct violation of our own interests.

In the course of the last three years, for example, the United States has loaned to the government of China, headed by General Chiang, no less than $90,000,000. Fifty million of this was for currency stabilization and two other sums, of $20,000,000 and $25,-000,000, were loaned to the Export-Import Bank to enable the Chinese to make purchases in this country.

Some interesting things have happened in respect to those loans. The last one, for example, was guaranteed by an American lien on Chinese shipments of tung oil and antimony. Consequently one of the first things that the Chinese did was to buy a fleet of American trucks to transport tung oil to French Indo-China for shipment to the United States in order eventually to liquidate the obligation. They have already paid back $4,000,000 of it through shipments to the United States.

In December 1939 the Japanese High Command announced a very successful bombing operation on the highway that leads from the Chinese Province of Yunnan down into French Indo-China and the port of Haiphong. The Japanese announced that a Chinese truck train had been successfully bombed out of the road and that three-fourths of its vehicles had been destroyed. It was a notable victory.

It just happened that that Chinese truck train was carrying tung oil bound for the United States to pay an installment of the interest on the then recently concluded loan of $20,000,000. So what was actually blown out of the road was not merely Chinese trucks (purchased in Detroit by a corporation organized in Chicago for that purpose) but the interest on American money.

Now the curious part of this Japanese victory was that the planes that did the bombing were copied from American blueprints, fabricated out of metal that had been rolled in Pennsylvania, powered by fuel shipped out of southern California; and the bombs that they dropped were made of scrap iron from New Jersey.

The whole Japanese attack on the Indo-China supply line, made possible by Japan's use of American materials, has been designed to destroy China's ability to communicate with the outside world, and particularly with the United States. In that campaign we have given material assistance to the Japanese determination to make our money investment in the Chinese Government worthless.

The paradox does not end there. The United States is also pouring millions of dollars into the Chinese Red Cross and other Chinese rehabilitation services. At the same time it is supplying to Japan the precise materials that make those services necessary and provide them with an increasing number of dependents. Americans very correctly wish to contribute to the Chinese services in aid of Chinese refugees. Yet it is American materials sold to Japan that have pushed that number of refugees up into the millions.

WE VIOLATE OUR OWN POLICY

The United States has given and is continuing to give financial aid to the government and people of China, and recognition to the sovereign Chinese State. We are specifically pledged to the recognition and support of General Chiang. Our ambassadors are maintaining a liaison with his friendly government. At the same time we are carrying out a program that is committed to the destruction of this government that we recognize and support.

Our recognition of the Chinese State, moreover, does not begin and end with the presence of Ambassador Nelson T. Johnson in Chungking. We made a point of that recognition as early as 1843; it has been repeatedly reiterated—not only to the Japanese but to all of the powers of the Western world. It has become an essential part of our treaty structure. It is not merely an emotional commitment, it is a legal commitment to which we are solemnly pledged.

Now, on the face of it, the American position becomes logically and legally intolerable. We cannot, with any pretense of honesty, continue the active support of a political and military campaign whose major object is to destroy a government to which we are so pledged, and in destroying it invalidate the commitments that we have made in the course of more than a hundred years. In other words, in the name of caution and non-involvement, we are participating in the progressive demolition of our own foreign policy in Asia.

Our support of China has also a moral basis. Both as a government and as individuals, America has afforded political leadership for the Chinese. We have undertaken to inculcate the belief in democracies. We have fostered the establishment of free institutions and we have assisted the promotion of free education. We have repeatedly undertaken to make the Chinese depend upon us for that very moral leadership that we believe is necessary to the building of a free, happy, and modern China.

In the course of the decades in which this has been going on it has been natural that there should have been hundreds of protestations of our essential high-mindedness. We have urged courses of action and repeatedly insisted that as a country and as individuals we had no axes to grind. We have told the Chinese that we wish to see their country free and strong and prosperous, and that we believe that we can assist in this development if our example is emulated and our friendship cherished.

We need not be surprised if the Chinese have taken these protestations seriously. The Chinese have had good reason to regard the United States as their best friend in the family of nations.

What becomes of our position, if, when this friendly government is threatened, we find it expedient, in the name of caution, to stand aside? What can we expect to be the effect on our moral position in China if we now say: "Yes, those were brave words. We probably meant them when we said them, but it now becomes inconvenient to live up to them."

What recourse can we have if the Chinese point out to us that we have within our power the ability to stop this assault on Chinese sovereignty, but that when the time comes to exercise that power we stand cynically aside and say that it will be dangerous and expensive?

Under the conditions that exist now the Chinese have given another demonstration of their amazing patience. We could have no complaint if in the length and breadth of China it were published on every billboard that the word "American" was a synonym for "hypocrite."

BLOOD ON OUR HANDS

This challenge to the American position leads us out of the field of logic and into the field of morals. At this point, too, there is good reason why the sensibilities of Americans should be outraged by the course of events in China.

We have repeatedly signed commitments and urged commitments against the bombing of open cities. Yet we have sat back smugly and supplied the materials for the raids on women and children in Hangchow, Canton, and Chungking. It may not be a sound basis for a judicious foreign policy, but the healthy American is inclined to be revolted by the spectacle of American volunteer doctors going to China to pick American shrapnel out of Chinese children.

It is an easy matter to sit off ten thousand miles away and read the casualty list: "10,000 civilians killed in forty-eight hours of raiding in the north district of Canton, 500 more students added today to the civilian victims of the Japanese raiding of Chungking."

There are so many people in China that a few hundred thousand out of those teeming millions may seem of little consequence. But those few hundred thousand are civilians in open cities, destroyed by American materials in deliberate violation of what we have repeatedly said are our moral convictions.

The American who even pretends to be sensitive to his own good name must have rightly felt a shudder of horror when he read the dispassionate announcement in May of this year that Japanese planes would continue to bomb Chungking daily until the spirit of Chinese resistance was broken. A spokesman for the Japanese High Command admitted quite frankly that Chungking was not a land objective and that there was no intention of attempting a campagin against it other than a campaign of demolition from the air.

The very phraseology of that announcement indicated without question that the objective was the Chinese civilian population. It did not take an attack on three universities in the third day of the raiding to demonstrate that any so-called military objectives were entirely outside Japanese consideration.

We have become so glib about "total warfare" in the last few years that we may too readily accept the theory that an aerial attack on the spirit of resistance is quite as much a part of warfare as the demolition of a prepared military position. There are still a lot of Americans who believe, however, that the presumption that "all is fair in war" does not include war on women and children.

Those raids and the policy that they represent are a part of the American contribution to the Japanese war on China. Whether we like it or not, the supply of war materials to Japan, when it is within our power to shut those materials off, has made us moral partners in Japan's aggression. That partnership implies not only our support of the announced Japanese intention of destroying a friendly government, but it also involves our participation in the peculiarly unsavory methods by which the Japanese have chosen to wage war.

That goes also for the narcotic traffic in China. Many Americans were shocked and a little stunned when they began to find out, a few months ago, that the Japanese army was paying its way in North China by peddling heroin and morphine. Of course, American officials had heard all about that, long before it became a matter of general public knowledge. There had been repeated protests to the Narcotic Commission of the League of Nations and it was perfectly apparent that there was not an ounce of sincerity in a carload of Japanese disclaimers. Nevertheless, the use of opium as a war material, on an organized and highly profitable scale, did not reach the conscience of the American public until early in 1940.

The United States is not suppyling drugs to the Japanese army, but it is supplying the fuel that makes drug transport possible. The Japanese army is peddling cocaine in North China today because the government of the United States is willing to leave the Japanese army in North China. This, of course, is only a side-light on the general moral indictment that Americans are beginning to bring against aggression.

Those who urge an immediate and effective embargo on war materials to Japan are conscious of these moral factors. They believe that our position in Asia is so important, our own moral self-respect so important, that caution no longer fits the case.

CAUTION VERSUS OUTRAGE

There is in the United States a very considerable body of persons who are still capable of a sense of outrage. The clash on the Japanese embargo is the clash between that sense of outrage on the one hand and the question of "Safety First" on the other. It is very largely a struggle between conscience and caution.

If popular polls are an indication, a large part of the American population at the present time is more outraged than cautious. On the other hand if the pigeon-hole technique in Washington is an indication, our policy makers are still on the caution side.

There is still another ground on which the question of embargo is discussed in some circles, quite apart from this clash between safety and morality. There are some who hold that the interests of the United States in China are so great, and so dependent upon the continuation of a free Chinese Government, that the United States would act only in enlightened self-interest if it undertook to check the Japanese assault.

They hold that it is not merely American property that is being damaged by Japanese planes, but America's future in China being menaced by Japanese aggression. They believe, for example, that our position in respect to the Chinese market may make the difference, some years from now, between poverty and prosperity in the United States. They believe that precisely as China stands in urgent need of the United States at the present time, so the day will come when the United States will stand urgently in need of aid from an independent China.

From this point of view the extent of Japanese control is a grave threat to the whole theory of independent states, upon which our relationship with Asia is based. It is a threat not merely to American political prestige but to the trade relationships made possible by that prestige.

If the Chinese, as Carl Crow and others have pointed out, are to be considered as four hundred million customers, there must be Yankee business men who will feel that it is not good tactics to supply the materials to shoot the customers on the present grand scale.

Not everyone believes, of course, that the United States has a great economic future in Asia. A great many persons do, and our policy in Asia, for more than fifty years, has been founded upon that assumption. If we look forward to increasing advantages from the progressive development of a great, friendly, awakening China, we would certainly do well to safeguard those interests by helping to assure that China is not stifled so soon after her awakening.

Some persons carry this point of view so far as to assert that a clash with Japan is inevitable. They point out that all that remains to be decided is the time and the place for the clash. The present situation makes Japan so vulnerable, they say, that the United States might as well take "preventive" action now.

Others do not go as far as this. They do not believe that an armed clash between the United States and Japan is inevitable. They believe, indeed, that it can probably be avoided only by depriving Japan of the opportunity to strengthen herself at the expense of China and other Asiatic countries, with the co-operative supply of our materials. They urge that the stronger we make Japan, at this point, the less careful will Japan be to avoid a clash with us. Persons who take this point of view believe that the United States should impose an embargo on Japan, in our own interest, and then thereafter proceed to an amicable settlement of certain outstanding economic causes of friction between the two countries.

These last few points of view have one thing in common; they take a long-range rather than an immediate look at the situation in the Far East. They are based on the belief that we have a position from which retreat is extremely unwise, if not impossible, and that we must defend that position as best we can. Our long-range position cannot possibly be improved by the Japanese domination of all of eastern Asia. In so far, therefore, as our supplies of materials make that domination possible we are acting against our own long-term interests.

The Chinese themselves take that position. They point out, with justice, that they have faithfully resisted aggression while the rest of the world was succumbing to it. They remind us that they have been our true allies in the fight for a free future.

CHAPTER XIII

JAPANESE EXPANSION AND AGGRESSION

U P UNTIL early 1940 there was some talk about the possibility of "localizing" the war in China. The place of that war in Japanese expansion and aggression was not clearly understood, nor had it been proclaimed in Tokyo. Expansion was recognized in a general way as a part of the Japanese program, but its exact character and its relation to future Japanese policy were sometimes obscure. The course of the China War, the repercussions from Europe, the entrenchment of Japanese Fascism and its now openly declared objectives have made it possible finally to separate some of the facts from the myths about the projected Japanese course.

The steady acquisition of neighboring countries has been a fixed part of Japanese policy since 1895. Formosa, Korea, the Mandated Islands, Manchukuo, North China, and Hainan form a clearly connected narrative. It is the logical prelude to the now admitted drive for the control of all of eastern Asia.

The major myth about this expansion concerns the immediate cause for it. It has been popularly and often sympathetically supposed in the United States that Japan was obliged to acquire new territories in order to send out an overflow of excess population from a small and crowded country.

Too small a proportion of the Japanese Archipelago proper is arable. The result is an enormous congestion of population, with the actual figure running over 800 to the square mile. Such a density—more than twice that of New Jersey, for example—would seem to be a good reason for expanding.

The Japanese people, moreover, are prolific. The American has come to think quite correctly of Japanese population expansion in terms of those million Japanese babies that are born every year. The case can be put dramatically, and it often is, since it makes excellent propaganda for sympathy. This population pressure should logically demand some type of outlet.

The curious fact is, however, that even with those million babies a year the Japanese are not good colonizers nor good pioneers. They have had Formosa for forty-five years and it is still underpopulated. They have had Korea since 1910, and there are still only a handful of Japanese in the country. Manchukuo was the greatest potential population outlet that they have had, and the Japanese have had to import Shantung coolies at the rate of a million a year to keep the land in cultivation. The population pressure has not resulted in any surge of emigration toward Manchukuo. On the contrary, the Japanese Government has been obliged to organize and subsidize in order to get any Japanese on to the land at all.

The Japanese had had free access to the Philippines for forty years until 1940's limitation was imposed. They say that recently their average entry has been 2,800 a year. Their colony is important in the Philippines, but it is not large. The Japanese have had access to Hawaii, and there are about 150,000 of them there altogether. At the present time they have the Mandated Islands, and those islands are not taking up any substantial part of those million babies a year.

And yet, throughout all of this area, Japanese influence rather than Japanese population is expanding. Key men in production and merchandising are trained and sent out. A position is taken in the productive life of some of these communities out of all proportion to the size of the Japanese population. Japanese are operating as important distributors and as major concessionaires, and as such they are channeling the wealth of these areas into Japan.

If population outlet were the cause for Japanese expansion on the mainland of Asia, for example, it would certainly be the height of folly to concentrate on the Yangtze Valley, already overpopulated.

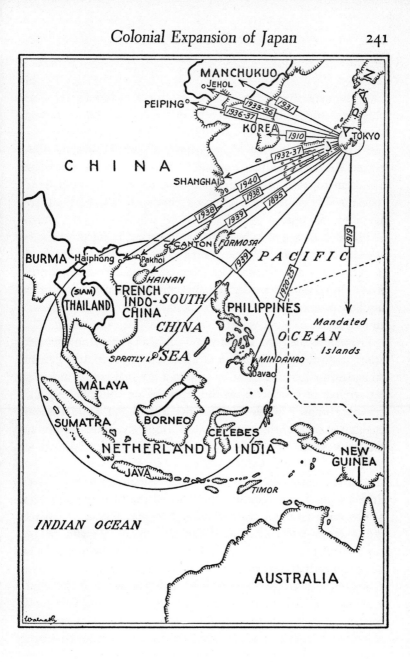

THE PRESSURE IS THERE

At the same time it would be short-sighted to suggest that population pressure in Japan does not exist. It does. But it is being solved just as in New York and Detroit, not by any movement toward frontiers but by a higher degree of industrialization and a greater dependence upon commerce. The Japanese, in a word, do not seem to want to colonize, but they do want to control. The urge for this control is not merely emotional and religious, it is soundly economic.

The high degree of industrialization required in Japan to support a dense and continually expanding population is necessarily dependent upon two things. The Japanese must have access to relatively cheap raw materials, and they must have a market for the finished products in whose fabrication this packed population is employed.

Precisely as the New Yorker who lives in a twenty-story tenement attempts to solve the problem of his overcrowding not by going to an agricultural frontier, but by getting a job that pays a cash wage for services or commerce, so the Japanese are concentrating their economy upon a production for the rest of the world that will enable the bulk of this population to live in the dense community that it prefers.

Earlier Japanese expansion was not so clearly economic. It is possible that the acquisition of Formosa was more a matter of establishing a political and military position off the coast of China than of obtaining essential raw materials. The later phases of Japanese expansion, however, such as the occupation of Manchukuo, and the control of North China, and the move into the South China Sea, are clearly traceable upon a raw materials chart.

The most desirable objective in Manchukuo was high-grade fuel, in which the Japanese Archipelago proper is deficient. The world's largest open-cut coal mine is at Fushan, just a few miles east of Mukden. The successful operation of this mammoth deposit suggested that other mineral resources of equal importance could be found and developed in the three northeastern Chinese provinces that constituted the area called Manchuria.

The Japanese had already developed a good technique of commercial progress in Manchuria through their control of the South Manchurian Railway. This railway was built and paid for with soy beans. Manchuria was the greatest soy-producing country in the world, and the outlet was over the South Manchurian Railway through Dairen. The Japanese were fully acquainted, therefore, with the commercial prospects in Manchuria and were ready to take advantage of them.

The move into North China had similar economic objectives. There were important coal and iron deposits in that part of the world and, moreover, North China was one of the best potential cotton producers in Asia.

The drive for markets has taken a more gradual and less dramatic form. It consists also in middleman operations that extend all over eastern Asia. The Japanese in this field have been at a disadvantage because of the intrenched position of the Chinese. The Chinese had gravitated toward profits. The biggest point of commercial exchange in southeastern Asia, as we have observed, is Singapore, and Singapore is the largest Chinese city outside of China. But wherever one goes throughout any of the Asiatic islands—Borneo, New Guinea, Celebes, Sumatra—wherever he wants to buy anything from a sewing-machine needle to a rear axle for a Chevrolet, he goes to a Chinese to buy it.

The Japanese, therefore, have had to face earnest and experienced competition. To do this they have had to rely upon low-cost merchandise, organized distribution, and the co-operation of the Chinese. The largest single product that they have to distribute is cotton textiles. But, in addition to that, they handle a large group of small manufactures that go into changes in standard of living. They are necessarily dependent upon Chinese middlemen for the distribution of a large part of these goods. And since the Chinese are capable of dealing them a severe economic blow through boycotts or other merchandising restrictions, the Japanese have felt from time to time that they were obliged to have political control in order to enforce their search for necessary markets.

The need for raw materials and markets to take care of the problem of a constantly expanding population gives a very sound case to the economic expansionists in Japan. It forms the basis for the large movement, from the time of the World War through 1931, in which Japanese industrialists assumed an increasingly important part in the economic and political life of the country. The men who were making Japanese policy were the men who directed the destinies of the House of Mitsui, Mitsubishi, and other great Japanese industrial empires. They were pushing their goods into all the markets in the world; they were developing a gigantic merchant marine. They were working, in a word, toward true economic expansion.

This met obstacles at many points. Quotas were imposed, restrictive tariff policies were adopted, and the Japanese economic empire faced an ever harder task in preserving the markets that already existed and in obtaining new ones. The most successful phase of this policy was the conclusion of commercial agreements with certain nations that controlled large markets. The most important of these agreements were in the field of textiles.

By committing themselves to certain purchases of raw materials, the Japanese were able to obtain an outlet for a considerable volume of cotton goods in both India and Java. Even as late as 1934, we have observed, they concluded with the United States the so-called "Gentlemen's Agreement" under which they were to share with the United States on an equal footing the cotton textile market in the Philippines.

IMPATIENT PATRIOTISM

There was in Japan, however, an increasing impatience with the restrictions put on Japanese goods by other countries, and with it an inability on the part of many persons to see that Japan's economic future could be assured through the peaceful means of barter and agreement. The representatives of this economic empire, moreover, formed that group in Japan that was interested in a higher degree of representative government and, indeed, in real constitutionalism. The peaceful expansion of Japanese interests, therefore, became synonymous with a non-military, and hence an unpatriotic, policy in many Japanese minds.

The more militant Japanese, backed by religion and tradition, had a somewhat different idea of Japanese expansion. Expansion was not conceived of necessarily as an outlet for surplus population or for the meeting of economic needs. It was a matter of the fulfillment of Japan's logical destiny as a world power. This political group was able to entrench itself firmly with the occupation of Manchuria, and since that time the political phases of Japan's expansion have been more important than the economic.

It is important, however, to stress these economic factors because the Constitutionalists had perhaps unwittingly given to the military group the soundest possible arguments in defense of an expansion policy. They could demonstrate, and demonstrate effectively, that some type of Japanese expansion was imperative. And so there was a ready-made front for the "New Order in East Asia."

THE TANAKA MEMORIAL

This political policy of Japanese expansion is no stranger to the world. Its basis is usually supposed to be the famous Tanaka Memorial, allegedly submitted to the Emperor of Japan by his then Prime Minister, Baron Giichi Tanaka, on July 25, 1927. This Memorial was a program primarily for the Japanese conquest of Manchuria and Mongolia, but it envisaged also the eventual defeat of the United States, and the subsequent accession of the Japanese to a position of paramount power in the world. Plans for the occupation of Manchuria and Mongolia, the building of railways, the establishment of industries, and methods of expansion by using Korean emigration as a front, were developed in great detail in this 10,000-word document. But it was the almost casual references to a plan of world conquest that attracted even more attention. The most important of these are contained in this passage, found near the beginning of the Memorial:

"For the sake of self-protection as well as the protection of others, Japan cannot remove the difficulties in eastern Asia unless she adopts a policy of 'Blood and Iron.' But in carrying out this policy we have to face the United States, which has been turned against us by China's policy of fighting poison with poison. In the future if we want to control China, we must first crush the United States, just as in the past we had to fight in the Russo-Japanese War. But in order to conquer China we must first conquer Manchuria and Mongolia. In order to conquer the world, we must first conquer China. If we succeed in conquering China the rest of the Asiatic countries and the South Sea countries will fear us and surrender to us. Then the world will realize that eastern Asia is ours and will not dare to violate our rights. This is the plan left to us by the Emperor Meiji, the success of which is essential to our national existence.

"The Nine-Power Treaty is entirely an expression of the spirit of commercial rivalry. It was the intention of England and America to crush our influence in China with their power of wealth. The proposed reduction of armaments is nothing but a means to limit our military strength, making it impossible for us to conquer the vast territory of China. On the other hand, China's sources of wealth will be entirely at their disposal. It is merely a scheme by which England and America may defeat our plans. And yet the Minseito [majority political party] made the Nine-Power Treaty the important thing and emphasized our trade rather than our rights in China. This is a mistaken policy—a policy of national suicide. England can afford to talk about trade relations only because she has India and Australia to supply her with foodstuffs and other materials. So can America because South America and Canada are there to supply her needs. Their spare energy could be entirely devoted to developing trade in China to enrich themselves. But in Japan her food supply and raw materials decrease in proportion to her population. If we merely hope to develop trade, we shall eventually be defeated by England and America who possess unsurpassable capitalistic power. In the end, we shall get nothing. A more dangerous factor is the fact that the people of China might some day wake up. Even during these years of internal

strife, they can still toil patiently, and try to imitate and displace
our goods so as to impair the development of our trade. When we
remember that the Chinese are our sole customers, we must be-
ware lest one day China become unified and her industries prosperous. Americans and Europeans will compete with us; our trade
in China will be wrecked. Minseito's proposal to uphold the Nine-
Power Treaty and to adopt the policy of trade towards Manchuria
is nothing less than a suicide policy.

"After studying the present conditions and possibilities of our
country, our best policy lies in the direction of taking positive steps
to secure rights and privileges in Manchuria and Mongolia. These
will enable us to develop our trade. This will not only forestall
China's own industrial development, but also prevent the penetration of European Powers. This is the best policy possible!

"The way to gain actual rights in Manchuria and Mongolia is to
use this region as a base and under the pretense of trade and commerce penetrate the rest of China. Armed by the rights already secured we shall seize the resources all over the country. Having
China's entire resources at our disposal we shall proceed to conquer India, the Archipelago, Asia Minor, Central Asia, and even
Europe. But to get control of Manchuria and Mongolia is the first
step if the Yamato race wishes to distinguish themselves on Continental Asia. Final success belongs to the country having raw materials; the full growth of national strength belongs to the country
having extensive territory. If we pursue a positive policy to enlarge
our rights in Manchuria and China, all these prerequisites of a
powerful nation will constitute no problem."

The Tanaka Memorial was made public by the Chinese. The
Japanese immediately declared, and have kept on declaring ever
since, that it was a Chinese forgery. They have pointed to certain
discrepancies in statements of fact, and have insisted that no responsible Japanese could possibly have made those mistakes.

For two short years the ghost of the Tanaka Memorial seemed
to be fairly effectually laid. When the conquest of Manchuria began, however, it was inevitable that Japanese progress should be
compared with this alleged program. The correspondence led
many persons to believe that they dare not disregard the Memorial,
no matter how loud the Japanese disclaimers.

STILL BEFORE THE PUBLIC

As late as April of 1940, Rear Admiral Joseph K. Taussig, testifying before the House Naval Affairs Committee, again cited the Tanaka Memorial, stated that he believed it to be an authentic and credible definition of Japanese policy, and urged that American naval armament be governed accordingly. The Navy Department promptly disavowed Admiral Taussig's opinion (he was on the retired list), and the Japanese Embassy in Washington followed up immediately with a reiteration of the fact that there were at least six major discrepancies in the text of the Memorial that should completely discredit it.

A debate on whether or not the Tanaka Memorial is a forgery would be fruitless. Two facts in respect to it, however, are important. The first is that its inability to die and the Japanese sensitivity to it suggest that it constitutes a background for some very important thinking, both Japanese and American, on the relationship of the two countries.

The second is the fact that Japanese military policy since 1930 has so closely followed the pattern of the Tanaka Memorial that, if it is a Chinese forgery, some obscure and anonymous Chinese is the greatest prophet since the days of Isaiah.

The Japanese have moved on to the Asiatic mainland precisely as the Tanaka Memorial said they would and should. Their so-called "New Order in East Asia" and their "Imperial Way" now openly proclaim that Japan's "manifest destiny" is a hegemony in eastern Asia that would form the stepping-off place for precisely the sort of world conquest that was set forth in this famous declaration of intent.

The most important thing in respect to this program of expansion is the fact that it has passed out of the hands of commercial-minded men and into the hands of the Japanese army and navy, using the rising tide of unified Japanese Fascism. So long as Japanese expansion was the problem of selling imitation batik in the fishmarket at Menado, there was a case to be made for it and a means of dealing with it. No right-minded person wanted those million babies a year to starve. Likewise, the fact that the Japanese could and would supply to countries of relatively low living standards a large volume of textiles and other processed goods that were within the purchasing reach of these populations was a good argument in favor of the Japanese.

When the Japanese acquisition of raw materials and markets, however, became a question not of buying and selling but of stealing, the situation changed its complexion. The military party had a hand-made program for taking quickly and without too much objection precisely the things the industrialists had suggested that Japan had to have, but that the industrialists had proposed to obtain over a considerable period of years and by rather too devious channels. The military party could therefore declare that it had been coerced into a direct course of action by the inability of foreign countries to recognize the gravity of the problem and by the unwillingness of the Chinese to co-operate in its solution.

A Declared Political Policy

But after we have accepted the necessity for Japanese expansion of some sort because of economic pressure, we face the question of expansion as a declared political policy. The case that the Japanese have finally made is not that they must meet certain needs but that they propose to assert certain rights. To understand this development fully we should trace and analyze the major theories of Japan's Asiatic conquest.

The early days of Japanese conquest were justified on the ground of self-defense. The most picturesque and the most famous phrase that came out of this whole era was that applied to Korea. The Japanese called it "the dagger pointed at Japan's heart." The proximity of the Japanese Archipelago to the Asiatic mainland and the narrowness of the Korean Strait gave a good deal of point to this argument. The Japanese, moreover, had carried on a national development through many centuries and had maintained their integrity and cohesiveness by isolating themselves from the continent. They felt very definitely that non-involvement in the affairs of the rest of the world was a guarantee of their own safety. When this isolation was broken down, partly through American influence and partly through improvement in the means of communication, the Japanese relationship to the mainland began to assume a much larger importance.

It is unlikely that the Japanese in recent years have ever felt that there was any grave danger of the conquest of Japan by China. When the Japanese talk about fighting the Chinese in self-defense, it is unlikely that they are thinking about military self-defense so much as economic self-defense. The Chinese are notably a pacific people, and there has been no move toward Chinese expansion for several centuries.

On the other hand, the Japanese have feared, and possibly correctly, the threat of Russian domination. The dagger pointed at Japan's heart was feared by the Japanese, not because it was in the hands of China, but because it might pass into the hands of Russia. Russia obviously had good motives for expansion. The eastern Siberian holding was rich, but it suffered from the relative lack of ice-free harbors. Vladivostok was the only port of importance. The Russian southward movement through Manchuria, therefore, was a natural one. Their hold on the Kwantung peninsula gave them a natural outlet at Dairen not only for the products of Manchuria, but for eastern Siberia as well. The Japanese felt that they must forestall a consolidation of Russian control on the mainland between Dairen and Vladivostok that would naturally take in Korea.

There is, moreover, a natural clash between Japanese and Russian economic interests in northeastern Asia. The fisheries off the Kamchatka peninsula are among the most valuable in the world and fish is one of the major items in the Japanese diet. The island of Sakhalin is geologically a part of the Japanese Archipelago and is the richest of all the Japanese islands in its deposits of oil. Russian and Japanese claims to this island, therefore, very naturally conflicted. They have been resolved by an artificial division of the island between the two powers, and while this affords a temporary modus vivendi, it adds to, rather than subtracts from, the causes of friction.

The development of the airplane has given an entirely new point to the Japanese idea of self-defense. Tokyo is only 600 miles from Vladivostok. The Japanese build their houses out of wood and paper, and the Russians have had some good practice recently with incendiary bombs. So when the Japanese talk about the danger from Russia, they are not manufacturing an artificial bugaboo. They are facing what they believe constitutes a very real danger. Russia is more than the hereditary enemy of Japan. Russia is the one country that might wish to strike hard at Japan's position in East Asia and would be in a position to do so.

For this reason Russian encroachment upon China and Russian influence in China have been viewed as a very real threat by the Japanese.

COMMUNISM OR RUSSIA?

There has been much confusion at this point because, for purposes of world consumption, the Japanese put their emphasis on an antipathy toward Communism. The early days of the China campaign were pictured as a crusade against Communist domination in China, and the Japanese never allowed this particular point to be forgotten.

As a matter of fact, the Japanese objection to Communism, as such, was largely window-dressing. What Japan was afraid of, in a word, was not Communism, but Russia.

The Japanese, therefore, have made it a part of their program on the Asiatic mainland to limit, to the best of their ability, any expansion of Russian influence and control. It is for this reason that so much of the Japanese campaign has been concentrated on Inner Mongolia, and for this reason that the Japanese have repeatedly stated that part of their program for China is the stationing of garrisons in these strategic provinces that form an accessible frontier between Russia and the rest of China.

While it would be an overstatement, probably, to declare that the Japanese fear of Russia is pathological, it is nevertheless true that the Japanese consciousness of a Russian threat affects all of Japanese policy. Most persons are probably agreed that if it had not been for the Hitler-Stalin pact the Japanese would have made their anti-Comintern connection with Germany and Italy into a working military alliance at the earliest convenient moment, not even waiting to see the outcome of the major battles in western Europe.

Japanese operations on the Asiatic mainland must be considered in part as the erection of more defensible frontiers against Russian encroachment. This position is neither illogical nor unreasonable. If the city of New York, for example, were within 600 miles of a well-equipped and hostile bombing base, we would have adopted drastic ideas about self-defense at a much earlier date and would have heard vastly less about "isolation."

Unfortunately, the Japanese feel that this particular phase of their self-defense program must be carried out at the expense of China. The Chinese Republican Government was definitely under Russian influence for a period, and Communism of a sort does have an important foothold in northwestern China and a large and intelligent following. The developments in the Chinese practice of democracy, however, have had a tendency to reduce the element of Russian leadership in this Communistic group. But at the present time the Japanese do not dare to take a chance on this reduction.

Perhaps a word should be said at this point as to the character of the Communist group in China. The actual degree of Russian leadership and Russian influence here cannot easily be determined. It is apparent that important advances are being made in the practice of democracy in the so-called Communist areas.

Some persons believe that there are such important differences between Russians and Chinese, and the Russian and Chinese ideas of Communism, that the danger of Communistic infiltration can be, and has been, greatly over-estimated. They point out that a necessary part of the Russian social organization is the nationalization or communization of land, and that this has not been a part of the Chinese program. Moreover, they urge that the Chinese is above all things a great individualist and that, while his sense of the family is very highly developed, his sense of the society is notably weak. It is believed, therefore, that the Chinese has a better sense of balance with which to approach the whole problem of instituting social organizations than the Russians could possibly have had, and that therefore so-called Communism in China cannot have the same connotations and the same effect that it has had in Russia. This boils down to a fixed belief on the part of many persons who have associated with them that the Chinese, man for man and family for family, have a more sensitive civilization than was possible in Russia, and that they can adapt themselves to new economic and social patterns without the abuses and distortions that were necessarily the result of major experimentation in Russia.

CHINESE NEW DEALERS

Persons who take this point of view assert that the Chinese Communist group is actually pledged to nothing more than a good working democracy. They declare that the difference between this point of view and the point of view held by Generalissimo Chiang Kai-shek is largely a matter of difference of opinion upon the time required to put democratic government into operation. The Chinese Communists, they point out, are simply asking that China do within three or four years what General Chiang and the Kuomintang believe will require at least a quarter of a century.

One of the persons who holds this point of view said to me a few weeks ago that he regarded the Chinese Communists, as far as political philosophy was concerned, as about twenty per cent more conservative than the United States New Deal. Applied to China, he said, that constitutes Communism.

This view is not shared by all students of the Chinese scene. It goes without saying that the Russians are making as much effort as they can to influence the political thinking and the social experiments of this important Chinese group. Persons who see in that control a great danger to China believe that it has possibly progressed much further than is sometimes thought.

The inability of Western observers to get into the province of Sinkiang (where Communist influence is strong) has naturally led to the supposition that there must be some things in Sinkiang that the Russians and the Chinese Communists want to conceal from the rest of the world. Those who are alarmed about the situation state that this thing that is being concealed is an enormously high degree of Russian penetration and influence.

There is confusion at this point, also, because this refusal to allow observation has given the anti-Communist propaganda an extraordinarily good lead and a free hand. In the newspaper business we were able to spot a number of stories about the devastating Russian influence in Sinkiang as coming directly from Japanese propaganda headquarters in Hong Kong. While one is naturally and correctly suspicious of such a source, the impenetrability of northwest China gives more than usual credibility to some of the stories that are being told.

It is also apparent that the Chinese Communist Party is wielding an increasing political influence. The capitulation of General Chiang to the Communists at the time of his celebrated kidnaping was in itself an indication that there was reason to reckon with the earnest and sincere political strength that the Chinese Communist Party represented. It has often been said that the Communists forced General Chiang's hand and dictated a course of resistance to the Japanese. In any case, they have co-operated very strenuously with the Kuomintang in its policy of stern resistance.

Those who are not alarmed by the appearance of a Communist party in China believe that this is far-sighted patriotism and that the Communists deserve all the credit that can be given to them for their very stout-hearted resistance. Those who are alarmed believe that the policy of Chinese Communist resistance is a policy of Russian rather than Chinese resistance to Japan, and that the Chinese Communists have taken this occasion to fight the battles of Moscow.

This, of course, is the position of the Japanese. They feel that Communist penetration in China is the spearhead of another movement that sooner or later threatens Japan.

There is another specific reason for the Japanese objection to Communism in China that the Japanese deny, and that every Chinese and most friends of China believe. The net result of the Communist alliance with the Kuomintang was enormously to strengthen Chinese unity and therefore the Chinese ability to resist Japanese conquest. Many persons believe that the Japanese conquest of China was precipitated by the fact that the Chinese had, for the first time since the formation of the Republic, shown real signs of being able to form a strong government. So long as General Chiang was busy fighting the Communists, there was little chance of first-class resistance to Japan. When that hatchet was buried, it is urged, the Japanese were put in a position of now or never striking at China.

It is probable that the correct appraisal of the Chinese Communist movement and its threat to Japan lies somewhere between the point of view of those who minimize its importance, and that of the Japanese, who insisted from the beginning that it was the most vital consideration in their Asiatic operation. The threat to Japan is there. That fact cannot be dodged.

If the Chinese can derive from Communist influence the good factors in democratization, and can resist pressure of Russia, the danger to Japan as such would disappear. On the other hand, such an assimilation would be a major factor in strengthening China, and the result would be a government that would resist a program of Japanese expansion on the Asiatic mainland. Either way, therefore, the Japanese have nothing to lose and everything to gain by fighting Communism in China, and they have much to gain in pleading their world cause by stating that this is the major reason for their operation.

"THE NEW ORDER IN EAST ASIA"

It is perhaps partly in the attempt to emphasize this phase of the Japanese program, as well as to put the best possible face on the Chinese invasion, that the Japanese coined the now famous phrase, "The New Order in East Asia." This is the official reason for the Japanese operations, and supposedly its complete justification to the outsider.

It is easy to coin synonyms for the new order. Most of the newspapermen whom I know simply call it "the new disorder." It is also called the "Japanese order," because obviously it bears the label "Made in Tokyo" from start to finish. It is hard to imagine the indiscriminate bombing of Canton and Chungking, the establishment of Japanese monopoly, the disruption of trade, the institution of worthless currency, and the peddling of opium as anything that could be called an "order," new or old.

After the first emotional rejection of the too bland Japanese explanations of what they have in mind when they so ambitiously announce the re-making of a large part of eastern Asia, it will be advisable to analyze this program. Just what does the "New Order in East Asia" mean?

There are three basic documents that give the authoritative story of the "New Order." The first is its proclamation, the second, the official Chinese reaction to it, and the third, the official American reaction.

"The New Order" was proclaimed on December 22, 1938, by Prince Fumimaro Konoye, who was then the Premier. In an official statement that had been approved three weeks earlier by the Japanese Imperial Conference, he said:

"The Japanese Government is resolved to carry on military operations for the complete extermination of the anti-Japanese

Kuomintang regime and at the same time to proceed with the work of establishing a new order in East Asia, together with those far-sighted Chinese who share our ideals and aspirations.

"A spirit of renaissance is now spreading over all parts of China, and enthusiasm for reconstruction is mounting ever higher. The Japanese Government desires to make public its basic policy for adjusting relations between China and Japan in order that its intentions may be thoroughly understood at home and abroad.

"Japan, China, and Manchukuo will be united by the common aim of establishing a new order in East Asia and, realizing the relationship of neighborly amity, a common defense against Communism and for economic co-operation.

"For that purpose it is necessary, first that China should cast aside all narrow prejudiced views of the past and do away with the folly of anti-Japanism and resentment regarding Manchukuo. In other words, Japan frankly desires China to enter of her own free will into complete diplomatic relations with Manchukuo.

"The existence of Comintern [Communist International] influence in East Asia cannot be tolerated. Japan, therefore, considers it an essential condition of the adjustment of Sino-Japanese relations that there should be concluded an anti-Comintern agreement between the two countries in consonance with the spirit of the anti-Comintern agreement between Japan, Germany, and Italy.

"In order to insure full accomplishment of this purpose Japan demands, in view of the actual circumstances prevailing in China, that Japanese troops be stationed at specific points during the time the agreement is in force and also that the Inner Mongolian region be designated as a special anti-Communist area.

"As regards economic relations between the two countries, Japan does not intend to exercise an economic monopoly in China, nor does she intend to demand that China limit her interests with those third powers who grasp the meaning of the new East Asia and are willing to act accordingly.

"Japan only seeks to render effective co-operation and collaboration between the two countries. That is to say, Japan demands that China, in accordance with the principle of equality between the two countries, should recognize freedom of residence and trade on the part of the Japanese subjects in the interior of China with a view to promoting the economic interests of both peoples and that in the light of the historical and economic relations between the two nations China should extend to Japan facilities for the development of China's natural resources, especially in the regions of North China and Inner Mongolia.

"The above gives the general lines of what Japan demands. If Japan's true object in conducting the present vast military campaign be fully understood, it will be plain that what she seeks is neither territory nor indemnity for the cost of the military operations. Japan demands only a minimum guarantee for the execution of her function as a participant in the establishment of a new order.

"Japan not only respects China's sovereignty but is prepared to give positive consideration to questions of the abolition of extraterritoriality and the rendition of foreign concessions and settlements—matters which are necessary for the full independence of China."

The Reply of General Chiang

The reaction of the Chinese to this purportedly generous offer, in which, later on, the Japanese were to emphasize above all else the "no territories and no indemnities" clause, was prompt and vigorous. They interpreted the "no territories" offer as meaning "no territories except all of China," and the "no indemnities" as meaning "no indemnities except all of China's economic future."

General Chiang Kai-shek made China's reply in a speech on December 26, 1938. The following paragraphs give the character of the official Chinese response:

"The Konoye statement may be called a complete exposure of the fantastic Japanese program to annex China, dominate East Asia, and further even to subdue this world. It is also a complete revelation of the contents of the enemy plan to destroy our country and exterminate our race. . . .

"Let all observe that what he meant by a China reborn was that independent China was to perish and in its place an enslaved China created, which would abide by Japan's word from generation to generation. The so-called new order would be based on the intimate relations that would tie the enslaved China to the Japanese-created Manchukuo and Japan herself. What is the real aim? Under the pretext of opposition to the 'Red Peril' Japan seeks to control China's military affairs; claiming to uphold Oriental civilization, Japan seeks to uproot China's racial culture; and by urging the elimination of economic barriers, she aspires to exclude American and European influence and dominate the Pacific. Again, the so-called 'economic unity' of Japan, Manchukuo, and China is the instrument she intends to use for obtaining a strangle-hold on China's economic arteries. Let us try to realize the immense evils with which the words 'creation of a new order in East Asia' are pregnant. In a word, it is a term for the overthrow of international order in East Asia, and the enslavement of China as the means whereby Japan may dominate the Pacific and proceed to dismember other states of the world.

"Our object in prosecuting this war of resistance is to complete the task of national revolution and secure for China independence, liberty, and equality. Internationally, our object is to support righteousness and justice, restore the prestige of treaties, and re-establish peace and order. This is a war between justice and force, and a war between an abider by the law and a breaker of it. It is also a war between righteousness and brute force."

THE UNITED STATES REACTION

Five days after General Chiang had put China on record, and just eight days after Prince Konoye had made his proclamation, the United States Government stated its position on the "New Order in East Asia." Naturally, the objection was first to the fact that the "New Order" proposed to dynamite the basis for the Nine-Power Treaty, that is, equal opportunity in China.

But the State Department went further than that and made a few remarks about Japan's assumption of the position of "agent of destiny." A note was delivered at the Japanese Foreign Office on December 31, 1938, two paragraphs of which read:

"The people and the Government of the United States could not assent to the establishment, at the instance of and for the purposes of any third country, of a regime which would arbitrarily deprive them of the long-established rights of equal opportunity and fair treatment which are legally and justly theirs along with those of other nations. . . .

". . . This Government does not admit, however, that there is need or warrant for any one power to take upon itself to prescribe what shall be the terms and conditions of a 'new order' in areas not under its sovereignty and to constitute itself the repository of authority and the agent of destiny in regard thereto. . . ."

The first phase of this "New Order" is an economic one. The Japanese have stressed repeatedly that they wished to break down the existing barriers between Japan and China and to bring those two countries and Manchukuo into a productive interchange of their products. Japan presumably is to be the major manufacturing center, with Manchukuo and North China supplying the bulk of the heavy raw materials and the remainder of China supplying the bulk of the needed market.

A corollary of this economic planning is the Japanese desire to reduce their dependence upon supplies and markets that are too far away from the homeland. This would be particularly advantageous, for example, in the matter of the supplies of raw cotton. If Japan can build up these supplies within a few hundred miles of Osaka, she can profit in time of peace by the elimination of the long trans-Pacific haul, and in time of war can enjoy the assurance that overseas supplies are not likely to be interrupted by blockade or embargo.

The reason for desiring a closer degree of economic unity than would be normally achieved in the rational intercourse of buying and selling is probably, in part, the desire of the Japanese to free themselves from the disadvantage of a currency that is subject to international valuation. In other words, it is not without good forethought that the Japanese have called their sphere of operation the "Yen Bloc." The reason for a yen bloc is, of course, that with a sufficient amount of currency control from the top the Japanese can disregard the primary conditions of stability. They can deplete their resources, drain their gold reserve, pile up their debt, manipulate to their hearts' content, and still dictate the value of their currency within a large producing and consuming area.

BEHIND THE "YEN BLOC"

The inability to do this, thus far, has proved embarrassing. One of the most interesting side-lights of the Chinese invasion has been the fact that smugglers could buy Japanese yen in Shanghai at an approximate parity with the Chinese dollar, which the Japanese in turn were so violently hammering down. If they could manage to run these advantageously purchased yen up to Kobe, they could repurchase foreign currency at a sufficient profit to give them their steamship fare and 200 per cent. It was a thorn in Japanese flesh, to say the least.

Theoretically, in a carefully managed yen bloc the value of currency would be dictated by Tokyo, and values would be fixed, not in relation to international credits, but in relation to the needs and desires of the Japanese Imperial Treasury.

This might be laudable as a very long-range objective if stability were thought to be the paramount consideration and if complete faith were reposed in the good will of the Japanese. In the course of the operations so far, unfortunately, Japanese-managed currency has been a polite way to camouflage the wholesale robbery of North China. The so-called Federal Reserve Notes have been issued for the benefit of the Japanese army. The army is obliged to defend this currency by the polite policy of shooting any unfortunate Chinese who still presumes to possess the authorized money of the Chinese Government. The result is to turn these Japanese notes into nothing more nor less than gigantic I.O.U.'s, issued at the point of the bayonet to the Chinese in return for goods and services.

The operations thus far have accordingly caused a certain amount of skepticism about the economic altruism of the Japanese and their desire to create a new economic order for the sake of Chinese stability.

It is this factor, of course, that makes the "New Order in East Asia" a definite "Get Out" sign for the Western world. The Japanese have pictured their motives as a desire to free the Chinese and other Asiatic peoples from the shackles of Western domination. The concessions of the Western Powers in major Chinese cities are pictured as an insult to the quality and dignity of the Chinese, and as a constant drawback upon the exercise of real Chinese sovereignty. The Japanese, therefore, are able to picture themselves as the Oriental rescuers of an important part of the Orient from Occidental domination.

The flaw in this otherwise convincing argument is the fact that the Chinese don't agree with it. As matters stand, the Chinese and the Malays would rather take their chance on winning equality from their Western "enslavers" than from their Japanese "liberators."

There has been no small amount of dust thrown in the world's eyes on the issue of Chinese extra-territoriality and the causes for Japanese aggression. We have already seen that before the Japanese had started to "free" Asia from Occidental domination the Western governments had begun to recognize that extra-territoriality was never more than a transitional phase, and that the assumption of its everlasting fitness made by some of the Old China Hands was short-sighted.

Chinese sovereignty was necessarily impaired by the existence of some of these extraordinary functions exercised on Chinese soil by foreign powers. The correct way to repair this damage to Chinese sovereignty would naturally be to afford that sovereignty the opportunity to develop the exercise of those functions so as to make foreign interference unnecessary. This obviously could be done only if a Chinese republican government were strengthened rather than weakened.

The concessions increase in importance precisely as the strength of the real Chinese Government goes down. For this reason the Japanese case of destroying the government of China in order to get rid of foreign administrative functions is fallacious from the beginning.

The foreign concessions in China have been, moreover, the out-

standingly important link between China and the rest of the
world. They have been China's way of making and keeping friends,
of relating her economy to that of other powers, of establishing
her currency and its values, of collecting revenues, and of the rub-
bing of shoulders that is necessary in good governmental intercourse. It is precisely this character of the concession that the
Japanese must destroy if the "Yen Bloc" is to function efficiently.

Obviously Chinese currency should have, from the Japanese
point of view, no international value except in relation to the yen.
Chinese trade should have no position in international relations
except as it was channeled through Japanese hands and diverted
for the benefit of the Japanese economic structures. For this reason
the "New Order in East Asia" must demand, on economic rather
than on sentimental grounds, the abolition of the Western concessions.

ORIENTAL "CULTURE"

Another aspect of the "New Order" is the important matter of
close cultural affiliation of the Asiatic peoples. The Japanese object
to the introduction of too many Western ideas. They dislike American missionary work particularly, and feel that the Asiatic will be
better off if he develops his own indigenous culture.

This field of argument is very hazy. It is extremely difficult to
quarrel with the Japanese point of view if one is willing to assume
that it is offered in entire good faith. There has been much Occidental blundering as the result of the misconception that there is
something inherently superior in the Western way of doing anything. The Orient does have its culture and a very important one.
A plea for that culture, based on its right to exist and on its essentially Asiatic character, is necessarily a sound one.

Before too much emphasis is given to it, however, it would certainly be a good idea to consult the Chinese and the Malays. The
assumption of the natural superiority of the Japanese concept of

culture may in the long run be just as fallacious as the assumption
of the natural superiority of Occidental culture. It is quite possible
that the Chinese might wish to orient their next centuries of
development on some point of interest other than Tokyo. "Asia for
the Asiatics" is a good cultural battle-cry, but until it is shown that
Asiatic culture is a cohesive unit threatened by the impact of the
outside world, it might be more sensible to suggest Japanese culture for the Japanese, Chinese culture for the Chinese, and
Malaysian culture for the Malays.

Political terms are being used here in their strictly cultural sense.
"Asia for the Asiatics" is not merely a cultural battle-cry—it is also
a political and military slogan. That leads us to the next phase of
the "New Order"—its growth into the now proclaimed "Asiatic
Monroe Doctrine" and the "Greater East Asia" policy.

"A Monroe Doctrine for Asia"

When the "New Order" was proclaimed, the European War
was still in the offing. Naturally, that order was presumed to apply
only to Japan, Manchukuo, and China. If the French position were
unimpaired, the British fleet capable of moving to and out of
Singapore, and the United States unperturbed by a European
threat, Japan could not hope to push farther south than Shanghai.
The "New Order" bit off just about what the Japanese thought
they could chew.

The Nazi victory in Flanders and the collapse of France accelerated the tempo of Japanese ambition. While "non-involvement"
was still one of the things that Japan was declaring, the Japanese
army was putting more and more pressure on the Foreign Minister to make a vigorous declaration of Japan's aims, from which
there would be no deviation and no retreat. The press began announcing that the basis of Japan's great Asiatic policy would shortly
be forthcoming.

After a week of feverish anticipation, the then Foreign Minister, who was shortly to lose his post for being too moderate, stepped in front of a microphone. This is the story of what he said, as told by Hugh Byas, Tokyo correspondent of the *New York Times*, under a June 29 date-line.

"Foreign Minister Hachiro Arita in a broadcast to the Japanese Empire this afternoon pictured a new vast aggregation of satellite States in East Asia and the South Seas revolving harmoniously around Japan. They would be stabilized by Japan's superior power but their individual characteristics, political, cultural, and economic, would be respected.

"In one significant phrase the Foreign Minister took a big step forward in outlining Japan's aims. Hitherto he has defined these as the maintenance of the status quo and Japan's military and economic interests. Today he declared: 'The uniting of all these regions (East Asia and the South Seas) in a single sphere was a natural conclusion.'

"A new world of great regions of super-States, each grouped around a dominant military power, was the theme of Mr. Arita's address, to which millions of Japanese listened. The press had told the public to expect a re-statement of Japan's 'Monroe Doctrine,' a declaration of East Asia's autonomy, but what the public got was neither an enlarged Monroe Doctrine nor a pronouncement on the European War.

"Mr. Arita's only reference to the European War was a repetition of Japan's non-involvement policy and a warning that any attempt to dispose of East Asia or the South Seas would be a matter of grave concern to Japan.

"In the broad abstract phrases into which the Japanese language naturally falls the Foreign Minister developed his idea of a new world order and explained its scientific and ethical foundations. He began with the Confucian maxim that in an ideal world all nations should find their proper places.

" 'All mankind longs for peace,' he went on, 'but peace cannot endure unless nations have their proper places. Since this is difficult in the present stage of human progress the next best thing is for peoples who are related geographically, racially, culturally, and economically to form spheres of their own.'

"It is in this spirit, Mr. Arita said, that Japan is now establishing a new order in East Asia. In a passage addressed to countries who oppose the use of force in creating the new order—obviously intended for the United States—Mr. Arita declared Japan was wielding 'a life-giving sword that destroys evil and makes justice manifest.'

"He then returned to his theme of regional groupings. He asserted East Asia and the South Seas formed such a group. In a few sentences, drafted with extreme care and capable of the broadest interpretation when they come to be translated into action, Mr. Arita then outlined a policy aimed at uniting those regions under single supreme authority, obviously Japan's.

" 'The countries of East Asia and the regions of the South Seas are geographically, historically, racially, and economically very closely related,' he continued. 'They are destined to co-operate and minister to each other's needs for their common well-being and prosperity.

" 'The uniting of all these regions in a single sphere on a basis of common existence, insuring thereby the stability of that sphere, is a natural conclusion. The idea of first establishing a just peace in the various regions and then establishing a just peace for the whole world has long existed in Europe and in America also.

" 'This system presupposes the existence of a stabilizing force in each region which as the center of the peoples within that region will secure their co-existence and co-prosperity as well as the stability of their sphere. It also presupposes that these groups will respect each other's individual characteristics—political, cultural, and economic—and co-operate to fulfill each other's needs for the common good.' "

A Reply from Washington

This was, ostensibly, an address to the Japanese people, and as such it called for no comment nor response. Its obvious invocation of the principle of the Monroe Doctrine, and its equally obvious avoidance of mentioning the name, put Washington on the spot. As it happened, there had been dispatched to Germany a note re-emphasizing the Monroe Doctrine and warning against any transfer of sovereignty in this hemisphere. When the German reply was received in Washington, just a few days after Mr. Arita had, by implication, invoked the Monroe Doctrine as a basis for

Japanese hegemony in East Asia, Mr. Hull had an opportunity, if not to kill two birds with one stone, at least to retort to two Foreign Ministers in one document.

Mr. Hull pointed out, in a statement on July 5, that there were Monroe Doctrines and Monroe Doctrines, and the part of his reply to the German plea of complete innocence of any idea of territorial aggrandizement in this hemisphere that was interpreted as applying equally to the Nazis and the proponents of a Japanese order in Asia went as follows:

"The Monroe Doctrine is solely a policy of self-defense, which is intended to preserve the independence and integrity of the Americas. It was, and is, designed to prevent aggression in this hemisphere on the part of any non-American power, and likewise to make impossible any further extension to this hemisphere of any non-American system of government imposed from without.

"It contains within it not the slightest vestige of any implication, much less assumption, of hegemony on the part of the United States.

"It never has resembled, and it does not today resemble, policies which appear to be arising in other geographical areas of the world, which are alleged to be similar to the Monroe Doctrine, but which, instead of resting on the sole policies of self-defense and of respect for existing sovereignties, as does the Monroe Doctrine, would in reality seem to be only the pretext for the carrying out of conquest by the sword, of military occupation, and of complete economic and political domination by certain powers of other free and independent peoples."

A "Spokesman" Out of Turn

Unfortunately, some of the force of Mr. Hull's unshakable position was taken away, the following day, by the entirely inexplicable second-hand statement by President Roosevelt, given out through his secretary-spokesman Stephen Early, to the effect that the President thought it quite logical that there should be a Monroe Doctrine for Europe, another for America, and another for Asia.

Mr. Roosevelt was quick to see that he, or his secretary, or both, had made probably the most significant and certainly the most unnecessary blunder in Far Eastern affairs in forty years, and he tried to correct the misapprehension the next day. But the fat was in the fire. The Tokyo press had already broadcast, with terrific enthusiasm, the President's "modification" of the Monroe Doctrine, and his obvious approval of Japan's aims.

Mr. Roosevelt's mild disclaimer was never printed in Tokyo, of course, and on July 10 the spokesman of the Japanese Foreign Office, Mr. Suma, acclaimed Mr. Roosevelt's benediction in a formal statement that read as follows:

"Regardless of whether or not President Roosevelt's statement on the Monroe Doctrine constitutes a new definition and modification of that doctrine, the fact cannot be disputed that the attitudes taken by the President and the Secretary of State of the United States on the question show that the United States government has converted the primarily passive and defensive character of the Monroe Doctrine into a positive one.

"Hitherto the Monroe Doctrine has been applied to prevent the extension of the European system of government to the Americas, as well as to forestall aggression of outside powers on the Western Hemisphere. Now, it is claimed, 'the United States very sincerely believes and maintains the position that the administration or ultimate disposition of such islands or territorial possessions should be and is properly a question to be decided by and among all of the republics of the Western Hemisphere.'

"If this is the real attitude of the United States, it naturally coincides with the idea of regional structures which has been recently suggested by Mr. Arita, the Foreign Minister. Did not President Roosevelt declare that 'The United States government wants to see and thinks there should be application of the Monroe Doctrine in Europe and Asia, similar to the interpretation and application of those principles in this hemisphere'?

"Here we cannot help feeling that Mr. Hull discussed the Monroe Doctrine, while Mr. Roosevelt dwelt upon a Monroe Doctrine applicable to all geographical areas including the Americas. This we wish to take note of with special interest."

SOME DIFFERENCES IN DOCTRINE

It is obvious that the distinction between "the" Monroe Doctrine and "a" Monroe Doctrine is one that the Japanese army will not be obliged to make. It was obvious to Mr. Hull, of course, that such a distinction had to be made, and he made it. It was not, unfortunately, obvious to the Presidential spokesman. But, lest confusion arise, that distinction between "the" Monroe Doctrine and an "Asiatic Monroe Doctrine," made by Mr. Hull in implication, should be emphasized.

In the first place the American Monroe Doctrine was inspired directly by the desire to preserve political independence in weak American states. The Doctrine was directed against attempts from the outside to overthrow existing political institutions, because it was feared that such an overthrow would result, as President Monroe said, in the loss of an independence that had just been achieved.

Not very many persons can honestly believe that the extension of Japanese control over East Asia in the name of an "Asiatic Monroe Doctrine" is similarly founded upon any desire for the preservation of the faltering independence of small Asiatic states.

Similarly, perhaps the most striking difference in the two interpretations is the fact that the Japanese are now using "Asia for the Asiatics" as the reason for the extension of their own sovereignty. This was not the American position in 1823, nor is it the American position at the present time. Indeed, the United States has been so anxious to correct the idea that the Monroe Doctrine was the basis for any extension of American control in this hemisphere that as recently as 1930 (but before the "Good Neighbor" became a campaign slogan) a specific document was drafted and published by our State Department, declaring that the Monroe Doctrine would not be used as the basis for intervention in the domestic affairs of any state in the American hemisphere.

This was going much further, indeed, than a mere declaration of non-intention to extend American sovereignty. It was going to the point of the United States' specifically eschewing what might be considered the normal function of protecting its nationals and their interests, in order that its position under the Monroe Doctrine might not be misunderstood. No similar disclaimer has ever come out of Japan. And in the light of what has happened at Mukden, Peiping, Nanking, and Haiphong, any such disclaimer seems extremely unlikely.

The Monroe Doctrine, in short, has never been made the basis for any conquests or any annexations. However unpalatable the means of acquiring Texas and California may be to the post-mortem student of history, the Monroe Doctrine was not involved in these transactions, and it is obvious that it will not be involved in any depredations in the future. For this reason the simile, however comforting to the Japanese, will not bear inspection.

The next thing that the "New Order in East Asia" and the Japanese "Monroe Doctrine" are supposed to involve is the extension of its hands-off policy to the Russians. The "New Order" must, as already shown, be anti-Communist. This particular part of the "New Order" program has had its ups and downs since the Hitler-Stalin alliance. Japan has had trouble in climbing on the Hitler band-wagon and avoiding sitting beside Stalin. For this reason the anti-Communist part of the "New Order" is important chiefly because it affords the reason for the insistence on those Japanese garrisons up in North China, and because it has given the Japanese their best propaganda abroad.

"Friendly" to Japan

Now we come to the heart of the "New Order in East Asia" program. The "New Order" means a declared system of relationships in which governmental attitudes are "friendly" to Japan. In other words, once there is a new order, there will be no more boycotts, no more quotas, no more restrictions, and no more "intransigent" armies. Anti-Japanism in China and in the area of the

South China Sea is the biggest Japanese bugbear. The "New Order" must end it forever.

In the first place, of course, this is what the Japanese mean by "peace." They mean freedom from the threat of economic interference and control on the part of the Chinese Government or any Western government of all elements that might be unfriendly to Japanese commercial policy. We have already seen the importance of the Chinese middleman throughout all of southeastern Asia, and we have also observed that on at least two different occasions Japanese policy was directly dictated by the Chinese boycott.

It has been extremely difficult for the outsider to accept at its face value the repeated Japanese declaration that the Japanese army and navy were bombing Chinese women and children for the sake of making friends with China. And yet this statement is literally true. It is the strangest paradox in the whole Chinese scene.

The resolution of the contradiction lies in the definition of the word "friendship." The Japanese are really determined to establish, throughout the Far East, governments that are officially "friendly" to Japan. They must be governments just strong enough to control any anti-Japanese leanings on the part of their nationals, and yet subservient enough to orient all their policies toward Tokyo. They must be governments that can declare against a boycott of Japanese goods and enforce their declaration.

So when the Japanese say that they must have "friendly" governments in China, in Indo-China, in Netherland India, Malaya, and the Philippines, they are telling the truth from their point of view, and their military operations are designed to eliminate what they regard as unfriendly governments. The real paradox is in the Japanese conviction that they can succeed by these tactics. This, of course, is explained in part by the fact that "friendship" is not conceived of by the Japanese as an equality, but as the acceptance of one will by another.

The "New Order in East Asia" can be regarded from two different points of view, depending on where one's sympathies lie. If it is taken at its face value, it is a far-reaching attempt to re-organize economic and political structures in the interest of closer trade ties, more alert political controls, and a cohesive and vigorous East Asiatic civilization. This is the best possible face that can be put on it, and it can be justified only if the methods that are employed in bringing it about do not over-reach the objectives. To justify it also presupposes that the Japanese have a better idea of what East Asia needs than do either the Chinese or the Western Powers. This presupposition is not difficult for Tokyo. It is a little bit hard to swallow in Chungking, Hong Kong, or Washington.

The chief difficulty in accepting this program at such an optimistic estimate is the fact that policy in Asia is not being dictated by liberal and conservative economists, but by the Japanese militaristic Fascists. One of the shrewdest observers of affairs in North China said to me a few weeks ago:

"It is extremely doubtful if, with a half-dozen exceptions, there is anyone in the Japanese army below the grade of colonel who ever even heard of economics."

The Japanese army has shown a capacity for direct action and for movement to an objective that often destroys a long-range view and habitually disregards any consideration of international relationships as they have been understood by qualified experts in that field in Tokyo.

WINDOW DRESSING FOR AGGRESSION

The skepticism in regard to the army's ability to comprehend, much less carry out, a "New Order in East Asia" leads therefore to the other point of view on this program. That point of view is that the whole thing is a lot of window dressing, designed to obscure rather than clarify the issues, and to put a front of respectability on naked aggression.

The time element, indeed, supports the latter point of view. The Japanese army had the bit in its teeth before the apologists could mobilize the dictionary. North China had been over-run and

Nanking sacked before anyone in Tokyo got around to thinking up the "New Order." The Japanese method of allowing the world to accept a fait accompli suggests at least that the altruistic economic and political theorizing is very largely ex post facto.

Once again the most accurate estimate of the situation would probably lie somewhere between these points of view. There are unquestionably serious-minded persons in the Japanese Government who are trying to make the best of a bad situation. They would undoubtedly like to see a "New Order" in which there was a greater degree of stability than has heretofore existed. Some of them may sincerely believe that the co-operation of the Western world with such an order would not be an impossibility.

Armies in the field, however, and army men in Cabinets, may change such points of view when they are translated into action. There is, undoubtedly, more than a little ground for the conviction that as matters stand, the "New Order in East Asia" means simply a Japanese order made by the High Command and enforced by captains in a predatory army.

It should go without saying that the accession of so much authority to the Japanese in so large a part of the world would necessarily invite grave abuses. The Chinese believe from past experience that the abuses could and would outweigh any theoretical altruism. Most of those to whom I have talked are agreed that they would rather take their chance on establishing an independent China in co-operation with the supposedly predatory Western Powers that have "exploited" China for a couple of centuries than turn their country over to the tender mercies of Tokyo.

We have now examined the two leading theories behind Japanese conquest on the Asiatic mainland. Both of them are Japanese in their origin and differ chiefly in the range of their plan. The first, the story of the dagger, is a matter of almost elementary self-defense. The second, the "New Order in East Asia," presupposes a degree of relatively far-sighted planning but perhaps a certain myopia toward the feeling of the other Asiatics.

The shift in emphasis from the "New Order," as it affects China, to the "Asiatic Monroe Doctrine," as it affects the whole of eastern Asia, suggests a third possibility for the China campaign. It is beginning to appear that the Japanese have been even more far-sighted than the "New Order" propaganda would indicate. Having forsworn the Tanaka Memorial, they are still following its pattern. The "Imperial Way" and Japan's "manifest destiny" are showing, all too clearly, that the economic and political conquest of China was a mere stepping stone on the path to Japan's fulfillment of her ultimate thrust for power. The campaign in China has assumed an entirely different perspective.

It is in the south and the southeast that Japan can acquire the raw materials not available even among the riches of China. In the Malay population to the south lies the potential market, already with a rising standard of living, spared the ravages of a war such as has been fought in China, and affording an even better outlet for Japanese goods than could be found with the coolies of the Yangtze or the peasants of Yunnan. As it becomes clearer that the southward movement to the control of the rich archipelagoes of the South China Sea is the real Japanese objective, the China campaign becomes nothing more than a minor holding operation to immobilize a possible enemy on the right flank while the main thrust of Japanese expansion goes southward.

The "New Order in East Asia" as it affects China fits into that picture admirably. A docile Chinese government, in which Western influence had been eliminated, would be expected not only not to furnish any opposition, but to look forward eagerly to a sharing of profits. A hostile Chinese government, on the other hand, would constitute not only a threat to Japan through this ever-present boycott weapon, but also a convenient base of operations from which other threatened powers could resist the Japanese invasion.

That this was in Japanese minds from the outset is shown by the fact that the Japanese did not expect a long war in China. It has been made abundantly clear that the Japanese civilian statesmen, as well as the Japanese army, believed that a rapprochement with China could be reached within six months. This would seem on the face of it to rule out the idea that the Japanese really planned the occupation of China. What they planned was its immobilization as a hostile power.

This basis for the China campaign will serve to explain why the Japanese have so consistently asserted that the conclusion of "the China affair" was the first essential tenet of foreign policy. That is quite correct. It is, and for now obvious reasons. The big Japanese drive cannot go forward until China is reduced.

The turn of European events, however, has made it possible for the Japanese to combine two elements of policy in the more recent stages of the China War. The necessity of cutting off supplies from General Chiang made a good case for putting the heat on France and Britain as soon as it became obvious that they were in no shape to defend their interests. The United States could hope to escape the same process only as long as it was clear that American interests would be defended.

During the past few years anyone who has said that Japan had an organized program for southward expansion and aggression has usually been called a war-monger. He has been accused of reviving the "yellow peril," misinterpreting the aims of the Japanese Government, and creating dangers of the imagination that do not exist in fact. The progressive course of the Japanese onslaught has now shown that the "war-mongers" were right. The world is gradually becoming convinced that when Tokyo set up a South Seas Bureau it meant business.

Until quite recently the Japanese kept up the front of the need for purely economic intercourse with these areas as the basis for policy. That front has now been dropped. A possibly legitimate commercial expansion has been transformed into a bald military aggression that requires the equivocal justification of a "Monroe Doctrine" to save even the Japanese face.

Russia in the Picture

Where does Russia fit into that picture? Obviously Russia fitted in beautifully when the Anti-Comintern Pact had more than lip service. Germany could be counted upon to immobilize a threat from Russia by pressure on the European flank. Japan in turn could take China out of the picture by a swift campaign that installed a "friendly" government.

The Japanese Nationalists were quick to point out that Germany's expression of disinterest in the fate of Netherland India constituted a "blank power of attorney" to Japanese expansion. Is it unreasonable to suppose that the Japanese had confidently hoped that that power of attorney would be given by Berlin while Chancellor Hitler still clung to his original thesis that Comrade Stalin was the scum of the earth?

The Russian-German alliance, therefore, had the effect of necessitating a much more vigorous and a much longer campaign in China. Russia is still the enemy; and the Kwantung army cannot be moved down from Manchukuo. China must now be not merely immobilized; China must be pulverized before the southward march can be completed.

It is certainly not to be expected that Russian altruism and Russian devotion to democracy will rise to defend the Malays (and their European mother countries) against the Japanese onslaught. It is not hard to imagine that Comrade Stalin might object to pulling capitalist chestnuts out of the fire. On the other hand, there is equally no reason for an optimistic hope in Tokyo that Russia would neglect an opportunity to embarrass Japan on the north if and when the Japanese had their hands full getting that Bridge to Borneo.

In this particular case, therefore, it would seem that the shrewd manipulation of Herr von Ribbentrop had helped turn the China "incident" into the China War, and had unwittingly strengthened the hands of the democracies. Russia is, proportionately, a greater menace to Japan as Russia herself is not menaced from Europe.

Nevertheless, this puts the Western defense of the South China Sea somewhat at the mercy of the whims of the Wilhelmstrasse and the Kremlin. When the Germans and the Russians again fall out—and few people believe that that shotgun marriage was made in heaven—the Japanese will again have the green light. Japanese fear of Russia will diminish when Russia again faces the danger of attack from the west. At that time the future of the United States in Asia and the future of the democracies in the South China Sea will depend to a large degree on how far the tatterdemalion battalions of Chiang Kai-shek have been able to bog down the Japanese tanks. The Chinese are fighting the battle on the Japanese right flank, and at the moment they also happen to be covering one of our most important defense salients in Asia.

Mr. Roosevelt was roundly booed when he intimated that the American frontier was on the Rhine. He was talking about the European frontier. The American Asiatic frontier for several years has been back on the Han River, in northern Hupeh, and on the Yangtze, above Ichang. And it has been at the bend of the Yellow River, where it turns up into Shansi. That frontier battle may be simply the preliminary outpost clash for the major operation that is still to come. Chinese women and children just happen by accident to have been in the American pillbox at Chungking for the Japanese demolition movement.

If Japan's immobilization program wins, and our outpost in China falls, the defense of our position and the democracies' position in the South China Sea will be enormously more difficult. If that outpost holds, there is still a chance that the status quo in Netherland India, the Philippines, Indo-China, Thailand, Malaya, Borneo, and even Australia may continue to be a matter for diplomatic negotiation rather than the dispatch of battle cruisers.

CHAPTER XIV

THE DEFENSE OF THE SOUTH CHINA SEA

By THIS time it should be obvious that, economically and militarily, someone is going to fight for the South China Sea. What can be done to defend it?

The American position is under the great disadvantage of distance. Charts of the vulnerability of the Philippines have all been drawn on this geometric scale of its distance from Hawaii and California. It has been repeatedly declared that the United States must withdraw from this salient because of the fact that even the best of navies could not operate to advantage in the South China Sea, 4,500 miles from its base at Pearl Harbor.

This theory assumes that such a problem would be posed under its most disadvantageous conditions. Those conditions are always stated: "Can the United States, single-handed, defend an important position on the other side of the world?"

That statement makes two assumptions that are still insufficiently justified. The first is that the defense of the South China Sea would be solely an American problem.

The events of 1940 in Europe have demonstrated, to the satisfaction of most Americans, that there have been other countries in this world, such as Britain, France, the Netherlands, Denmark, Belgium, and Norway, with whose interests we are inextricably linked. The destruction of these countries, or serious invasion of their interests, by another economic and political philosophy, has been seen as a direct threat to the safety and interest of the United States.

If this is true in Europe, it is even more true in Asia where the interests of the four Western colonies have an astounding parallel. In the South China Sea we are dealing not with four widely separated colonies but with a geographical and political unit, bound by the strongest ties of production and commerce and fused by the presence of the same outside danger.

It is impossible to conceive of a threat to the interests of the United States in southeastern Asia that would not be equally a threat to the interests of a revived France, Britain, and the Netherlands. One can even go further than that: it is impossible to conceive of a threat to the United States that would not be equally a threat to the safety and well-being of the Filipinos, Annamese, Chinese, Cambodians, Malaysians, and Javanese. Common danger should create for the United States at the outset a group of allies embracing whatever remains of the Western democracies and virtually the whole Malay race. We already have an ally in the Chinese.

That factor changes immediately the second part of the supposition, that the defense of the South China Sea would be an American naval operation based on Hawaii. On the contrary, it would undoubtedly be a naval, air, and land operation based on a half-dozen ports in at least four countries.

If the history books tell us the truth, when Admiral Dewey sailed the *Olympia* into Manila Bay in 1898 he was not cruising out of Honolulu or San Pedro. He brought the *Olympia* in from Hong Kong. There is no reason to assume that in future operations of the United States the local stations of friendly or actually allied powers will be closed to us.

This puts a different complexion on the defense of the South China Sea. Instead of being an excessively long-range naval operation, it becomes a short-range, closely-knit naval, air, and land operation based on a polygon of defense posts that are still strong if we are willing to use them.

Five Naval Bases

It was observed that the South China Sea has six great harbors. It has also five important naval bases.

At the north there is British Hong Kong. This is a strongly fortified position, a good intermediate base, and at a strategic point. Any plan of attack on the South China Sea would necessarily involve at the outset the reduction of Hong Kong. It is presumed that this would be accomplished by encirclement, three phases of which—the occupation of Canton, the occupation of Hainan, and the closing of access to the immediate mainland—have already taken place. The base itself, however, is admirably prepared for siege, and, in conjunction with other defense positions, would prove a salient to the north that should show great strength. Undoubtedly the Japanese got a bad shock when the British evacuated their women and children from Hong Kong, thus indicating their conviction that this base could and would be defended.

Flanking the two sides of the South China Sea are two other bases that are of great naval importance. These are the American station at Cavite in Manila Bay on the east and the French station at Cam-Ranh on the coast of Annam on the west.

The American establishment in the Far East has for many years been relatively small. The Asiatic fleet normally does not have capital ships. It has one heavy cruiser, the flagship, one light cruiser, a destroyer flotilla, a submarine flotilla, some river gunboats and some auxiliary ships. This fleet, of course, is capable of large-scale expansion and the base on which it operates can accommodate a major battle force.

The American position has been strengthened in recent months by the replacement of vessels already in location by some of superior type. The submarine flotilla has been increased and improved. Even more important, the navy has augmented its small force of fighting planes by bringing in a squadron of heavy patrol bombers. This patrol squadron assigned for "neutrality" purposes has been operated on a replacement system so that the personnel has been trained in Philippine operations.

The position at Cavite is strongly defended by the island of Corregidor at the entrance to Manila Bay. This position is often called the Gibraltar of the East, and it is undoubtedly the strongest coast defense position under the American flag. Like Hong Kong, it is prepared to withstand long siege, and until it is reduced, access by sea to Manila Bay is impossible.

The French naval base at Cam-Ranh is a relatively new Asiatic operation. At the time that it was started—about 1936—it was declared that it would be made one of the strongest positions in the French Empire. The exact character and extent of the operations that were carried out were, of course, military secrets. The natural facilities, however, are excellent and its strategic position extremely valuable for the side that gets there first.

Even after the French collapse there was a sufficient naval force in Indo-China to give a higher degree of stability than was at first supposed. Apparently the colonial French did not take orders from the Nazis to make themselves defenseless in the Far East. They made concessions to the Japanese, but they did not disarm.

Directly to the south of the South China Sea is the most important of the Netherland overseas naval bases. This is at Surabaya on the northern coast of the eastern end of the island of Java. This is a strong defense position because it commands three straits as well as the overland communications with the whole of eastern Java.

This base is the home of the Netherland Indian naval establishment. That establishment, under normal conditions, consists of three cruisers, one of which is a very modern light cruiser; eight destroyers; a sizable submarine flotilla whose exact number is not revealed by *Jane's Fighting Ships*; eight minelayers and escort vessels; eight minesweepers and six auxiliary ships. Presumably this force has been augmented by as much of the Netherland navy as was able to escape the German attack. But the importance of

Surabaya is not so much the current strength of its naval force as its location as a strategic base of operations.

There is another naval station in Java at the other end of the island. This is at Tandjong Priok, northeast of Batavia.

The other naval base commanding the South China Sea is the largest one in the world, the British base at Singapore. The position at Singapore is of the utmost importance because of its location and because of the fact that it commands the approaches not merely to the Straits Settlements but to Netherland India itself. Singapore is the defense position for western Java and for Sumatra. It is the key to operations from the Mediterranean and from Africa. It controls the whole British life-line to eastern Asia and is monitor, indeed, over the northern approaches to Australia.

Like these other bases, Singapore is more important positionally than as a current naval establishment. If events in Europe should cause the transfer of British naval strength from its bases in the British Isles, the Singapore establishment might become a gigantic operating outpost for the Empire as well as a defense position.

The defense of the South China Sea, therefore, is well planned from the point of view of naval stations. It is not a weak position; it is a very strong one.

STRENGTH OF THE AIR ARM

Changes in modern warfare have emphasized the importance of the air arm of a military force.

The potential air defense of the South China Sea has been based in part, up to the present time, upon the development of commercial air lanes and commercial landing fields. This means necessarily the development of emergency fields. There are more than a hundred in the Philippines alone. There are at least a score in Netherland India. There are a number in French Indo-China. There are also important fields in Malaya.

There are, in addition, already in operation, fixed air establishments in all of these possessions. The Hong Kong base is of course more important for seaplane operation than for land planes.

In the Philippines, however, the balance is about equally drawn. There is a strong American military air base at Nichols Field, south of Manila, and a smaller air base at Fort Stotsenburg, ninety miles north of Manila. These Philippine bases are only 600 miles from Hong Kong. They can command the approaches to the South China Sea both from the north and through the middle of the Philippine archipelago at San Bernardino Strait. At the present time these air bases are not overwhelmingly strong. They are not adequately defended by anti-aircraft guns, and they have not yet been completely bomb-proofed. They are capable, however, of large-scale expansion and could be made as important as defense plans required. The number of planes now on station there is, of course, a military secret.

The French have had an air base in connection with the Cam-Ranh naval station and have also an air base at Saigon to the south.

How strong these French forces are, since the French collapse, cannot be known, but it is known that France had begun making them considerably stronger before the European war started, and that a special Indo-China armaments tax, designed to yield about $7,000,000 annually, made the colony partially independent of the mother country for its defense program.

The emphasis in that program was on air defense. The French Minister of Colonies, in a report to the President of France in July 1939, described in general terms new plans for the defense of Indo-China and stressed not only the early doubling of the soldiery but a large planned increase in the air arm. Fifty planes were to be purchased from the Netherlands immediately, but there was to be prompt industrial development to make the colony independent of defense shipments from Europe. The introduction of airplane and motor manufacturing was the most important phase of this plan.

Gnome-Rona undertook to build a plant with an annual output of 150 planes and 400 motors in Indo-China.

At the time of the Minister's report the French Air Force in Indo-China consisted of six squadrons and this was subsequently greatly increased. Likewise the number of air fields was rapidly multiplied on a scale entirely unjustified by developments in civil aviation.

There are facilities for air defense in Indo-China, which, as part of a larger defense program, might prove to be important and useful.

The air establishment of Netherland India has made very rapid strides in the last three years. Large orders have been placed and filled for American planes for combat purposes, while training planes are being built in two establishments in Java. Koolhoven planes are being built at Tandjong Priok and Walaven ships are being turned out at Bandoeng.

The Netherland Indian air force has its naval air arm at Surabaya, where a large concentration is being increased. The army has its own organized air forces with three major military airdromes. These are located at Andir, Tjililitan and Kalidjati. The service maintains its own workshops and is engaged in construction.

The United States has become the major source of the supply of military aircraft to this government. From 1933 to 1936 approximately 300 planes were imported, the United States supplying 86 of them. In 1937 airplane armament began on a larger scale when 318 planes were imported. Of these the United States supplied 171 and the Netherlands 147. The year 1938 was the largest in this program. In that year Netherland India acquired approximately 1,200 new aircraft. Of these the United States supplied 1,108.

This air establishment is not yet large, but it is growing. It has had the important stimulus of the tremendous Netherland operations in commercial flying. K.L.M. has penetrated to every part of the South Seas and has made Netherland India air-conscious. It is extremely likely, moreover, that the shift in the center of gravity for the time being in the Netherland Empire from the homeland to Netherland India will have the effect of concentrating more and more attention on air strength in the colony.

The Royal Air Force maintains its Far East unit at Singapore. There is a major air base at Singapore distinct from the great naval station. It has been the largest British colonial air operation.

The British air position is strengthened also by the presence of the Indian station to the west and the Australian air establishment to the south. The course of the war has brought the British Empire air operations into increasing importance and it is by no means rash to suggest that the Commonwealth of Australia will eventually provide the major production hinterland for Britain's Singapore air base.

Like the naval stations, the air bases surrounding the South China Sea constitute a formidable defense when they are considered as a unified positional establishment rather than individual and isolated outposts.

There is less unity in the various land forces at the disposition of the Western Powers. Indo-China and Netherland India are in relatively stronger positions here than the British and the Americans.

French Colonial troops in Indo-China number at least 100,000, are of a relatively high order and have demonstrated their ability in the past. They are well trained and well led. Their resistance, however, is now a political rather than military problem.

The Philippine establishment is only beginning to take form. It can be very important under the proper leadership.

The Netherland establishment is large and growing. Like the force in Indo-China, the Netherland Indian army is an object of native pride; it is a native organization under strong outside leadership.

The strength and character of the British land forces in the Far East are very largely a matter of Britain's occupation elsewhere. The British necessarily have withdrawn some of their strength from the China coast during the present war. There is, however, an excellent British nucleus remaining.

Avoiding an "Understanding"

It is obvious that the successful defense of this position in the South China Sea is a matter of joint operation, with the United States playing the strongest part; and the question has been raised repeatedly in the past twenty years as to the possibility of an understanding over defense plans among the countries involved. Yet, because of political considerations, this has been one of the touchiest of subjects. At any time in the past twenty years, if an American or a Netherlander were asked about the possibility of an understanding with the British and the French on South China Sea defense, he would run from the question as from the plague.

The necessity of an interchange of information and a joint plan of operation is apparent. Such an alignment, however, has been carefully avoided in the past.

Anyone who looked at a map would know that the defense plan of Netherland India must be completely dominated by the British position at Singapore. Singapore is only four hours by sea from the nearest Netherland possession, or about forty minutes by air. It is inconceivable that this fact should not have been taken into consideration in all of Netherland India's defense problem. It has been a matter of good politics, however, to avoid any mention of the fact, and no British or Netherland staff officer would have dared to admit, up to May 1940, that there could possibly have been any formal exchange of information.

The position of the United States has been even more delicate. American naval units have paid courtesy calls at Singapore and their courtesy has been returned. I have counted at one time as many as thirty-six British ships in Manila Bay. Yet the official position of this country and of Great Britain has been that its responsible naval officers exchange visits back and forth with their eyes blindfolded, their ears stuffed, and a gag in their mouths.

Almost every student of the Far Eastern political scene has had occasion at one time or another to ask American officers, "What kind of understanding exists between the British and Americans on the defensive interchange between Manila and Singapore?" In every case the indiscreet question has been met with a frightened look and a run for cover.

When an American naval officer declared, three years ago, that there were circumstances in which a wink was as good as a treaty, there were reverberating disclaimers in Washington and Whitehall. Yet it must be obvious that the necessity of a joint action in an emergency cannot possibly have escaped every naval officer in the Far East.

The reason for this conspiracy of silence is the pathological American fear of anything that could be called an alliance. Our diplomacy has been obliged at times to go out of its way to avoid action that would seem to be parallel to the British and French in the Far East, and yet it is perfectly obvious that if we propose to defend our position, the action has to be not only parallel but joint. Moreover, it is now equally obvious that the United States will have to bear the brunt of it.

Whether this joint action is accomplished by some sort of formal alliance or merely by a completely informal but thoroughgoing understanding with a necessary exchange of information, is a matter of dialectics. If and when we are forced to defend the South China Sea, we shall be defending it with the British, and whatever is left of the French and Dutch, regardless of what anybody says about entanglements.

An Ode to Chestnuts

The sacred shibboleth of isolation has already been shattered beyond repair. It seems inevitable that the fantastic slogan "pulling British chestnuts out of the fire" will also lose its point.

It has been assumed for about twenty years that the United States could not take vigorous action in the Far East except in the interest of the British Empire. Consequently every suggestion of such an action was attributed to domination of American policy by the British Foreign Office and there developed a fixed school of thought that insisted that whatever we did east of the Alleghenies and west of the Rockies would in some measure or other redound ultimately to the glory and honor of Whitehall, through our own naïveté or stupidity.

This word-worship in the United States reached the point that if someone even suggested that the lives of Americans should be protected on the 180th meridian, he was accused of pulling British chestnuts out of the fire.

Quite apart from the fact that it may be folly to talk about who owns the chestnuts when the whole house is ablaze, it is beginning to be realized that the British Empire is not the only political entity in the world that owns chestnuts. It is also beginning to be realized that not all of the American chestnuts are within the continental limits of the United States. We may eventually realize that they are not all within the Western Hemisphere.

One of the American chestnuts, for example, is freedom to import more than half of the world's supply of rubber and tin. Another is our foreign trade with southeastern Asia that runs a little over a half-billion dollars a year; another is the safety and security of sixteen million Filipinos for whom we are still responsible; another is a fixed property investment in Asia of several hundred million dollars. Still another is continued access to some of the world's most important deposits of mineral wealth.

Another one is the steadfastness of American treaty structures and American treaty commitments.

These are not imaginary creations of the British Foreign Office for the purpose of entangling the United States into the defense of the British Empire. They are real American chestnuts in a real Asiatic fire.

The American public has rapidly come around to the position that there is no good reason why we should not assist, in one way or another, in the defense of the interests of the resisting French, British, and Dutch. Americans are beginning to see that inherent in every one of these interests is a vital interest to the United

States. We came very quickly to realize, for example, that the British navy itself was the very biggest American chestnut in the European fire.

But quite apart from this, American interests themselves are so great that we need no excuse of altruism or chivalry to undertake their defense with the best means at our disposal. We are, indeed, fortunate in the fact that enlightened self-interest dictates a policy of friendly co-operation with the few remaining powers that are friendly to us. It is quite as important for us at the moment to ask Britain and the Netherland and French colonies to put their facilities at our disposal to help pull the American chestnuts out of the Asiatic fire as it is to rush to their defense.

This possibility, however, presumes a complete change in the direction of American policy. It presumes our active participation, either militarily or otherwise, in the clash in which the world is now engulfed. It presumes that we quit standing on the sidelines and get into the game.

To a Dynamic Policy

Our policy in Eastern Asia for the past twenty years has been primarily a static policy, when it was not actually a policy of retreat. The Washington Conference, for example, undertook to freeze the military situation. Our treaty commitments to China, to the Netherlands, and to the Japanese are all based on the preservation of a balance and upon the willingness of all of the contracting parties to avoid taking action.

That policy has already been destroyed. We have continued in the presumption that a static position can be maintained after one party to these commitments has taken a dynamic stand.

The world picture has changed so rapidly within the last year that it is obvious that a policy of inaction will no longer defend our interests. We must now meet movement with movement.

How would such a policy read, translated in terms of the Far East and specifically in terms of the South China Sea?

Its application on the other side of the world would, of course, depend in part on the degree to which our forces would have to be put at the disposal of the British Empire. We have already seen, however, that the European conflict is not without its strong Asiatic repercussions and that a part of American assistance to Western democracy will have to be given in the Far East.

How, then, could this aid be given?

As a prelude to the adoption of a dynamic Far Eastern policy more than one person has suggested that the United States should first of all repeal the Japanese Exclusion Act. Such a course of action would serve to clear our decks and clear our consciences. It would, from the beginning, indicate that our shift in ground was not anti-Japanese but pro-American. It would correct one of the mistakes of our past and put us in a more justifiable moral position at a time when moral positions will have to count.

The next necessary item of business would be to clear the confusion out of the Philippine situation. This would have to be done first of all by the declaration that outright political and military independence for the Philippines within the next quarter of a century would be completely unthinkable. The United States could, at the same time, obtain the enthusiastic support of the vast majority of the Philippines for a program designed to give the highest degree of autonomy and at the same time a maximum degree of protection. The formula for the Philippine compromise could be found quickly if bad faith were disposed of on both sides. That would mean an embargo on pressure groups in the United States and an embargo on irresponsible petitioners in the Philippines.

The next imperative step would be the transport of a sufficient amount of American naval and air strength to the Far East to make it plain to all hands that we meant business. That would mean basing some capital ships on Manila and not on Hawaii. It would mean a declaration that we had a position in southeastern Asia, that we proposed to defend it, and that we were able to defend it.

When these preliminary steps have been taken the United States may be in a position to assert its influence on the side of its conscience in the Chinese-Japanese War. We may then be in a position to render effective aid to China by considerably larger advances of credit than have been discussed up to the present time and by a real supply of war material, whether the Japanese like it or not.

By this time a good many Americans have realized that Chiang Kai-shek's army back on the Yangtze has been fighting America's battle precisely as the British navy has been fighting it on the other side of the Atlantic.

By the time these other steps have been taken, and taken quickly, the United States will be in a position to impose its embargo on war materials to Japan. Almost all of the argument against the embargo is based upon the presumption that we will continue a static policy. Once the policy is changed the argument against the embargo falls to the ground.

It is inconceivable that if we recognize the danger to our interests and prepare to meet it vigorously, we should continue to augment that danger while we are in the process of defending ourselves from it. If we believe that we have no future in Asia we can well afford to be indifferent to the outcome of the Japanese-Chinese struggle and the Japanese move toward the South Seas, providing we can still our conscience. If we do believe that we have a future in Asia and that that future is threatened and challenged, we can hardly commit ourselves to the incredible folly of continuing to arm the enemy.

WE ARE NOT HELPLESS

But what is most important is that this possibility of an embargo changes our position from one of weakness into one of strength. At the moment that is not sufficiently understood.

We have been so appalled at the progressive demolition of free governments in Europe that we have assumed that every ounce of our energies must be expended to defend our mere continental limits or, at most, a part of the Western Hemisphere.

The fall of France was the signal for an immediate cry for "appeasement" of the Japanese. Presumably we had to take part in an Asiatic Munich in order to be able to build tanks in the United States. So we watched the Japanese grab toward French Indo-China and the peremptory demands on Britain with the frightened assumption that there was nothing we could do about it.

As a matter of fact, the Japanese dependence upon the United States for the major part of the war materials needed in the southward march is precisely what makes it possible for this country to defend its own interests, and those of the other democracies, against this aggression. Even if the amount of assistance that we can get from the other countries in the South China Sea area is reduced to virtually nothing except the use of their facilities, we can still hold the whip hand over Japan through our control of the resources of war.

Even if we admit that our blindness has exceeded that of a Chamberlain, a Henderson, or a Gamelin, in continuing to supply to the Japanese the materials that were to be turned against us and our interest, we can still stand our ground, for those materials are still necessary to Japan.

Our greatest peril is not the danger of fighting a naval war too far from our shores. It is that we should resign ourselves to defeat without putting up a fight. We are being subjected on all sides to a war of nerves. It is designed to persuade us to accept two immobilizing conclusions: first, that nothing is worth fighting for, and second, that we are unable to fight, even if we wanted to. Both of those are lies.

In the past we have not seen how great are the stakes. Now we are concentrating too vigorously on our weaknesses rather than on our elements of strength.

It is now imperative that we realize not only that we have a great future in Asia, but that we can defend it if we will.

In the course of the last few months we have seen an intolerably high price paid for the sins of smugness and complacency. We have seen nationalities and even civilizations disappear because they refused to face the facts. We have finally awakened to the challenge to our own security. We have come to understand that there are two international ways of life in terrific collision in the world at the present time. We have already been faced with the necessity of making our choice between those two ways.

We have discovered that there is no possibility of our disinterest in what happens in Europe. We hope that we have discovered it in time.

We will shortly discover that there is equally no possibility of our disinterest in Asia. Our future as a nation will once more depend, as it has depended in the past, upon our frontiers. We lost our frontier on the Rhine, we lost our frontier on the Somme and the Loire, and we spent the summer of 1940 in terrifying suspense as to whether or not we would lose our frontier defense in the British navy.

We still have our frontier in southeastern Asia. We can defend it if we will. But not all frontiers are peaceful.

The South China Sea is the battle-ground for our future in Asia.

INDEX

INDEX

Abaca, 127. *See also* Manila hemp
Abrogation of 1911 Treaty, 206, 228
Administration of the Admirals, 50
Airplane bases, 282–5
Airplanes, 23, 206, 211, 251, 283–5
Alaska, 31, 58, 62, 151
Aluminum, 20
"American character," 61
American Department of Commerce (1938 report), 34
American export market
  balance, 25, 147
  cotton textiles, 23, 43, 44, 149
  dependent on freedom of trade, 66–7
  development, 23–7
  French Indo-China, 25
  future in China, 184, 189–90, 193–6
  increase due to wars, 23
  Malaya, 25
  Netherland India, 23–5
  Philippines, 23, 149–50
American import market
  balance, 25
  influx of Philippine goods, 96–8
"American mind," 61
American Samoa, 145
American self-sufficiency questionable, 8–12, 14, 16–7
American trade
  Chadbourne Plan, 39
  cotton textile struggle, 43–4
  effect of embargo on, 222–3
  effect of "Empire mind" on, 62–3
  effect of Japanese aggression on, 32–4
  effect of Japanese dumping on, 43–5
  effect of market crash on, 41–2
  expanding, in Pacific, 55
  expanding, in Philippines, 147–50, 164
  in Hemisphere, 66
  Japan protests limitations, 139

needs access to markets, 64–6
needs Far Eastern policy, 63
raw materials, 9–27, 38–9
with China, 29–30, 183, 196
with French Indo-China, 25, 32, 34
with Japan, 17
with Malaya, 25
with Netherland India, 23–5
with the Philippines, 25, 30–1, 157–8
Andir, 284
Annam, 50, 280
Annamese, 32, 51, 72, 279
Annamese Code, 51
Antimony, 2, 20, 29, 38, 230
Aparri, 154
Argentina, 4, 149, 212
Arita, Hachiro, 89, 265–6
Asahi, 207
Asbestos, 21, 153
Asia
  American retirement from, 58–9
  raw materials, 2, 8–23
  Tanaka Memorial, 254–8
  United States defense materials, 19–20
  United States market in, 23–5
"Asia for the Asiatics," 264
Asia Minor, 247
Asiatic Fleet, 221, 280–1
Asiatic Monroe Doctrine, 133, 264–71, 274–5
Assam, 37
Australia, 65, 120, 149, 249, 277, 282, 285
Automobile trade, 10, 24
Aviation, 144–5
Axis, 87

Bain, H. Foster, 151
Bali, 34, 35
Balik Papen, 34
Bandoeng, 284

Batangas, 15
Batangas Bay, 123
Batavia, 2, 35–7, 77, 144, 282
Batik, 34
Belgium, 171, 278
Benguet Consolidated, 151
Berlin, 276
Bismarck, Otto von, 173
Bolivia, 18, 19
Borneo, 243
    boundary of Philippines and, 47
    division of, 47
    oil, 34
    rubber, 11
    threat from Japan to, 54, 85, 277
Borobadur, 34
Boxer Indemnity, 184
Boxer Rebellion, 184
Brazil, 4, 10, 11, 14, 16, 149
Bristles, 30, 187
British Residents, 52
Brussels Conference (1937), 175
Bryan, William Jennings, 56, 105
Buitenzorg, 35
Burma, 7, 18, 32, 37, 71, 83
Burma border, 194
Burma Road, 67, 82
Byas, Hugh, 265
Bynkershoek, 173

Cagayan Valley, 30
California, 202–3, 270
Cambodia, 50
Cambodians, 32, 279
Camphor, 21
Cam-Ranh, 280, 281, 283
Canada, 14, 65, 120, 149, 161, 246
Canton, 28, 29, 34, 183, 194, 234, 256, 280
Capitalism, 57
Capitalist system, 58
"Cash and carry" basis for war materials, 217
Cathay, 194
Cavite, 142, 144, 221, 280–1
Celebes, 20, 34, 35, 243
Central Asia, 247
Ceylon, 37
Chadbourne Plan, 39–40
Chamberlain, Neville, 292
Charner, Admiral, 50
Chemical specialties, 24
Chiang Kai-shek, 73, 89, 193, 230, 253–5, 258–9, 275, 277, 291
Chihli, Gulf of, 221
China, 1–3, 20, 34

American missionaries to, 185, 192–193, 218–20
    "awakening of," 193
    blockade by Japan of, 81–2
    Boxer Rebellion Indemnity, 67
    Communism in, 251–5
    Consular Courts in, 187
    economic penetration of, 183–4, 189–90
    educational development of, 192–3
    evacuating Americans from, 220
    extra-territoriality in, 187–9
    government of, 230, 232–3, 236
    loans to, 190, 230–1
    narcotic traffic in, 235
    nationalism in, 184–9
    New Order in East Asia, 256–74
    Nine-Power Pacific Pact, 171–5
    Open Door policy, 169
    partition of, 183
    potential markets of, 194–6
    relation to French Indo-China, 72–73
    Republic of, 183, 185
    Tanaka Memorial, 245–8
    Twenty-one Demands on, 185, 202
    United States moral obligation in, 232–3
China War
    China "incident," 175, 215
    effect on cotton textile struggle, 45
    effect on extra-territoriality, 188–9
    effect on industrialization, 191
    effect on Japanese politics, 224–5
    effect on U.S.-Japan relations, 204–205, 213–4
    effect on United States trade, 23
    "Holy War," 205–6
    narcotics as weapon in, 235
    Neutrality Act, 215–6
Chinese, 7, 37, 137, 218, 232–5, 243, 262–3, 279
Chinese Red Cross, 231
Chromite, 2, 20, 151–3
Chromium, 38, 159
Chungking, 232, 234, 256, 272
Cigarettes, 149
Cigars, 30, 96
Cinchona bark, 35
Cinnamon, 28, 36
Cloves, 36
Coal, 242–3
Cocaine, 235
Cochin China, 50
Coconut oil excise tax, 101–3, 108–9
Coconuts, 15–17, 40, 61, 96, 97, 100, 107

Index

Coffee, 9, 35, 36, 38, 148
Comintern, 257
Communism, 251–5
Congress of the United States
attitude toward "empire," 56
on defense of Philippines, 128
on Japanese relations, 203, 209, 214
on Philippine independence, 106–8,
141, 160, 163
Constitutionalists (Japan), 224–6
Consular Courts (China), 187
Continental limits (U.S.), 4, 8–9, 59, 62
Copper, 153, 210
Copra, 2, 17, 21, 30, 36, 38
Cordage, 30, 40, 61, 97, 98, 108
Corregidor, 128, 141, 179, 281
Cotabato River, 156
Cotton, 16, 139, 211, 260
Cotton textiles, 23, 31, 41, 43, 45, 65,
137, 149, 243
Crisis Decrees, 71, 76
Critical materials, 21
Crow, Carl, 236
Cuba, 13–4, 36, 39, 107, 149, 158
Cutch, 21

Dairen, 243, 250
Davao, 84, 137, 143
Davis, Dwight F., 69, 95, 97
Defense Ministries (Japan), 224
Denmark, 278
Department of Commerce, U.S. (1938
report), 34
Derris root, 28
Dewey, Admiral, 279
Diet, Japanese, 225
Djokjakarta, 34
Dominion status (Philippines), 161
Dong Nei River, 32

Early, Stephen, 267
Economic frontier, 1
Economic position of United States,
25, 63–5, 156–8
in relation to China, 183 ff.
Electric machinery, 24
Embargo, 181, 206 ff., 291
international repercussions, 227
Japanese economics, 213
moral embargo, 211
Neutrality Act, 215–7
political repercussions, 224–6
reprisals, 217–22
Embroidery, 30–1
Empires
British, 1, 28, 57, 282, 290
effect on living standards, 66–70
exploitation by, 64

French, 1, 54
Japanese, 54, 225, 265
moral defense of, 70
Netherland, 1, 54
New York students on, 58
relation to each other, 46–7
relation to South China Sea area,
46–7
the word "empire," 56
threat from Japan to other, 54
United States functions of, 164
Essential materials, 20–1
Ethiopian campaign, 153
Europe, 247
European War
American attitude, 210
effect on Far Eastern stability, 46
effect on Japanese expansion, 264
effect on nationalist movement,
Netherland India, 77
effect on United States trade with
Japan, 210–1
Japanese non-involvement, 265
Export-Import Bank, 230
Extra-territoriality, 187–9, 200, 258,
262

Farm Bureau, 108
Fascism (in Japan), 225, 248, 272
Fascist Revolution, 2
Fearn, Dr., 193
Federal Reserve notes (Yen Bloc), 261
Federated Malay States, 52
Ferrograde, 20
Fiji, 145
Filipinos
attitude toward Japanese domina-
tion, 136
defense of Philippines by, 122 ff.
demand independence, 104 ff.
diet, 96
politically self-conscious, 53
politicians, 117–8
purchasing power of, 149
standard of living, 65
Fish, 38, 250
Flores, 35
Foreign policy in Asia, American, 232,
289–91
Foreign Relations, Senate Committee
on, 214
Formosa, 54, 239, 240
Fort McKinley, 141, 143
Fort Stotsenburg, 141, 144, 283
France, 230, 278, 286, 292
effect of collapse, 3, 72, 80, 209,
264, 275, 281, 283, 292

France *(Continued)*
  Far Eastern threat to French Empire, 54
  Nine-Power Pacific Pact, 171
  relation to French Indo-China, 49–51
  stake in the Far East, 27
  treaty with Japan regarding Hainan, 81
Franco, General Francisco, 3
Freedom of trade, 66
French Indo-China, 1, 3
  air base program, 283
  area, 7
  Japanese demands on, 72
  Japanese threats to, 54, 80, 231, 271, 277, 281, 292
  nationalist movement, 72
  population, 7
  rattan, 22, 32
  relation to France, 49–51
  rice granary, 32, 97
  rubber, 10–11
  tin, 18
  trade, 32, 34
Fushan, 242

Gambier, 23
Gamelin, General, 292
Gentlemen's Agreement (textiles), 44–45, 244
  first Gentlemen's Agreement (immigration), 201
Germany, 120
  effect of victory on Asia, 79, 85, 87, 264
  holdings in Asia, 202
  Japan's understanding with, 87, 227, 252, 257, 276–7
  note on Monroe Doctrine, 266
  war materials, 207
Gnome-Rona, 283
Goh, Baron, 224
Gold, 2, 31, 133, 150–1, 159
Gomez, Guillermo, 113
Grant, President, 181
Great Britain
  agreements with Japan, 42
  attempted monopoly, 39
  British Empire, 1, 28, 57, 282, 290
  division of Borneo and New Guinea, 47
  economic relation to colonies, 65
  economic relation to United States in Asia, 287 ff.
  Far Eastern threat to, 54
  investments in China, 184, 190
  Japanese pressure against, 82, 225, 275
  labor control in Malaya, 74
  London naval commitments, 177–9
  navy, importance, 59, 66, 79, 123, 209, 264, 282, 286, 289
  Nine-Power Pacific Pact, 171
  oil interests, 39, 212
  Open Door policy, 169
  relation to Malaya, 52
  relation to United States in Asia, 279
  stake in Far East, 27
  Tanaka Memorial, 246
  trade in Asia, 9
"Greater East Asia," 78, 80, 82, 264
Guam, 179, 196
Gums, 24, 32

Hague, The, 2, 77
Hainan, island of, 3, 80, 280
Haiphong, 34, 81, 231, 270
Haiphong-Yunnan Railway, 34, 72, 81
Hangchow, 234
Hangkow, 183
Hanoi, 80
Hardwood, Philippine, 42, 96
Hare-Hawes-Cutting Bill, 101, 160, 161
Harris, Townsend, 179, 198–9
Harrison, Francis Burton, 94
Hata, Shunroku, 87
Hawaii, 58, 62, 106, 145, 146, 221, 279
Hay, John, 169, 184
Hemisphere defense, 4, 59
Hemisphere frontier, 4
Hemp, 137, 156
Henderson, Sir Nevile, 292
Heroin, 235
Hides, 189
Hitler, Adolf, 276
Hitler-Stalin alliance, 252, 270, 276
Hong Kong, 29–30, 37, 45, 54, 80, 82, 85, 144, 157, 254, 272, 280, 283
Honma, General, 217
Honolulu, 279
Hoover, Herbert, 176
Hull, Cordell, 67, 85, 167, 267–9

Imperialism, 63 ff., 105
"Imperial Way," 90, 205, 248, 274
India, 32, 42, 65, 68, 71, 74, 244, 246, 285
Indo-China. *See* French Indo-China
Industrialization (Japan), 242
Industrial machinery, 24, 149
Insular Government (Philippines), 98–9, 126

International Settlement (Shanghai), 187
Intervention, 3
Iron, 21, 31, 38, 42, 151, 159, 243
Ishii, Viscount, 170, 185, 202
Italy, 123, 153, 171, 207, 209, 227, 252, 257

Jane's Fighting Ships, 281
Japan
  Asiatic Monroe Doctrine, 264 ff.
  attitude toward Netherland India, 85-8
  charges of "dumping" against, 43
  closing of Haiphong-Yunnan Road, 34
  cotton textile struggle, 43-5
  demands in French Indo-China, 72
  economic expansion, 242-4
  embargo, effect on, 224 ff.
  Emperor of Japan, 199, 205, 246
  Empire, 54, 225, 265
  fear of Communism, 251-2
  fifth column activities in Philippines, 140
  government control over cotton exports, 44
  "Holy War," 205
  "Imperial Way," 90, 205, 248, 274
  industrialization of, 242
  penetration of Philippines, 84
  political structure of, 224-5
  population pressure, 239-42
  proclaims New Order in East Asia, 256 ff.
  protests Philippine limitation, 141
  purchase of ores, 151, 153
  raw silk trade, 17
  rise of military power, 245 ff.
  Russian relations, 227-9, 276
  self-defense motives, 249-51
  southward expansion, 274
  tactics of friendship, 269-70
  Tanaka Memorial, 245 ff.
  threat to China, 185
  threat to Far East, 54
  threat to Malaya, 82-4
  trade agreements with South America, 211-2
  trade growth in exports, 41-3
  treaty with France regarding Hainan, 81
  treaty with Thailand, 83
  Twenty-one Demands on China, 185
  understanding with Germany, 87
  United States handing wealth to, 158

violations of Pacific treaties and commitments, 169 ff.
war materials, 89, 210 ff.
Japan and the United States, 197 ff.
  economic factors, 213
  embargo and reactions, 206 ff.
  first Gentlemen's Agreement, 201
  first treaty, 199
  non-treaty basis, 204
  Open Door, 200
  Pacific treaties, 203
  Russian complications, 227-9
  second Gentlemen's Agreement, 44-45, 244
Japanese-Argentine Trade Pact, 212
Japanese Cabinet, 224
Japanese Exclusion Act, 203
Japanese expansion
  economic and political penetration, 136
  hostility to, 203
  MacArthur's statement on Philippine independence and, 129-30
  need of markets, 133
  population pressure, 239 ff.
Japanese High Command, 231, 234
Java, 7, 10, 13, 34-6, 39, 42, 77, 244, 279, 282
Johnson, Nelson T., 232
Jolo, 30, 154
Jones-Costigan Law, 40

Kalidjati, 284
Kamchatka Peninsula, 250
Kapok, 21, 28
Kellogg-Briand Treaty, 175-7, 182, 215
King, William H., 104
K.L.M., 144, 284
Kobe, 261
Kokumin, 218
Konoye, Prince Fumimaro, 256-9
Konoye Government, 73, 80, 89, 208, 225-6
Koolhoven, 284
Kopal, 23
Korea, 239, 240, 245, 249, 250
Kowloon, 29
Kuomintang, 253-5, 257
Kwangchow Bay, 50
Kwangchow-wan, 50, 80
Kwantung Peninsula, 250

Labor, 13, 64, 74, 108, 201
Lake Lanao, 156
Lansing, Robert, 170, 185
Laos, 50
Lead, 21, 153
Liberal Party (Japan), 224-5

Lingayan Gulf, 123
Living standard
as affected by empires, 60 ff.
in China, 190, 194
in Japan, 243
in Netherland India, 48
in the Philippines, 68–9, 97, 121, 150
Loans to China, 190, 230
Luzon, 123, 136, 140, 151

MacArthur, Douglas, 122 ff.
Mace, 23
Machinery, 24, 149, 190
Machine tools, 206
Madrid, 3
Malacañan Palace, 125
Malampaya Sound, 142–3
Malaya, 1, 2, 7, 8, 10–2, 18, 19, 37, 42, 52, 71, 73–4, 82, 271, 277
Malays, 7, 8, 54, 73 ff., 263, 274, 279
Malay States, 52
Manchukuo, 72, 239–40, 264
Manchuria, 176, 224, 245–7, 250
Mandated Islands, 84, 143, 202, 239, 240
Manganese, 20, 38, 151, 159
Manila, 30–1, 37, 68, 137, 139, 143, 144, 145
Manila, Post of, 141
Manila Bay, 128, 279, 281, 286
Manila hemp, 2, 20, 30, 38, 42, 96
Marco Polo Bridge, 215
Market crash (1929–30), 41–3
Mekong Delta, 32
Menado, 248
Merchants Protective Association (Manila), 43
Military needs (of U.S.), 17, 19, 20, 167
Mindanao, 143, 151, 155–6
Ministry of Colonies
France, 50, 283
Great Britain, 52
Ministry of Marine (French), 50
Minseito, 246, 247
Missionaries (to China), 185, 192–3, 218–9
Mitsubishi, 244
Mitsui, 244
Moluccas, 35
Mongolia, 245–7, 251, 257
Monroe, President, 269
Monroe Doctrine, 265–70
Morphine, 235
Mother-of-pearl and shell, 30
Mount Apo, 156

Mukden, 242, 270
Munich, 3
Munitions board, 19
Murphy, Frank, 95, 125
Mussolini, 3

Nanking, 177, 218, 270, 273
Narcotic Commission, 235
Narcotic traffic, 235
National defense, 19, 20, 58–9, 89, 105–6, 152, 164, 166, 207, 230
National Development Company (Philippines), 151
Nationalist movements
effects of European War on, 78
effects of Indian, 74
effects of Japanese threat on, 78
in British Malaya, 52, 73–4
in China, 184–9
in French Indo-China, 72
in Netherland India, 75–8
in Philippines, 77
in southeastern Asia (1935), 71
National Socialist Revolution, 2
Naval stores, 24
Nazis, 3, 173, 213
Netherland India, 1, 2, 7, 10, 11
air bases, 284
area, 7
effect of German conquest of the Netherlands, 85–9
import of automobiles, 24
import of planes, 23
import of steel mill goods, 24
nationalist movement, 75–8
naval stations, 281–2
population, 7
ports, 34–5
raw materials, 2, 8–18, 21, 22, 23, 34, 35, 36
relation to the Netherlands, 35, 47–9
relation to the United States, 167
Singapore, connection with, 37
threat from Japan, 54, 271, 277
trade, 19, 42–3, 212
Netherlands
conquest by Germany affects colonies, 85–9
division of Borneo and New Guinea, 47
Far Eastern threat to Netherland Empire, 54
Nine-Power Pacific Pact, 171 ff.
relation to living standards, 60
relation to Netherland India, 35, 47–9

Netherlands *(Continued)*
relation to United States in Asia, 279, 286, 292
sovereignty questioned in Netherland India, 75–6
suggested air routes to Philippines, 144
Neutrality Act, 215–7
New Deal, 91
New Guinea, 35, 47, 243
"New Order in East Asia," 139, 195, 248, 256–64
New York, 252
Nichols Field, 283
Nickel, 20
Nine-Power Pacific Pact, 171–5, 182, 186, 203, 246–7, 259
Non-intervention, 3
Non-Participation in Japanese Aggression, Committee for, 208
Norway, 278
Nutmeg, 23

Oil. *See* Petroleum
Olongapo, 142
Open Door policy for China, 169, 184–6, 200
Opium, 235, 256
Opium War, 169, 183
Oriental Exclusion Act, 201
Osaka, 195, 260
Osmeña, Sergio, 161

Pabst, General J. C., 87
Pacific Naval Pact, 177
Pact of Paris, 175–6
Palawan, 142, 143
Palembang, 62
Palm oil, 21, 22
Panama, 58
Panama Canal Zone, 143
Pan American Airways, 144
Pan-Asiatic policy, 208
Paper and pulp, 9, 24
Peace in the Far East, 47, 54
Peanuts, 34
Pearl Harbor, 146
Peiping (Peking), 183, 187, 194, 270
Peking Union Medical Center, 194
Penang, 18, 52
Pepper, 22, 28, 34, 35
Perry, Commodore, 179, 197–8
Petroleum, 2, 9, 21, 34, 37, 38, 39, 153, 190, 207, 210, 212, 250
Philippine-American Committee, 102
Philippine Assembly, 99, 103
Philippine Commonwealth, 69, 71, 96, 124, 138, 153, 159, 162, 164

Philippine Constabulary, 124
Philippine Constitution, 102
Philippine Department of Agriculture, 84
Philippine independence, 40, 53, 85, 91 ff.
Philippine National Bank, 94
Philippines, 1, 2, 4, 7, 8, 10, 11, 13, 14, 15
agricultural wealth, 155
area, 7, 8
army, 122 ff.
boundary of North Borneo and, 47
centralization of government, 98–9
Commonwealth. *See* Philippine Commonwealth
Constabulary, 124
crops to Japan, 139
defense. *See* Philippines, defense of
democracy in embryo, 53
dominion status, 161
economic asset to the United States, 147 ff., 157 ff.
effect of independence on, 54
effect of Japanese agreements on, 41–5
effect of Spanish-American War on, 56
"empire" exploitation in, 64
face-saving formula, 161–2
franchise to foreign aircraft, 144
independence. *See* Philippine independence
Japanese economic penetration in, 84
Japanese expansion in, 240, 244, 271, 277
living conditions and public health in, 68–70
mineral resources, 150–4
population, 7
public health, 67–9, 99
quota limitations, 40
raw materials, 8, 10, 11, 13, 14, 15, 16, 17, 19, 20, 21
reasons for American retirement from, 58–60
restriction on Japanese "dumping" in, 43–5
tariffs on Japanese goods, 43
trade, 2, 4, 19, 20, 21
trading post in Asia, 25
value of, 134, 147 ff.
Philippines, defense of, 122 ff.
air bases, 144
conflicting views on, 146

Philippines, defense of *(Continued)*
  economic penetration of Japanese, 137
  Japanese threat to, 127 ff.
  MacArthur on, 129–30
  naval and military bases, 141–3
  program and procedure of, 122–6
  Sayre on, 127
  value of Islands, 134
Philippine Scouts, 124
Pittman, Key, 124
Political position of United States in Far East, 26, 157, 184, 196
Population pressure (Japan), 239–44
Portugal, 171
Post of Manila, 141
Puerto Rico, 13, 62
Pulo Brani, 83

Quezon, Manuel, 102, 103, 123, 127, 140, 141, 159, 160, 161, 162
Quezon, Mrs. Manuel, 125
Quinine, 2, 20, 22, 28, 35, 38, 148
Quota limitations
  coconut oil, 39–40
  effect of market crash on, 41–3
  rubber, 39–40
  sugar, 39–40
  tin, 39–40

Ramie, 28
Rattan, 22, 28
Raw materials, 2, 9–23, 133, 148, 207, 242–4, 274
  related to defense program, 19, 20
  related to empire structure, 64
  United States access to, 60
Rayon, 45
Residents, British, 52
Residents-General (French Indo-China), 51
Resins, 24, 32
Ribbentrop, Joachim von, 276
Rice, 2, 32, 38, 96–7
Roosevelt, Franklin D., 102, 267–8, 277
Roosevelt, Theodore, 201
Roosevelt, Theodore, Jr., 95
Roxas, Manuel, 161
Royal Air Force, 285
Royal Dutch-Shell, 34, 39, 42, 212
Rubber, 2, 9–13, 20, 22, 32, 35, 37, 38–9, 148, 195, 288
Russia, 227–9, 251–5, 276–7
Russian Revolution, 57
Russo-Japanese War, 200, 246

Sago (tapioca), 22, 36, 38
Saigon, 32, 283
Saito, Deputy, 225
Sakhalin, 250
Samoa, 145
San Bernardino Strait, 283
San Diego, 146
San Pedro, 196, 279
Sayre, Francis B., 127–8
Schwellenbach, Lewis B., 214
Scrap metal, 206–8, 211
Shanghai, 54, 72, 187, 194, 217, 261
Shansi, 194
Shantung Province, 195, 202, 240
Shellac, 21, 28, 32
Shimonoseki, 200
Ship lanes, 82, 83, 183
Shoes, 43, 137
Shogunate, 199
Siam. *See* Thailand
Silk
  Chinese, 190
  raw, 9, 17, 222–3
  substitutes, 223
Singapore, 10, 12, 16, 18, 26, 37–8, 52, 82, 83, 167, 285–6
Sinkiang Province, 254
Sino-Japanese relations, 257
Sisal, 23
Socony-Vacuum, 218
Soong, T. V., 208
Soong sisters, 193
South Africa, 65
South America, 4, 10–1, 59, 149, 151, 211–2, 246
South China Sea area
  area, 7
  defense of, 278 ff.
  empires with holdings in, 46 ff.
  exports, value of, 28
  harbors, 28–9, 30–2, 34–5, 37
  importance, 9
  Japanese threat to, 54
  joint operation of empires necessary, 286–8
  market for United States exports, 23, 25
  monopolies in, 39
  naval bases in, 280–1
  new dynamic policy for, 289–91
  new order in East Asia, 265–6
  plane bases in, 282–5
  population, 7, 8
  preservation of stability in, 53–4
  raw materials of, 9–23, 28
  relation of United States to, 55
  relation to Western World, 1, 2

South China Sea area *(Continued)*
  status quo in, 1, 2, 3, 46
  threat of changes in, 54
  value of exports, 28
  wealth of, 2, 8, 9, 21
Southeastern Asia. *See* South China
  Sea area
South Manchurian Railway, 243
Sovereignty
  American, 219
  degrees of, 161–5
  Japanese, 204
  recognition by self-exile, 62
  removed from Philippines, 85, 158
  threat to Chinese, 186, 191, 204,
    233, 258, 262
Soviet Union, 57, 227–9
Soy bean, 16, 243
Spain, 3, 56, 94
Spanish-American War, 55, 105
Spratly Island, 3, 84
Stability in Far East, 53–4
  and German conquest in Europe,
    85–7
  and nationalist movements, 71 ff.
  and threat of aggression, 79
  and United States, 55
Stalin, 270, 276
Standard Oil Company, 153, 219
State Department, 44, 153, 215–6, 259,
  269
Steel mill manufactures, 24
Stimson, Henry L., 95, 176–7, 208
Straits Settlements, 52, 53, 282
Strategic materials, 19–20, 167
Subic Bay, 142
Suchow, 183
Sugar, 9, 13–4, 21, 31, 34, 36, 38–40,
  106–7, 138, 148
Sultan of Sulu, 47
Sulu Sea, 143
Suma, Yakichiro, 204, 268
Sumatra, 10, 22, 37, 243
Sun Yat-sen, 185
Superior Council (French Indo-
  China), 51
Supreme Court, 162
Surabaya, 34–5, 281–2
Surigao Province, 151
Sydney, 145

Tai Ping Rebellion, 169
Tanaka, Baron Giichi, 245
Tanaka Memorial, 245–8, 274
Tandjong Priok, 282, 284
Tariffs
  on Philippine products, 96, 101

to meet Japanese "dumping," 43
Taussig, Admiral Joseph K., 248
Tea, 23, 34, 36, 38, 148, 183, 190
Thailand (Siam), 8, 11, 18, 32, 37, 71,
  83, 277
Three Principles (of Sun Yat-sen),
  185
Tibet, 194
Tientsin, 187
Timor, 35
Tin, 2, 9, 18, 19, 32, 38–40, 42, 288
Tjililitan, 284
Tobacco, 22, 24, 30, 96, 100
Tokyo, 251, 261, 264, 271, 273
Tongking, 50
Tongking, Gulf of, 3, 80
Treaty of Commerce and Navigation
  (1911), 179–81
Treaty of 1911, abrogation of, 206,
  228
Treaty of Portsmouth, 200
Treaty ports, 187
Tung oil, 29, 38, 189, 231
Tungsten, 2, 20, 28–9, 38, 189
Twenty-one Demands on China, 185,
  202
Tydings-McDuffie Law, 91, 102, 130

Underwood Tariff Act, 96
Unfederated Malay States, 52
United States
  advantages of remaining in Far
    East, 147 ff.
  air bases in Philippines, 144–5
  and China, 183 ff., 230 ff.
  as Asiatic power, 184
  as empire, 55 ff.
  co-operation with Western Powers
    in Asia, 146, 286 ff.
  defense of Philippines, 122 ff.
  dynamic policy necessary, 289
  economic interest in Asia, 8, 9
  economic lifeline in Singapore, 10
  evacuation of nationals, 220
  export markets, 23–7, 44–5, 65, 67,
    149, 183, 190, 194–5
  frontiers, 4
  import markets to, 24–5, 96
  Japan and United States, 197 ff.
  military and naval defense mate-
    rials, 19–20
  national defense, 19–20, 58–9, 89,
    105, 152, 164, 166, 207, 230
  on New Order in East Asia, 259
  ore reserves, 152
  Pacific treaties and commitments,
    169 ff.

United States *(Continued)*
  Philippine venture, 91 ff. .
  position in South China Sea, 278
  preserver of stability in Far East,
    54, 79, 90
  relation to empire holdings in
    Asia, 46
  replies to Asiatic Monroe Doctrine,
    266
  reply to Japan on Netherland In-
    dia, 85–6
  stake in Far East, 24–7
  trade, 2–4, 9–25, 28–45, 157–8
United States Army, 105, 125, 128,
  141, 162
United States Empire, 55 ff.
United States Navy, 66, 105, 128, 142,
  162, 208–9, 221, 248, 278 ff.
United States War Department, 164
Uruguay, 4

Vandenberg, Arthur, 101
Vegetable oils, 2, 9, 14–7, 28, 30
Vienna, 4
Virgin Islands, 62
Vladivostok, 250
Volksrad, 49, 71, 76

Walaven, 284
Wang Ching-wei, 177, 188, 217
War materials, 45, 207 ff., 22, 235,
  291 ff.
Washington Naval Disarmament Con-
  ference, 171, 186, 202, 289
Western Powers, union of interests,
  279
Whangpoo, 187
Wheat flour, 149
Wolframite, 29
Wood, General Leonard, 94, 112, 163
World trade, 38–43, 48
World War, 39, 96, 176, 185, 202, 244

Yamato, 247
Yangtze, 4, 173, 194, 274, 277, 291
"Yellow Peril," 202, 275
Yen Bloc, 260–3
Yonai, Admiral, 88
Yunnan, 195, 231, 274

Zambales, 152
Zamboanga, 156
Zanzibar, 36
Zinc, 153

Date Due

3360	Jan22		
"	Feb5		
6383	Mar13		
6499	Apr 1		
4875	Apr15		
6014	May 1		
6561	May14		
6490	Jul10		
6989	Aug21		
7373	Dec21		
6802	Feb 1		
7578	Jul17		
7625	Apr20		
APR 7 '53			
FEB 4 '55			